D1796974

Contemporary Approaches in Literary Trauma Theory

Also by Michelle Balaev
THE NATURE OF TRAUMA IN AMERICAN NOVELS

Contemporary Approaches in Literary Trauma Theory

Edited by
Michelle Balaev

palgrave
macmillan

First published 2014 by
PALGRAVE MACMILLAN

Palgrave Macmillan in the UK is an imprint of Macmillan Publishers Limited,
registered in England, company number 785998, of Houndmills, Basingstoke,
Hampshire RG21 6XS.

Palgrave Macmillan in the US is a division of St Martin's Press LLC,
175 Fifth Avenue, New York, NY 10010.

Palgrave Macmillan is the global academic imprint of the above companies
and has companies and representatives throughout the world.

Palgrave® and Macmillan® are registered trademarks in the United States,
the United Kingdom, Europe and other countries.

ISBN 978-1-349-47395-3   ISBN 978-1-137-36594-1 (eBook)
DOI 10.1057/9781137365941

A catalogue record for this book is available from the British Library.

Library of Congress Cataloging-in-Publication Data
Contemporary approaches in literary trauma theory / edited by Michelle Balaev.
pages cm
Summary: "Contemporary Approaches in Literary Trauma Theory showcases
some of the leading scholars in literary criticism who take trauma studies in a
new direction by broadening the theoretical foundations and future directions of
the field through innovative analyses of trauma in literature and culture. Trauma
causes a disruption, but the values attached to this experience are influenced by
a variety of individual and cultural factors that change over time. Trauma may at
times forever silence one, yet trauma can equally at times reorient consciousness
in an adaptive fashion that eschews pathology. This collection of essays argues that
trauma in literature must be read through a theoretical pluralism that allows for an
understanding of trauma's variable representations that include yet move beyond
the concept of trauma as pathological and unspeakable"— Provided by publisher.
Includes bibliographical references and index.
ISBN 978-1-349-47395-3
1. Psychic trauma in literature.   I. Balaev, Michelle, editor.
PN56.P93C65 2014
809'.93353—dc23   2014025702

Typeset by MPS Limited, Chennai, India.

increscunt animi, virescit volnere virtus

Contents

Acknowledgments

I would like to thank the following people for their support and guidance: Kathy Boardman, Peter Christenson, Valerie P. Cohen, John Cozma, Kai Erikson, Patti Fitchen, Will Hamlin, Michael Hanly, Jon Hegglund, James Hans, Paula Kennedy, Karen Kilcup, Steve Kroll-Smith, Mrs. Pauline Lumeng, Carole Lesley, Michael Mays, Paul Peppis, Herman Rapaport, Scott Romine, Debra Sommerville, Helen Southworth, Barry Stampfl, Anne Wallace, Eric Wirth, and the anonymous reviewers of the manuscript. I am grateful to my spouse Mikhail Balaev who has supported my research and writing for more than a decade and provided invaluable insights on this topic and many others.

Notes on Contributors

Paul Arthur is Professor of Digital Humanities at the University of Western Sydney, where he leads the UWS Digital Humanities Research Group. He was previously Deputy Director of the ANU Centre for European Studies. He has published widely in fields of history, literature, communication, and cultural studies, and is inaugural President of the Australasian Association for Digital Humanities. He also serves on the executive committee of the International Auto/ Biography Association and the advisory board of the Australasian Consortium of Humanities Research Centres.

Michelle Balaev is Assistant Professor of English at Washington State University. Michelle is the author of *The Nature of Trauma in American Novels* (2012) as well as numerous articles on twentieth-century American literature, trauma studies, psychology and literature, Asia Pacific literature, ecocriticism, and contemporary fiction. She has published articles, interviews, and reviews in such journals as *PMLA, American Literature, Studies in the Humanities, and ISLE*. Her current book explores tragedy in contemporary literature.

Greg Forter is Professor of English at the University of South Carolina. He has written extensively on trauma and literature, especially in U.S. fiction, and is the author of *Murdering Masculinities: Fantasies of Gender and Violence in the American Crime Novel* (2000) and *Gender, Race, and Mourning in American Modernism* (2011). Forter has edited a special issue of *The International Journal of Applied Psychoanalytic Studies* and is co-editor with Paul Allen Miller of *The Desire of the Analysts: Psychoanalysis and Cultural Criticism* (2008). His current project seeks to link the traumatic history of the Black Atlantic with that of the Indian Ocean/subcontinent, and is tentatively titled "Atlantic and Other Worlds: Critique and Utopia in Postcolonial Historical Fiction." Portions of this work have appeared in Raritan, *Contemporary Literature, and Slavery and Abolition*.

Herman Rapaport is Reynolds Professor of English at Wake Forest University and has published numerous articles on psychoanalysis, literature, and culture. *Between the Sign and the Gaze* (1994) considers psychoanalytic theories of fantasy and their application to film, literature, photography, and performance. His most recent book is *The Literary Theory Toolkit (2011)*.

Barry Stampfl is an associate professor of English and Comparative Literature at San Diego State University, Imperial Valley Campus. His primary research interest is exploring the relationship of two topics that hitherto have not been brought together: trauma and Charles S. Peirce's concept of abduction, a third form of logic responsible for the creation of new ideas. Stampfl has published essays on literary theory, Ernest Hemingway, Henry James, and Joseph Conrad in peer-reviewed journals such as *Modern Fiction Studies, Criticism, The Journal of Literary Theory,* and *The Henry James Review.* He has published four essays on trauma and abduction in issues of the Semiotic Society Yearbook/Annual (*Semiotics* 2008, 2009, 2011, 2013).

Laurie Vickroy is Professor of English at Bradley University. Her scholarship has focused on trauma studies, particularly the interrelationship of trauma, society, narrative, and identity. She is the author of *Trauma and Survival in Contemporary Fiction* and co-editor of *Critical Essays on the Works of Dorothy Allison* with Christine Blouch. She has written on a number of contemporary authors including Margaret Atwood, Toni Morrison, Dorothy Allison, Jeanette Winterson, Pat Barker, Marguerite Duras, Reinaldo Arenas, and Larry Heinemann. Her work has appeared in *Mosaic, The Comparatist, MELUS, Modern Language Studies, Women and Language, Obsidian II,* and *CEA Critic.*

Irene Visser is Senior Lecturer in Modern English Literature in the Department of English Language and Culture at the University of Groningen, The Netherlands. Her interests include the interdisciplinary relationships between literatures in English, postcolonial theory, cultural theory, and anthropology. Current research themes are trauma theory and postcoloniality, with a special interest in the developing relationality between cultural trauma studies and postcolonial literary studies. Recent publications have appeared in *Journal of Postcolonial Writing, English Studies, and The Contemporary Pacific.*

1
Literary Trauma Theory Reconsidered

Michelle Balaev

The field of trauma studies in literary criticism gained significant attention in 1996 with the publication of Cathy Caruth's *Unclaimed Experience: Trauma, Narrative, and History* and Kali Tal's *Worlds of Hurt: Reading the Literatures of Trauma*.[1] Early scholarship shaped the initial course of literary trauma theory by popularizing the idea of trauma as an unrepresentable event. A theoretical trend was introduced by scholars like Caruth, who pioneered a psychoanalytic poststructural approach that suggests trauma is an unsolvable problem of the unconscious that illuminates the inherent contradictions of experience and language. This Lacanian approach crafts a concept of trauma as a recurring sense of absence that sunders knowledge of the extreme experience, thus preventing linguistic value other than a referential expression. For Caruth's deconstructive criticism in particular, the model allows a special emphasis on linguistic indeterminacy, ambiguous referentiality, and aporia.[2] The unspeakable void became the dominant concept in criticism for imagining trauma's function in literature. This classic model of trauma appealed to a range of critics working outside of poststructuralism as well due to the notion of trauma's irreversible damage to the psyche. The assumed inherent neurobiological features of trauma that refuse representation and cause dissociation were significant to arguments that sought to emphasize the extent of profound suffering from an external source, whether that source is an individual perpetrator or collective social practice.[3] While the model is useful to forward claims regarding language's inability to locate the truth of the past, it was quickly accompanied by alternative models and methodologies that revised this foundational claim to suggest determinate value exists in traumatic experience.

The evolution of trauma theory in literary criticism might best be understood in terms of the changing psychological definitions of trauma as well as the semiotic, rhetorical, and social concerns that are part of the study of trauma in literature and society. The allure of the classic model exists in the pairing of neurobiological theories regarding the processes of the mind and memory together with semiotic theories regarding the processes of language, associations, and symbolization. Yet if the psychological basis of trauma is reexamined, then the classic model fails to fit the laws of structural and post-structural linguistics. This is to suggest that the traditional Lacanian approach only works if the psychological definition of trauma conforms to a particular theoretical recipe that draws from Freud to portray traumatic experience as a pre-linguistic event that universally causes dissociation. In many ways the thrill of the classic model is the apparent marriage of psychological laws that govern trauma's function to the semiotic laws that govern language's meaning.

The history of the concept of trauma is filled with contradictory theories and contentious debates, leaving both psychologists and literary scholars the ability to work with varying definitions of trauma and its effects.[4] Some alternative approaches start with a definition of trauma that allows for a range of representational possibilities. Alternative models challenge the classic model's governing principle that defines trauma in terms of universal characteristics and effects. Critics such as Leys, Cvetkovich, and myself who establish a psychological framework apart from the classic model thus produce different conclusions regarding trauma's influence upon language, perception, and society.[5] Beginning from a different psychological starting point for defining trauma than that established in the traditional approach thus allows critics a renewed focus on trauma's specificity and the processes of remembering. Understanding trauma, for example, by situating it within a larger conceptual framework of social psychology theories in addition to neurobiological theories will produce a particular psychologically informed concept of trauma that acknowledges the range of contextual factors that specify the value of the experience. This stance might therefore consider dubious the assertion of trauma's intrinsic dissociation.

Much of the newest criticism employs psychoanalytic and semiotic theories that restructure how we understand trauma's function in literature. Recent scholarship is more likely to explore the rhetorical uses of pathological dissociation or silence instead of working through psychological research that will unlikely provide a consensus regarding the empirical validity of trauma's universal pathologizing effects. By focusing on the rhetorical, semiotic, and social implications of trauma, contemporary critics have developed neoLacanian, neoFreudian, and new semiotic approaches. In this collection one finds a neoLacanian approach in Herman Rapaport's chapter, Greg Forter pursues a neoFreudian analysis, and Barry Stampfl elucidates a Peircean semiotic model. This shift in literary trauma theory has produced a set of critical practices that place more focus on the particular social components and cultural contexts of traumatic experience.

There are a number of ways to classify the different approaches that utilize alternative trauma models. These contemporary approaches are wide ranging but could be generally referenced under the umbrella term of the pluralistic model of trauma due to the plurality of theories and approaches employed. Many critics who address the rhetorical components of trauma explore both how and why traumatic experience is represented in literature by combining psychoanalytic theory with postcolonial theory or cultural studies. For example, critics like Rothberg and Forter work within a neoFreudian and postcolonial framework. Critics such as Luckhurst, Mandel, Yaeger, and Visser address the social and political implications of trauma within a variety of frameworks. In this collection Irene Visser employs a social psychology model of trauma within a postcolonial analysis, while chapters by Laurie Vickroy and Paul Arthur situate rhetorical concerns of trauma within a cultural studies framework.

The range of pluralistic models showcased in this collection moves away from the focus on trauma as unrepresentable and toward a focus on the specificity of trauma that locates meaning through a greater consideration of the social and cultural contexts of traumatic experience. The focus on the specificity of trauma is paired with an analysis that assumes greater skepticism regarding a universal pathological concept of trauma, thus generating more diverse views regarding the relationship between language and experience. Critics who diverge from the classic model may well be called revisionist. The revisionists, however, are not simply forging ahead along the path laid out by the early trauma theorists. Instead, revisionist critics either move away from Freud and Lacan altogether or take up certain Freudian or Lacanian theories while hewing a new theoretical paradigm in analyses that achieve a starkly different destination. In this fashion the scholars in the following chapters challenge the traditional concept of trauma as unspeakable by starting from a standpoint that concedes trauma's variability in literature and society.

Taking into consideration the variety of approaches to studying trauma in literature, this collection broadens the parameters of literary trauma theory by suggesting that extreme experience cultivates multiple responses and values. Trauma causes a disruption and reorientation of consciousness, but the values attached to this experience are influenced by a variety of individual and cultural factors that change over time. Rather than viewing literature as a closed psychoanalytic system, the scholars in this book employ theoretical approaches and critical practices that suggest trauma's function in literature and society is more varied and curious than first imagined by early theorists. The idea that knowledge of the past, not just any past but a particular type of past experience, can never be known or remains forever unclaimed by either the individual or society is being challenged by critical approaches that elucidate other possibilities regarding the value of trauma in terms of psychological, linguistic, and social mechanisms. The pluralistic model of trauma suggests that criticism may explore trauma as a subject that invites the study of the relationship between language, the psyche, and behavior without assuming the classic definition of trauma that asserts an unrepresentable and pathological universalism.

The collection thus demonstrates the methodological diversity within literary trauma theory that moves the field beyond a restrictive analysis by demonstrating trauma's varying representations. Criticism within this framework may function to acknowledge the impact of suffering on individuals and communities, to consider the role of literature in a violent world, or to analyze the ways language conveys extreme experiences. Some approaches in the following pages, as mentioned above, pursue a neoLacanian approach that extends the notion of trauma's silence in new directions. Still other approaches in the subsequent chapters challenge the central notion that trauma is a special pathogenic entity that uniquely ruptures knowledge, thus furthering the debate over the relationship between experience, language, and knowledge—a relationship that has vexed theorists for centuries.

Adhering to the dominant concept of trauma as a universal absence furthers certain ethical and aesthetic concerns but severely restricts the exploration of others. Understanding trauma beyond these monikers produces a greater range of questions regarding experience, representation, and value that this book explores. Authors here consider the multiple meanings of trauma that may be found within and between the spheres of personal and public worlds, thus providing views of both the individual and society, rather than consolidating the experience of trauma into a singular, silent ghost. The following chapters demonstrate the changing landscapes of literary trauma theory which has moved away from the early psychoanalytic methods to a theoretical position that advances a different set of issues, questions, and consequences that arose in part through the interdisciplinary approaches informed by psychoanalysis, cultural studies, and postcolonial theory. In a sense the book's critical reach suggests that literature is more diffuse, varied, and less programmatic than the classic model affords.

* * *

Trauma as the ultimate unrepresentable in the classic model maintains a tropological hegemony in literary criticism in part due to the theoretically appealing quality of this model to raise larger questions about the relationship between violence experienced by individuals and cultural groups, or the relationships between victim, perpetrator, and witness.[6] For example, in understanding trauma in Freud and Lacan's terms as both the return of the repressed and a sense of absence, Caruth writes in *Unclaimed Experience* that "trauma is not locatable in the simple violent or original event in an individual's past, but rather in the way that its very unassimilated nature—the way it is precisely *not known* in the first instance—returns to haunt the survivor later on" (4). Caruth's classic trauma model utilizes psychoanalytical referents for a literary criticism that establishes claims about the repressive, repetitive, and dissociative nature of trauma. The claim highlights one of the significant arguments in the book that connects individual trauma to cultural/historical trauma, which is achieved partly by relying upon a particular neurobiological approach in psychiatry that insists upon a causal definition of trauma.[7]

The innate causality between trauma and dissociation, the idea that an extreme experience directly produces a dissociative consciousness wherein the truth of the past is hidden, supports Caruth's claim that history functions the same as trauma insofar that "history can be grasped only in the very inaccessibility of its occurrence" (18). And further, "For history to be a history of trauma means that it is referential precisely to the extent that it is not fully perceived as it occurs" (18). At the end of the first chapter Caruth writes that "trauma is never simply one's own" (24). Although the book aims to create connections between the traumatized individual, society, and the historical past, this position rests upon the sacred assumption that trauma is inherently dissociative. The dissociative model of trauma here further supports the claim that "one's own trauma is tied up with the trauma of another" which forwards the notion of transhistorical trauma (8, 141). The claim that trauma "is not known in the first instance" and that trauma "returns to haunt the survivor later on" narrowly conceptualizes the psychological dimensions of trauma and the range of traumatic experience and responses. Psychological research indicates that amnesia, dissociation, or repression *may* be responses to trauma but they are not exclusive responses.[8]

Another problem within the classic model accompanies the dependence upon defining trauma as a deferred, recurrent wounding because this traumatic formulation removes determinate value from the experience. The theoretical binary of the traditional model rotates around an assumed paradox: "that the most direct seeing of a violent event may occur as an absolute inability to know it" (Caruth 92). This view disallows a specific determinacy of trauma on rhetorical, psychological, and social levels, while at the same time embraces an undying pathological influence on consciousness. One result of trauma's classic conundrum accordingly removes agency from the survivor by disregarding a survivor's knowledge of the experience and the self, which restricts trauma's variability and ignores the diverse values that change over time. In contrast, the pluralistic trauma model that allows determinate value and social specificity, even when a survivor like me had little agency in the moment of violence, thus acknowledges the variability of trauma in its definition and representations, and may emphasize the active potential for meaning in the moment of harm. Although the classic notion of trauma as a silent haunting or an absolute indecipherable is theoretically useful for certain ends, for example it underscores the damage done, the pluralistic approach highlights the ranging values and representations of trauma in literature and society, emphasizing not only the harm caused by a traumatic experience but also the many sources that inform the definitions, representations, and consequences of traumatic experience.

The different ends achieved by contemporary literary approaches underscore another limitation of the classic model that often moves away from the fact of the lived experience of trauma. Rather than claiming that language fails to represent trauma, pluralistic approaches consider linguistic relationships but not at the expense of forgetting that trauma occurs to actual people, in specific bodies, located within particular time periods and places. The above claim that "trauma is never simply one's own," and that "we are implicated in each other's trauma" (Caruth 24), produces a problem involving the assignment of responsibility for violence as well as understanding the relationship between direct and indirect action. The attempt to include everyone as victims of trauma runs the risk of including everyone as perpetrators. Although this was unlikely the intent, the claim veers toward universalizing the experience of trauma as well as collectivizing the instigator of violence, of which both implications serve to make anonymous the actor and recipient of violence. Obviously, actions produce consequences that are experienced directly or indirectly, but the danger of making collective the specific experience of a group or individual in the past is to create an unspecified action and effect as well as an indeterminate meaning of experience. Theoretically expanding the identification of action from a direct experience to indirect experience conflates cause and effect, and thus conceals questions of responsibility and agency.[9] Even with some of the theoretical restrictions of the classic model, it has been important for exploring the specter of a haunting absence and for renewing an interest in the limits and possibilities of language and literature.[10]

Contemporary pluralistic approaches in literary trauma theory are more likely to acknowledge both the neurobiological and social contexts of the experience, response, and narratives, as well as the possibilities that language can convey the variable meanings of trauma. Paying attention to the specificity of trauma does not exclude the fact that social, semantic, political, and economic factors are present in the experience and recollection of trauma. The knowledge that social practices are part of the context of even the most private violence differs from the claim that everyone is implicated in each other's (absent) trauma because the former position accepts the multiple contextual factors of trauma while also indicating that trauma is a lived experience, one that is identifiable to a greater or lesser degree.

If the larger social, political, and economic practices that influence violence are the background contexts or threads in the fabric of a traumatic experience in the first place, then trauma's meaning is locatable rather than permanently lost.

This collection demonstrates an array of theoretical approaches that include insights from social psychology, cultural studies, and digital culture, as well as from psychoanalytical, semiotic, and post-colonial theories. A single conceptualization of trauma will likely never fit the multiple and often contradictory depictions of trauma in literature because texts cultivate a wide variety of values that reveal individual and cultural understandings of the self, memory, and society. The scholars in this collection further the critical discourse on trauma, literature, and culture by demonstrating diverse methodologies of literary trauma theory. Each chapter indicates the need to examine the monolithic concept of trauma's inexpressibility in order to produce a more rigorous theory and criticism, thus expanding the interpretive potential of trauma theory. The varied values of trauma in literature and the critical regard for the classic model is a common thread among all chapters.

The book begins with an engagement of semiotic theories, followed by chapters that engage postcolonial and cultural theories. The chapters are thematically paired insofar that Stampfl and Rapaport's chapters advance semiotic concerns and poststructural theory, Forter and Visser's chapters extend the growing discourse in postcolonial theory and political contexts, and Vickroy and Arthur's chapters address trauma's social contexts within a cultural studies framework. In chapter two "Parsing the Unspeakable in the Context of Trauma," Barry Stampfl examines the status of trauma in literary criticism and demonstrates the significance of Peirce's theories on the abductive process of thought to understand traumatic experience in semiotic terms. Stampfl analyzes central contemporary concepts such as Mandel's rhetoricity of trauma and Forter's signification trauma alongside Peirce's abductive reasoning. Stampfl shows that Forter's non-punctual model of trauma that emphasizes the "retrodetermination" at work in a traumatic experience, complements Peirce's theories on abductive reasoning, which allows for a more nuanced understanding of the relationship between conciousness, trauma, and language. The chapter considers the formation of a unitary self and the "possibilities of recuperation and growth" in the moment of trauma.

In the third chapter, "Secondary Thinking and Trauma: Dostoevsky's *Notes from Underground*," Herman Rapaport analyzes trauma's signification in Fyodor Dostoevsky's novel. Rapaport amends Lacanian theory with André Green's theories on secondary thinking to argue that traumatic experience contains an active vitality that is represented as a "split discourse" which affirms a social identity despite mutual contradictions. Rapaport demonstrates that the "associative irradiation," which produces the double discourses of trauma, creates a recursive and malleable process of subjectivity in which the traumatized victim may "claim that experience over and over again." The recursive and repressed nature of trauma does not remove its expressive potential, but rather these elements allow trauma to be articulated.

Greg Forter in chapter four, "Colonial Trauma, Utopian Carnality, Modernist Form: Toni Morrison's *Beloved* and Arundhati Roy's *The God of Small Things*," extends the boundaries of postcolonial and psychoanalytical theories. Forter argues that novels employ modernist techniques to convey a concept of trauma, contrary to the traditional psychoanalytical view, in which remembrance of the past does not produce a repetitive foreclosure of knowledge but rather produces understanding and healing within a modern postcolonial reality. Forter's analysis indicates that the psyche is positioned dialectically to historical factors that "insist the condition of traumatic healing is a *social* amelioration by which the causes of past injuries cease to be operative in the present." The novels of Morrison and Roy indicate the equal importance of locating the traumatic past and utopian future which is a process embedded in a type of social amelioration of suffering.

Irene Visser argues in chapter five, "Trauma and Power in Postcolonial Literary Studies," that anthropological and sociological theories that emphasize the cultural-historical specificity of individual and collective trauma are better suited to analyze postcolonial literature because these theories allow for a differentiated understanding of trauma in indigenous narrative traditions. Employing postcolonial, sociological, and anthropolical theories, especially the grid-group theory of cultural thought styles by anthropologist Mary Douglas, Visser indicates that collective trauma, even when creating disruption, can also enable social solidarity and cultural identity rather than inherently fracturing the self. Through an analysis of Zakes Mda's novels *Ways of Dying* and *The Heart of Redness*, along with Witi Ihimaera's *The Whale Rider*, Visser demonstrates that trauma may function as a source of community when traumatic wounding is situated in relation to mechanisms of power and tribal authority.

In chapter six, "Voices of Survivors in Contemporary Fiction," Laurie Vickroy explores the social contexts of traumatic experiences and the narrative strategies writers employ in trauma fiction to engage readers in the ethical dilemmas of trauma. Informed by cognitive psychology, narrative and cultural theories, Vickroy argues that trauma in fiction produces three significant effects: the awareness of the multidimensionality of an extreme experience and particularly the social influences that shape the survivor's personality, the textual modeling of the social aspects of the individual's mind, and the ethics of reading that compel a compassionate correspondence between reader and survivor. The chapter demonstrates these findings through an analysis of novels by Margaret Atwood and Jane Smiley.

Paul Arthur in chapter seven, "Memory and Commemoration in the Digital Present," argues that online memorials reveal the gaining importance of digital media in performing social rituals that allow new freedom and forms of experience. Arthur considers the contemporary depictions of trauma that move from the physical sites where emotional suffering is expressed, such as a gravesite, to a modern internet space for feeling and communicating traumatic loss. The chapter shows that memory and trauma are conceived in various digital mediums and specific online sites to allow for the "normalization of death through continuing bonds." The essay considers the ways that cyberspace memorials (such as Facebook and MySpace) establish a type of digital self and digital trauma that allows the experience of loss to be attenuated in an ongoing past that paradoxically allows for a sense of closure of traumatic memories and a limit to the grieving process. Trauma is understood by locating its meaning in the new space of the internet—cyber space—that redefines the meaning of traumatic memory and its impact on identity.

The collection signals a shift from the field's inception when it first imagined trauma as inherently indecipherable to a view of trauma as multiply configured with diverse representations in literature and far reaching effects in culture. Today literary trauma theory displays an expansive range of values by allowing the definition of trauma to be contested. The contradictions of trauma reflect the cultural ambivalence regarding the meaning of trauma in society, how to evaluate the aspects of a lived experience of trauma that are both idiosyncratic and to a certain extent collective, and the ongoing theoretical debate regarding trauma's meanings in literature. The variety of theoretical models and critical practices of literary trauma theory that are found in this book demonstrate the broadening borders of this innovative field.

Notes

1. Elaine Scarry's *The Body in Pain: The Making and Unmaking of the World* (1985) and Caruth's anthology *Trauma: Explorations in Memory* (1995) were significant as well.
2. Freud's traumatic repetition, Lacan's absence, and deMan's distended referentiality figure prominently in Caruth's *Unclaimed Experience*. See also Shoshana Felman and Dori Laub's *Testimony: Crises of Witnessing in Literature, Psychoanalysis, and History* (1992) for a psychoanalytic poststructural model.
3. See Deborah Horvitz's *Literary Trauma: Sadism, Memory, and Sexual Violence in American Women's Fiction* (2000) and J. Brooks Bouson's *Quiet As It's Kept: Shame, Trauma, and Race in the Novels of Toni Morrison* (1999).
4. See Ruth Leys, *Trauma: A Genealogy* (Chicago: Chicago UP, 2000). See also Mark Micale and Paul Lerner, *Traumatic Pasts: History, Psychiatry, and Trauma in the Modern Age, 1870–1930* (New York: Cambridge University Press, 2001). See in sociology Kai Erikson's *Everything in Its Path: Destruction of Community in the Buffalo Creek Flood* (1976).
5. For example, Ann Cvetkovich's *An Archive of Feelings* begins with a skeptical regard for the idea that trauma is inherently pathological to argue through a cultural studies and feminist framework that traumatic experience is not relegated to the catastrophic, pathologic, or unspoken.
6. See for example the work of such scholars as Shoshana Felman, Dori Laub, J. Brooks Bouson, Suzette Henke, and Deborah Horvitz. See also *The Future of Trauma Theory* (Oxon: Routledge, 2014).
7. The causality between trauma and dissociation, trauma and repression, or trauma and amnesia has been contested by psychiatrists and psychologists starting with Pierre Janet's doubt about his early conclusions to current psychological debates articulated by Laurence Kirmayer, Bessel van der Kolk, and Richard McNally. A thorough analysis of this debate can be found in Ruth Ley's *Trauma: A Genealogy* (Chicago: University of Chicago, 2000). See Mark Micale and Paul Lerner's *Traumatic Pasts: History, Psychiatry, and Trauma in the Modern Age, 1870–1930*. New York: Cambridge University Press, 2001. See, for example, Bethany Brand, et al., "Where Are We Going? An Update on Assessment, Treatment, and Neurobiological Research on Dissociative Disorders as We Move

Toward the *DSM-5" Journal of Trauma and Dissociation* 13.1 (2012): 9–31. See Ellert Nijenhuis and Otto van der Hart, "Dissociation and Trauma: A New Definition and Comparison with Previous Formulations," *Journal of Trauma and Dissociation* 12.4 (2011): 416–445. See Judith Herman, *Trauma and Recovery* (New York: Basic Books, 1992).

8. See for example the research of Laurence Kirmayer, Frederic Bartlett, Colin Ross, Craig Piers, and Derek Summerfield. See John Briere and Catherine Scott, *Principles of Trauma Therapy: A Guide of Symptoms, Evaluation, and Treatment* (Thousand Oaks: SAGE, 2006). See Salah Qureshi, et al, "Does PTSD Impair Cognition beyond the Effect of Trauma?" *The Journal of Neuropsychiatry and Clinical Neurosciences* 23.1 (2011): 16–28. See Richard McNally, et al, "Does Early Psychological Intervention Promote Recovery from Posttraumatic Stress?" *Psychological Science in the Public Interest* 4.2 (2003): 45–79. See Nigel Hunt, *Memory, War, Trauma* (Cambridge, Cambridge University Press, 2010).

9. To a certain extent the conflated claims act as a wish fulfillment to imagine a better world where the solitary experience of victimization could be shared with others. The results of violent acts, however, are distinctly different for the victim than the perpetrator, and the individual survivor endures a specific violence within a particular sequence of actions which produce certain consequences.

10. Cathy Caruth's recent publication *Literature in the Ashes of History* (Baltimore: Johns Hopkins University Press, 2013) continues exploring these issues.

Bibliography

Bartlett, F.C. *Remembering: A Study in Experimental and Social Psychology.* New York: Macmillan, 1932.

Becker, David. "The Deficiency of the Concept of Posttraumatic Stress Disorder When Dealing with Victims of Human Rights Violations." *Beyond Trauma: Cultural and Societal Dynamics.* Eds Rolf Kleber, Charles Figley, and Berthold Gersons. New York: Plenum Press, 1995. 99–110.

Bouson, J. Brooks. *Quiet as It's Kept: Shame, Trauma, and Race in the Novels of Toni Morrison.* New York: State University of New York Press, 1999.

Briere, John and Catherine Scott. *Principles of Trauma Therapy: A Guide of Symptoms, Evaluation, and Treatment.* Thousand Oaks: SAGE, 2006.

Brand, Bethany, Ruth Lanius, Eric Vermetten, Richard Lowenstein, and David Spiegel. "Where Are We Going? An Update on Assessment, Treatment, and Neurobiological Research on Dissociative Disorders as We Move Toward the *DSM-5" Journal of Trauma and Dissociation* 13.1 (2012): 9–31.

Caruth, Cathy. Ed. *Trauma: Explorations in Memory.* Baltimore: Johns Hopkins University Press, 1995.

Caruth, Cathy. *Unclaimed Experience: Trauma, Narrative, and History.* Baltimore: Johns Hopkins University Press, 1996.

Culbertson, Roberta. "Embodied Memory, Transcendence, and Telling: Recounting Trauma, Re-establishing the Self." *New Literary History* 26.1 (1995): 169–195.

Cvetkovich, Ann. *An Archive of Feelings: Trauma, Sexuality, and Lesbian Public Cultures.* Raleigh: Duke University Press, 2003.

Deprince, Anne and Jennifer Freyd. "Dissociative Tendencies, Attention, and Memory." *Psychological Science* 10.5 (2000): 449.

Erikson, Kai. *A New Species of Trouble: The Human Experience of Modern Disasters.* New York: W.W. Norton, 1994.

———. *Everything in Its Path: Destruction of Community in the Buffalo Creek Flood.* New York: Simon and Schuster, 1976.

Felman, Shoshana and Dori Laub. *Testimony: Crises of Witnessing in Literature, Psychoanalysis, and History.* New York: Routledge, 1992.

Forter, Greg. *Melancholy Manhood: Gender, Race, and the Inability to Mourn in American Literary Modernism. Cambridge: Cambridge University Press, 2011.*

———. *Murdering Masculinities: Fantasies of Gender and Violence in the American Crime Novel.* New York: New York University Press, 2000.

Granofsky, Ronald. *The Trauma Novel: Contemporary Symbolic Depictions of Collective Disaster.* New York: Peter Lang, 1995.

Hartman, Geoffrey. "On Traumatic Knowledge and Literary Studies." *New Literary History* 26.3 (1995): 537–563.

———. *The Longest Shadow: In the Aftermath of the Holocaust.* Bloomington: Indiana University Press, 1996.

Henke, Suzette. *Shattered Subjects: Trauma and Testimony in Women's Life-Writing.* New York: St. Martin's Press, 1998.

Herman, Judith. *Trauma and Recovery.* New York: Basic Books, 1992. Horvitz, Deborah. *Literary Trauma: Sadism, Memory, and Sexual Violence in American Women's Fiction.* Albany, SUNY Press, 2000.

Hungerford, Amy. *The Holocaust of Texts: Genocide, Literature, and Personification.* Chicago: University of Chicago Press, 2003.

Janet, Pierre. *Psychological Healing: A Historical and Clinical Study.* (1919) Trans. E. Paul and C. Paul. New York: Macmillan, 1976.

Kirmayer, Laurence. "Landscapes of Memory: Trauma, Narrative, and Dissociation." *Tense Past: Cultural Essays in Trauma and Memory.* Eds Paul Antze and Michael Lambek. New York: Routledge, 1996. 173–198.

Leys, Ruth. *Trauma: A Genealogy.* Chicago: University of Chicago Press, 2000.

Luckhurst, Roger. *The Trauma Question.* London: Routledge, 2008.

Mandel, Naomi. *Against the Unspeakable.* Charlottesville, University of Virginia Press, 2006.

McNally, Richard. *Remembering Trauma.* Cambridge: Belknap Press, 2003.

McNally, Richard, Richard Bryant, and Anke Ehlers. "Does Early Psychological Intervention Promote Recovery from Posttraumatic Stress?" *Psychological Science in the Public Interest* 4.2 (2003): 45–79.

Micale, Mark and Paul Lerner. *Traumatic Pasts: History, Psychiatry, and Trauma in the Modern Age, 1870–1930.* New York: Cambridge University Press, 2001.

Nijenhuis, Ellert and Otto van der Hart. "Dissociation and Trauma: A New Definition and Comparison with Previous Formulations," *Journal of Trauma and Dissociation* 12.4 (2011): 416–445.

Piers, Craig. "Remembering Trauma: A Characterological Perspective." *Trauma and Memory*. Eds Linda Williams and Victoria Banyard. Thousand Oaks: SAGE, 1999. 57–67.

Qureshi, Salah, Mary Long, Major Bradshaw, Jeffrey Pyne, Kathy Magruder, Timothy Kimbrell, Teresa Hudson, Ali Jawaid, Paul E. Schulz, and Mark E. Kunik. "Does PTSD Impair Cognition Beyond the Effect of Trauma?" *The Journal of Neuropsychiatry and Clinical Neurosciences* 23.1 (2011): 16–28.

Ross, Colin. *The Trauma Model: A Solution to the Problem of Comorbidity in Psychiatry*. Richardson: Manitou Communications Press, 2000.

Rothberg, Michael. "Decolonizing Trauma Studies: A Response." *Studies in the Novel* 40.1/2 (2008): 224–34.

———. "Race, Visuality, and Identification in Fanon and Kluger." *Wasafiri* 24.1 (2009): 13–20.

Scarry, Elaine. *The Body in Pain: The Making and Unmaking of the World*. New York: Oxford University Press, 1985.

Summerfield, Derek. "Addressing Human Response to War and Atrocity: Major Challenges in Research and Practices and the Limitations of Western Psychiatric Models." *Beyond Trauma: Cultural and Societal Dynamics*. Eds Rolf Kleber, Charles Figley, and Berthold Gersons. New York: Plenum Press, 1995. 17–29.

Tal, Kali. *Worlds of Hurt: Reading the Literatures of Trauma*. New York: Cambridge University Press, 1996.

Van der Kolk, Bessel A., Alexander McFarlane, Lars Weisaeth. *Traumatic Stress: The Effects of Overwhelming Experience on Mind, Body, and Society*. New York: Guilford P, 1987.

Vickroy, Laurie. *Trauma and Survival in Contemporary Fiction*. Charlottesville: University of Virigina Press, 2002.

Yaeger, Patricia. "Testimony without Intimacy." *Poetics Today* 27.2 (Summer 2006).

Young, Allan. *The Harmony of Illusions: Inventing Post-Traumatic Stress Disorder*. Princeton: Princeton University Press, 1995.

2

Parsing the Unspeakable in the Context of Trauma

Barry Stampfl

The unspeakable is an ancient, highly serviceable rhetorical device classically associated with romantic love, the sacred, and the sublime. Formally, its identifying feature is the explicit admission of the inadequacy of language in a given case. The lover insists that words cannot describe the beauty of the loved one. The religious poet runs changes on the inability of language to do justice to the divine. The majestic mountain range cannot be adequately described in human speech.

In our own modern/postmodern era, the trope of the unspeakable has attained particular prominence within trauma studies. In the wake of Adorno's influential pronouncement that there can be no poetry after Auschwitz, it has positively reigned in Holocaust studies, from which vantage it has exerted a pervasive influence in the new literary trauma studies descending from, among others, Shoshanna Felman and Dori Laub (1992), Cathy Caruth (1995, 1996), Marianne Hirsch (1997), and Geoffrey Hartman (1995). Of course, even when the distinctive emphases of this interdisciplinary initiative were still in process of being shaped, voices already were raised—by Dominic LaCapra (2001) and Michael Rothberg (2000), for example—to argue that the horror of the Holocaust and of other overwhelming events *can* be researched, mentally digested, and expressed. Still, the alleged unrepresentability of the traumatic event widely was accepted as a starting point of discussion, and has continued to be regarded as an intellectually respectable position even by those who disagreed with it.

Today, as we traverse the second decade of the twenty-first century, the larger project of literary trauma studies seems to be reaching a crisis that in part is signaled by changing critical attitudes with respect to the unspeakable. On one hand, the unspeakable increasingly is viewed as being linked with—and perhaps even as shorthand for—a constellation of positions definitive of the once provocative new trauma theory of the 1990s, now ossified into the received wisdom of a dominant paradigm. A more-or-less measured impatience with this paradigm is evident in much recent work in trauma studies.[1] On the other hand, despite sometimes scorching criticism, the unspeakable remains very much with us, just as do assumptions regarding trauma bequeathed to us by scholars such as Caruth, Felman, and Hartman. Thus, even as Roger Luckhurst seeks to question and revise the definition of the trauma novel pioneered by Anne Whitehead (2004) and Laurie Vickroy (2002), he continues to retain as a component of his larger approach their emphasis on the narrative transmission of the deferred impact of the traumatic event, attesting to the continuing robustness of a theory imbued with the unspeakable (2008: 87–116).[2] How, then, should we evaluate the significance of the unspeakable as it has figured in the context of trauma? And what can we imagine to be the future of this trope?

The key to the exploration of these questions in my view is the realization that we err from the start when we conceive of the unspeakable in the singular: as *the* unspeakable, as if there were only one. My starting point definition of the unspeakable as a trope, a particular kind of linguistic expression, is meant to be suggestive of the broad range of meanings potentially associated with this bit of rhetorical strategy. But "trauma" itself is the name of a realm of experience large and diverse enough to require a pluralistic conception of the unspeakable, one that recognizes the trope's alternative or even antithetical possibilities. In this essay, I will seek to begin the making of this inventory by zeroing in on the commonsensical idea that the unspeakable may be merely a phase in the process of traumatization, not its predetermined endpoint. Were it not for the accumulated weight of literary trauma studies' insistence on the unspeakable as trauma's distinctive, core characteristic, this thought would probably seem quite obvious, especially since all I wish to suggest is that traumatization need not *necessarily* conclude in a state of involuntary, deeply conflicted silence. As it is, the taking up of this seemingly simple thought is replete with theoretical complications, which I will explore in three stages.

First, I will consider at some length a text that articulates contemporary grievances against the unspeakable with maximal force and focus, Naomi Mandel's *Against the Unspeakable* (2006). Better than anyone else, Mandel makes clear the extent of the dominion of the unspeakable in trauma theory, even as she repudiates this ascendance and seeks to move beyond it. Very much taking her argument to heart but worrying that it falls prey to oversimplification in its description of the role of the unspeakable, I move on to consider an alternative theoretical framework proposed by Greg Forter apropos his readings of William Faulkner. Seeking to provide an alternative to what often is thought of as the Caruthian understanding of trauma assumed by the dominant paradigm, Forter elaborates a two-phase model of "signification trauma" that complicates and diversifies our understanding of the unspeakable. Finally, building on ideas from Forter but breaking from the psychoanalytic which informs his thinking, I briefly will describe a way of theorizing trauma in terms of Charles Peirce's concept of abduction. This semiotic perspective allows us to further elaborate the role of the unspeakable in the context of trauma.

* * *

While many have criticized the unspeakable, Naomi Mandel stands alone for putting this theme at the center of a sustained inquiry ambitiously working out a new path for contemporary trauma studies. In *Against the Unspeakable: Complicity, the Holocaust, and Slavery in America* (2006), Mandel cuts through "Holocaust piety" (Rose 1996: 41) in order to provide a rather fierce judgment: that those who wield the rhetoric of the unspeakable are both showing off and putting themselves on, posing moralistically while taking the easy way out. Though her argument is complex and sophisticated, defying easy summary and including thoughtful caveats that ought to be taken seriously, Mandel undeniably is firm in concluding that evoking the unspeakable in the context of trauma simply is not respectable.

I find that I have mixed feeling as I try to respond to this. On one hand, I suspect that Mandel is basically right in her negative description of how the unspeakable actually functions in many instances of its employment within the discourse of trauma. I say this all the more readily since, having had my consciousness raised by her book, I am able to recognize in my own mind a kind of unholy joy rising from the contemplation of the unspeakable. On the other hand, however, in some respects her argument appears to me to be flawed. It occurs to me that what Mandel denounces as the unspeakable would be better understood as a special case of the unspeakable: the unspeakable in arrested development, as it were.

Asking what it is that the unspeakable enables writers, artists and critics to *do*, Mandel identifies the taking of "the moral high ground" as its underlying purpose (2006: 23, 64). The rhetorical evocation of the limits of language in the context of atrocity becomes, according to Mandel, an expression of solidarity with the suffering of victims. This is because one of the assumptions underlying the unspeakable specifically in the context of atrocity is that "the cognitive categories marshaled to make sense of horror inevitably misrepresent it; this misrepresentation can do violence, cause harm, or perpetuate injury—effects that call for critical intervention" (4). Moreover, "this reverence toward the victim's subjective experience is wedded to an analogous reverence toward history's objective fact" (6), as in the injunction against ever forgetting the Holocaust. Combining, then, the most exquisite sensitivity and respect for the inner world of the wounded ones with an austere insistence upon the impartial study of the events which wounded them, the unspeakable subtly and yet powerfully imparts to its employers an aura of righteousness. Such compassionate and yet rigorous thinkers must be morally good. The absence of such commingled compassion and rigor, by contrast, would be bad. Thus, the presence or absence of rhetorical gestures deferentially acknowledging the limits of language becomes the criterion which determines the moral authority, or lack thereof, of commentary upon atrocity.

Overlooked in this ascendance is the trope's essential duplicity. Mandel writes, "What is unspeakable evokes the privileges and problems inherent in speech while actively distancing itself from them, performing a rhetorical sleight of hand that simultaneously gestures toward and away from the complex ethical negotiations that representing atrocity entails" (5). Seeming to figure as the ultimate instrument for facing-up-to and coming-to-grips-with, the trope of the unspeakable actually gives permission to turn away. For Mandel, this duplicity becomes clear in two of the trope's interrelated implications: its tendency to suppress awareness of the body, the suffering corporeal presence of the victims of atrocity, and its finessing of our sense of complicity, our recognition "that all of us, literary authors and critics alike, are the producers and products of our culture and hence always already complicit in the ugliest aspects of our histories" (24). The role of the body is minimized when the unspeakable turns its searchlight on the question of what can or cannot be expressed, a redirection of attention that effects an unintended sublimation, causing the physical to retreat to the background.[3] Complicity is evaded when the artist/critic mounts to the moral high ground seductively offered by the unspeakable. We rise up like spirits from the spectacle of degradation, our wholeness and purity in inverse proportion to the violation and fragmentation that we imaginatively witness/don't witness via the trope of the unspeakable.

For what it is worth, I am willing to testify to my own susceptibility to this syndrome. Looking back now after reading Mandel's book, I see that my reaction to an essay written by Lisa Garbus, "The Unspeakable Stories of *Shoah* and *Beloved*," may be taken to illustrate Mandel's point. When I first encountered Garbus' essay shortly after its publication in 1999 it seemed to me to crystallize the attractions of the concept of trauma for literary interpretation and theory, attractions inextricable from the trope of the unspeakable. In Garbus' discussion, the unspeakable provides not only the overarching explanation for the structural features of Lanzmann's film and Morrison's novel but is central to the definition of literature in general. As Garbus quotes from Roland Barthes: "We refuse to come to terms with the absolute lack of parallelism between the real and language, and it is this refusal, perhaps as old as language itself, that produces—as an endless agitation—literature" (1999: 53–54; Barthes 1978: 21–22). Positing the unspeakable quality of the real as the paradoxical necessary condition for literary expression in general provides a framework for Garbus to seamlessly interweave with her readings of Lanzmann and Morrison the story of her own real-life visit to Poland to visit the place of her mother's suffering as a child-victim of the Holocaust. The surfacing of the personal here, so characteristic of trauma-centric literary criticism, for me exponentially multiplied the emotional impact of Garbus' essay, which otherwise might have seemed to be a relatively bloodless exercise, only just another fabrication of clever readings for ambiguous texts. Reading Garbus' essay in the last hours of the twentieth century, then, I seemed to discover in the unspeakable a kind of magic carpet, an instrument for passing smoothly and convincingly from the universal to the specific, for connecting with history—at last—while remaining firmly within the domain of literary study, and at the same time honoring the claims of both heart and mind. In the flush of these appreciative realizations, any worries about my own personal complicity with the ugliness of culture, American slavery, or German genocide, certainly were driven far from my thoughts.

Thus, I cop to Mandel's charge: I got high on the unspeakable. But though willing to plead guilty for myself, I would exonerate Lisa Garbus, the author of the essay I found to be so inspiring. For even though there is, palpably, a vein of exhilaration running through her essay, for her the dynamic of the situation must be understood quite differently. As the child of a Holocaust survivor, she is engaged in a process of recovery crucial to her own psychological well-being; the exhilaration in her essay, then, I read not as the righteousness that comes from taking the moral high ground but as the relief—verging, perhaps, upon joy—attendant upon escaping from a potentially imprisoning psychological low ground.

In making this distinction between victim (Garbus) and witness-reader (myself), I reiterate an insight developed by Mandel when she contrasts "the survivor's inability or unwillingness to speak, on the one hand, and the rhetorical work of the unspeakable, on the other" (Mandel 2006: 100). Clearly, in Mandel's moral calculus, the former is far less problematic than is the latter:

> For if the Holocaust's survivor's experience is, by her, unspeakable (which is different from claiming that the Holocaust itself is unspeakable), survivor testimony to that experience speaks the unspeakable, a speech informed by acute silences and epistemo-logical gaps that reflect the impact of a traumatic experience on the speaker's psyche. *Representations* of survivor testimony are repre-sentations of such speech, not of the (presumably unrepresentable) Holocaust, not of the (too often sacralized) survivor. They stand, therefore, in a different relation to representation's limits than the evocations of the unspeakable I have examined thus far, in which the limits of language, representation, and thought were assumed to be objective qualities of the subject matter, not the product of its apprehension (100; Mandel's emphasis).

But a generalized sense of the Holocaust's ineffability, I would argue, cannot be neatly severed from the testimony of victims; rather, the intuition of event-specific unspeakability grows out of, and is supported by, the accumulation of individual narratives. This is to say that Holocaust victims, as well as survivors of other atrocities, *typically* insist that words cannot convey the enormity of their experiences. Nor is there any easy way of disambiguating the blurred lines intrinsic to the victim/witness distinction. For victims naturally are crucially concerned with bearing witness to their own victimizations, while witnesses separated from atrocity by time and space nonetheless may be vulnerable to secondary traumatization.[4] In short, while it is more problematic to say "The Holocaust is unspeakable" than it is to say "I cannot tell you what happened to me at the Nazi death camp," the two statements are obviously closely related. Speaking about the two statements as if they were qualitatively different—and then rejecting the first while honoring the second—does not make a lot of sense, and this incoherence is writ large, finally, in the elaboration of Mandel's argument as a recommendation to "eschew" or "abandon" the unspeakable (24, 219). For the question thus arises: if we *were* to relinquish rhetorical evocations of the unspeakable, would this not be detrimental to our attempts to investigate, communicate, and commemorate traumatic events? No, it would not, answers Mandel, for alternative rhetorical strategies articulating "an ethics of complicity" in opposition to the unspeakable show promise of being "both ethically and critically productive" (24).

But I would insist that it is important to remain focused on the survivor's predicament, succinctly described by Judith Herman as "a conflict between the will to deny horrible events and the will to proclaim them aloud" (Herman 1992: 1), even if alternative rhetorical strategies prove to be ever so productive. In the context of the survivor's predicament the unspeakable's potentially positive function as an enabler and enlarger of cognitive/affective response in the aftermath of trauma most clearly comes into focus. For, of course, the traumatized survivor evoking the unspeakable in fact has begun to speak. Expressing the thought that the experience in question cannot be conveyed in words feels like a natural or even necessary first step: how else break the silence? The rhetorical trope of the unspeakable serves to lower expectations in auditors—who are warned not to expect a snappy, "well-shaped" account—while in the same breath also points to the overwhelming, soul-destroying quality of the experiences that have been undergone: compared to which, what could be more salient? Moreover, the assertion that language cannot possibly do justice to the enormity of atrocity in itself creates a tension likely to summon forth further attempts at exploration and communication. Evocations of the unspeakable often give rise to paradoxical attempts to speak the unspeakable, as when the lover, after all, continues to try to describe the loved one, even though (or because) he/she has just said it cannot be done, or when the seeker after the divine produces parables or allegories in an attempt to indicate indirectly and partially what cannot be directly and fully comprehended. A key aspect to be considered in the evaluation of the unspeakable in the context of trauma, then, must be the nature of the larger cognitive/affective process of which a particular evocation of the unspeakable makes up a part. The unspeakable Mandel identifies arguably deserves to be rejected because it has become a mandatory destination, and thus a kind of conceptual stagnant pool. But recourse to the unspeakable may make up an important way station in the course of an ongoing cognitive/affective process leading to the reintegration of the traumatic event.

In the next section, I will review a recent theoretical intervention performed by Greg Forter by way of solidifying a sense of the unspeakable's plurality in the context of trauma. Forter develops a two-phase of model of traumatization based on Freud's early work in two closely related essays.[5] Because Forter's model neatly catches characteristic emphases of the new revisionist thinking in (post) modern trauma studies, it makes a natural point of reference for my inquiry. What becomes of the unspeakable when we think of it in terms of Forter's revisionist two-phase approach?

* * *

Forter takes his point of departure from what he calls Caruth's "punctual" model of trauma, which he sees as being derived from Freud's later theorizing inspired by the carnage of the First World War and featuring repetitions enforced by the death drive. According to Forter, Caruth's theory of trauma stipulates "a punctual blow to the psyche that overwhelms its functioning, disables its defenses, and absents it from direct contact with the brutalizing blow itself" (2011: 98–99; 2007: 259). Such assaults can be delivered only by "historical events of … singularity, magnitude and horror" (2007: 259; 2011: 98), real-life catastrophes epitomized by the Holocaust. Again, this is a conception of trauma that evidently is imbued with the unspeakable, insofar as the absenting of the psyche from direct contact with the brutalizing event renders the event unrepresentable to the traumatized one.

While some notable critics of this dominant paradigm have responded to Caruth's influential model with downright ferocity,[6] Forter, by contrast, does not reject it wholly; applied to singular, horrific events, it produces "accounts of historical violence that are both socially specific and psychologically astute" (2011: 98; 2007: 259).[7] However, pivoting from expressions of appreciation, Forter quickly moves to consideration of the punctual model's "central limitation" (2011: 100): its inability to account for "those forms of trauma that are *not* punctual, that are more mundanely catastrophic than such spectacular instances of violence as the Holocaust" (2011: 100; 2007: 260). By way of correcting this deficiency, Forter proposes a model extracted from Freud's early thinking emphasizing that the sexual trauma originates from the witnessing of the primal scene. In this account, a specific historical occurrence that could not be comprehended by the infant at the time of its occurrence becomes— subsequent to the repression of the polymorphous sexual energies of infancy and their reconstitution, in puberty, around the genitals— "retrospectively significant and potentially pathogenic" (2007: 263). As Forter describes this second phase:

> A word, an observation, a sensory perception, a feeling—something in a person's present life sets off a chain of associations that lead to the first scene's unconscious "understanding," giving rise to intense anxiety precisely by making that scene *significant* and rendering it traumatic *for the first time.*

> (2007: 264, Forter's emphases)

Far from being an extraordinarily terrifying event akin to armed assault or train wreck, the original occurrence may not even have been experienced as unpleasurable—until its retrodetermination,[8] in the second moment, as a distinctly traumatic event.

Thus, in its way Forter's approach is well-attuned to the postcolonial turn in contemporary trauma studies, as exemplified, for example, by Michael Rothberg's *Multidirectional Memory* (2009), Stef Craps and Gert Buelens' essay on Michael Chabon's *The Final Solution* (2011), and, indeed, much of the special issue of *Studies in the Novel* on the topic of

"Postcolonial Trauma Novels" that appeared in 2008.[9] Even though Forter's focus on canonical American modernism—and, of course, his allegiance to traditional western thought leader Sigmund Freud— might seem to be incompatible with the project of "decolonizing trauma studies" (Rothberg 2008), Forter puts his finger on the very issue that Rothberg identifies as being of utmost importance to the decolonizing revisionists: the chasm between "an event based model of trauma" versus one which could "account for ongoing, everyday forms of traumatizing violence" (Rothberg 2008: 226). Forter's two phase model is precisely an attempt to answer the demand for a theoretical alternative that is sensitive to the mundane, quotidian processes of traumatization that Laura Brown influentially described as being "insidious" (Brown 1995). Forter's compatibility with postcolonial trauma studies is validated, moreover, by his deter-mination generally to assert trauma's social, political, and cultural dimensions. Boldly reinterpreting the witnessing of the primal scene as "nothing less than a way of describing the more or less pathogenic confrontation that each of us must make" with "the emphatically social inscription in the psyche of power relations that precede any given self" (266), Forter understands the model of trauma he proposes to depict the initiation of every individual into cultural systems of patriarchal and racial oppression.

   This rehearsing of Forter's intervention leads to my question: what happens to our understanding of the unspeakable when we attempt to follow its vicissitudes in the Forter model? For starters, we must appreciate that the answer is not simple. First, as we have seen, Forter does not deny the relevance of the punctual model to traumatic reactions inspired by extreme, singular events, so the Caruthian concept of deferred impact, with its intimate linkage to the unspeakable, remains viable in Forter's view with respect to such terrifying phenomena as train wrecks and armed assaults. But, sec-ond, even within the two-phase model devised by Forter to supple-ment the punctual model, the fate of the unspeakable is by no means clear. Let us try to break down the possibilities. What becomes of the unspeakable in each of the two phases of Forter's non-punctual model?

   Since the first phase initiated by observation of the primal scene is one of dormancy, there can be no description of the causes of psy-chic disturbance during this period. This is true whether we think of the primal scene in terms of Freud's definition (the child's first observation of real or imagined sexual intercourse, especially by parents) or in Forter's socialized version (the primal scene as an allegory of "*history*," meaning of "the forces of signification and sexuality that ... come to inhabit the child before h/she has the equipment for making sense of them" [2011: 105]). Clearly, the period of dormancy is incompatible with the rhetorical definition of the unspeakable as the formal expression of the thought, "Language cannot express the reality I have in mind." There can be no struggle to do verbal justice to a "reality" that has not yet become an object of attention, that evidently does not even particularly stand out in memory. At the same time, in a different sense one might say that the quality of being unspeakable positively reigns during the period of dormancy, as the trauma-to-be "gestates" in the psyche of the one-in-process-of-being-traumatized. The real life causes of the trauma-in-progress are never so inaccessible to consciousness, conceptualization, and linguistic expression as during this period.

Similarly, but even more radically, the second moment in Forter's two-phase non-punctual model arguably bears a mixed relationship to the trope of the unspeakable. For, on the face of it, it might seem that Forter directly attacks the assumption that unspeakability makes up the core of traumatization when he makes *significance* the *sine qua non* of non-punctual traumas. Signification would seem to be the opposite of that absenting of the psyche from the brutalizing event which Caruth defines as the heart of trauma; through signification, however faultily, the psyche gains a kind of access to the meaning of the event. Thus, when Forter observes that the non-punctual trauma is not really traumatic until the second phase of his two-phase model— in Freud, the oedipalized moment of retrodetermining epiphany—he seems to make *realization* the core of trauma. A moment's reflection will convince us, however, that the conception of trauma as a darkly transformative epiphany is not necessarily antithetical to the idea of the unspeakable but may actually be quite exquisitely compatible with it. For—again—if we think of the unspeakable as a trope, a certain way of speaking, we must recognize that the unspeakable is always already (paradoxically) part of a universe of discourse, a form of signification.

Forter's references to episodes of retrodetermination in Faulkner's novels help us to approach this paradox more closely. Here in the interest of space I will review only Forter's climactic example: the "affront" offered to young Thomas Sutpen at the door of a local plantation. An adolescent boy who has lived in the socially and racially stratified Tidewater area of Virginia for only two years, Sutpen is sent to the plantation by his father one day to deliver a message. He is rebuffed by a black house-slave at the door for using the front entrance, and warned never to make that mistake again. Faulkner evokes Sutpen's turbulent inner experience of the occurrence as follows:

> Before the monkey ... who came to the door had finished saying what he did, he [Sutpen] seemed to kind of dissolve and a part of him turn and rush back through the two years they had lived there like when you pass through a room fast and look at all the objects in it and you turn and go back through the room again and look at all the objects in it from the other side and you find out you had never seen them before, rushing back through those two years and seeing a dozen things that had happened and he hadn't even seen them before ... [He saw] his own father and sisters and brothers as the owner, the rich man (not the [slave]) must have been seeing them all the time—as cattle, creatures heavy and without grace, brutely evacuated into a world without hope or purpose for them, who would in turn spawn with brutish and vicious prolixity
>
> (Faulkner 1936: 186–190; Forter 2011: 112)

Sutpen has already looked at "the objects in the room" (his "primal scenes") but without really seeing them. They have made a sensory impression on him that has for a time lain dormant. Forter writes:

> It is, therefore, only through a second event—through Sutpen's affront at the hands of the plantation-owner, for whom the slave serves merely as medium—that the humiliating content of his initial impressions becomes both *conscious* and retrospectively *significant*. This second event ... takes impressions of inferiority and shame that might never have crystallized as inferiority and shame, and through an act of historical determination gives them a significatory content that constitutes the core of Sutpen's subsequent sense of self.
>
> (2011: 113).

As opposed to sensory stimuli associated with being in a train wreck or other explicitly life-threatening "punctual" events, the sights, sounds, smells, and tactile sensations associated with the revelation on the plantation's porch seem relatively mild and non-threatening. It is only as these stimuli become in a flash emblematic of meanings supported by "intertwined systems of private property, slavery, and the subjugation of women" (2011: 112) that they acquire pathogenic potency, upsetting Sutpen so much that he flees from the doorway without delivering his message, retreating to a forest hideaway he figures to himself as a "a kind of cave" (188). Here in this private sanctuary, and then, later that night, as he broods sleeplessly on the pallet that comprises his customary bed, Sutpen attempts to come to terms with the implications of the revelation he has received. Ultimately, the acute, short-term crisis is resolved when his shattered self is reassembled around a new ego ideal accepting of the value judgments inherent in the hegemonic social order. As Forter explains, Sutpen "incorporates not his actual father but a version of what Lacan calls the Symbolic father—an idealized, socially affirmative, and necessarily abstract or unincarnatable 'imago' of the very man who affronted him" (2011: 115). Precisely because the interval between the affront at the doorstep and the reconstitution of Sutpen's personality in terms of the Symbolic father is characterized by splitting and depersonalization, this interval stands as the locus of the unspeakable par excellence. But, as Forter makes clear, in contrast to the unspeakable criticized by Mandel the version of the unspeakable that here becomes evident in Faulkner's representation is above all dynamic, a transitional phase between traumatic break and psychological reconstitution wherein nothing as yet has been definitively decided. For Forter insists that the reproduction of slavery and patriarchy ultimately accomplished in the reconstitution of Sutpen's personality did not have to play out in the way that it did, but might have taken a far more healthy and politically progressive direction.

Retreating to his "cave," Sutpen experiences not "a blissful state of (re)union, but rather a psychic bifurcation: a splitting of the self into two distinct parts, from both of which he feels dissociated" (115). Sutpen himself does not speak, but listens passively to "the two of them inside [his] body ... arguing quiet[ly] and calm[ly]" about what to do (188). For several pages, the argument advanced by the two voices is fixated on the proposal made by one simply to kill the owner of the plantation. *But I can shoot him*, this voice suggests, with embellishments (189–191). The other voice patiently keeps insisting that this would not do any good. The corrupt social order fetishizing material possessions and making powerful, invidious distinctions on the basis of race and gender as well as class would be left in place even if this particular plantation-owning individual were eliminated, the real source of Sutpen's newly discovered shame thus left entirely untouched. Finally, a third voice emerges, the voice of Sutpen's "innocence," to argue that Sutpen must fight fire with fire; must acquire the wherewithal to compete with the plantation owner according to the rules of the existing social system. The psychological free fall in the aftermath of the affront comes to an end when Sutpen himself, not one of the voices, is able to endorse this analysis by saying "Yes." The return of Sutpen's own voice in the quote below, along with "the closing repetition of the first person 'he'" (2011: 116), signal the completion of a stunning conversion experience. Sutpen has been dramatically transformed: from hillbilly slacker to highly motivated and magically effective go-getter, destined now (evidently) to become rich and powerful. But this impressive integration has been achieved at the price of a catastrophic inner hollowing:

> It was like ... an explosion—a bright glare that vanished and left nothing, no ashes nor refuse: just a limitless flat plain with the severe shape of his intact innocence rising from it like a monument: that innocence instructing him as calm as the others [the other two selves within him] had ever spoken.... "You got to have land and niggers and a fine house to combat them with. You see?" and he said Yes again. He left that night. He waked before day and departed just like he went to bed: by rising from the pallet and tiptoeing out of the house. He never saw any of his family again. (192)

If Sutpen's transformative reverie is inhabited by several hallucinatory speakers, in what sense can it be said that this reverie exemplifies the moment of the unspeakable? Isn't it positively full to the brim with speaking? Yes, but this speaking is the paradoxical speaking of the unspeakable, a fact that is made manifest precisely by the outré nature of the psychological experience Faulkner brings before us. Sutpen's sense of self and of his own everyday world suddenly has been disrupted—not so much by an "event," since the transaction on the porch is so banal as scarcely to amount to such, in ordinary parlance—but by a burst of meaning that exceeds Sutpen's assimilative capacities: what Forter calls "signification trauma." The revelation at the plantation door has brought home to him not just his low social status in the hegemonic world order but the affective significance of this low status. The enormity of the blow is registered by the extremity of its psychological consequences: the splitting of the self, including especially the absenting of all power of volition from the "I" for the duration of the hallucinatory episode. For again, that shard of self we must think of as Sutpen himself, the central core of his identity, passively takes in the discussion carried on by the voices until, following the advice proffered by "innocence," we witness the emergence of "a newly coherent 'I' ... that has reintegrated the split-off selves" (2011: 116). The emergence of this new "I" is contingent upon the crafting of a plan of action that is commensurate to the psychological emergency initiated by the revelation of shameful inferiority: "You got to have land and niggers and a fine house to combat them with." Whatever its deficiencies— which, obviously, are considerable, as the coherence made possible by the new way of looking at things is "highly rigid and compulsive" (2011: 116)—this plan is clearly superior to the only alternative articulated by the voices, the simplistic proposal to shoot the plantation owner. Thus, Faulkner's text implicitly defines the moment of the unspeakable as a search for new conceptual moorings— new, viable ways of understanding world and self—following the destruction of the familiar assumptive world.

This interpretation depends crucially on the insight conveyed by Forter's insistence that "there is nothing necessary or inevitable about the dynamic" in terms of which Sutpen is transformed from unpretentious hick to overbearing slavemaster (117):

> The trauma Sutpen suffers is ... one he perpetuates by rigidifying his innocence and incorporating the man who humiliates him. But Faulkner also suggests that the trauma *need not* lead in this direction. Sutpen *chooses* the oedipally structured reproduction of slavery rather, say, than a course of political resistance. The traumatic recognition of his social insignificance could equally issue in a revolutionary yearning to level the hierarchies that traumatize him as in the urge to perpetuate those hierarchies. (117)

Forter is right to suggest that a decision to level the hierarchies logically would answer to the dilemma Sutpen confronts in the aftermath of the traumatic recognition as well as does the decision he actually makes, to compete with the plantation owner and his ilk on their own terms. Notably, though, this is an option that simply does not come up for "discussion," when Sutpen's "voices" hash out the situation in the cave and on the pallet. Sutpen "chooses" the reproduction of violent white planter masculinity without consciously considering the alternative of political resistance. But if this alternative *had* come up in course of the protracted intra-psychic debate, who is to say that Sutpen might not have found an entirely different life path? "Faulkner emphasizes this sense of possibility through the very fact of having Sutpen retreat to the cave and debate his response—the condition of such deliberation being, of course, that more than one response is conceivable" (2002: 117). Thus, for Forter, "the model of trauma as retrodetermination ... gives us a conceptual starting point for approaching the question of how we might *resist* traumatic subject-formation" (2007: 280). From this more hopeful perspective, Sutpen's melancholic plunge into the unspeakable might appear as a necessary phase in a process of working through, "metabolizing," and truly overcoming the toxic aftereffects of trauma.[10]

I will build on Forter's thinking to suggest that his non-punctual model aptly might be recoded as an abductive process of thought. As I hope my overall argument makes clear, the point of my departure from Freud's theoretical framework in favor of Peirce and semiotic theory is not a repudiation of psychoanalysis but its supplementation.[11] By clarifying the underlying logic of Sutpen's traumatic realization, this reference to Charles S. Peirce's idea of abduction as a third type of logical inference supports Forter's intuition that the model of trauma as retrodetermination potentially opens upon political resistance.

* * *

There are many scattered references to sign theory in trauma studies, especially in literary trauma studies, but relatively few system-atic attempts to think through the nature of trauma in semiotic terms. Semiotic references in trauma studies appear to be especially undeveloped if we are interested specifically in the Peircean tradition of semiotics, as opposed to Saussaurean semiology.[12] The emergence of the phrase "signification trauma" in Forter's essays as a synonym for the non-punctual model derived from Freud's early work is a good example of how concepts from semiotics occasionally surface in trauma studies, but without being integrated within a thorough-going, consistently semiotic approach to the study of trauma. Forter's use of the phrase is perfectly intelligible, as we have seen, as a way of emphasizing the centrality in non-punctual traumas of a moment of revelatory retrodetermination, in which signifiers previously experienced as neutral or benign suddenly come to be experienced as traumatogenic. But, does Forter mean to imply that punctual traumas, by contrast, do not involve signification? Julie Rea Harper, a semiotician who happens herself to be a survivor of major trauma, shows how untenable such an implication would be when she writes of posttraumatic stress disorder (PTSD):

> Among the numerous problems which stem from [PTSD] lies a common denominator, the alteration of prior reactions to signs. In any PTSD sufferer lie the altered images of particular pictures and sounds, and emotional responses, which were associated through the traumatic experience(s). It is central to our discussion here to consider PTSD as a condition that causes hyper and irrational responses to situations or "signs"—responses, which *seem* unmerited in a given context—as the normative population would experience it. (2005: 378)

Car wrecks and armed assaults impact upon the nervous system through signification, resulting, in cases diagnosed as PTSD, in a pathogenic "alteration of prior reactions to signs." But, let us set the semiotic underpinnings of punctual traumas aside to focus on Forter's preferred model. In fact, Forter's concept of signification trauma, especially as illustrated by Faulkner, serves admirably as a vehicle for introducing not merely a semiotic analysis of trauma but one that is keyed specifically to Peirce's category of abduction.

For of course, it would be possible—and probably strategic—to develop a semiotic account of trauma that does not rely on abduction. Peirce's long development of the controversial idea is characterized by multiple shifts in terminology,[13] many tensions and ambiguities, and one major, deliberate revision marking a sea change between his earlier and later work on the topic.[14] Nathan Houser describes the concept of abduction as "slippery" (2005: 499); Daniel J. McKaughan tellingly remarks that Peirce's use of abduction "slides around ... different though potentially compatible senses" (2008: 446); Tomas Kapitan, among others, is skeptical that Peirce ever managed to give a coherent account of abduction. Why not evade these controversies by focusing elsewhere, since other concepts from semiotic theory—for example, the idea of the "umvelt," featured in Harper's essay—seem promising for the study of trauma, offering us a way to deepen our understanding of "the potentiality of sensitivity to signs" (Harper 379)? In part, an answer to this question may be found in the remarkable interdisciplinary ascension of the idea of abduction since the middle of the twentieth century, to the point that it now appears to be the case that a positive consensus with respect to the value of abduction has begun to take shape: "many [now] … contend that abduction, construed as inference to the best explanation, is an essential part of scientific and everyday reasoning" (Psillos 1999; Magnani 2001; Thagard 2007: 232). Still, the growing prominence of abduction in philosophy and the philosophy of science and in the cognitive sciences, as well as in other disciplines, would be of little consequence to our purposes if there were not inherently something about abduction that answered directly to issues raised by trauma. Forter's model featuring retrodetermination highlights the very aspects of traumatization that abduction appears to be naturally suited to speak to, and to account for: trauma's profound connection to creativity and discovery.

Abduction is Peirce's answer to the question, where do new ideas come from? Determined in his later writings to sharpen the distinction between abduction and the other two types of inference, especially induction, Peirce repeatedly asserted that it is exclusively the province of abduction to originate hypotheses, while deduction and induction perform tasks of clarification and evaluation. Thus, abduction is "the type of reasoning through which creativity manifests itself not only in science and in art but also in everyday life" (Santaella 2005: 189; *CP* 2.5.171, *CP* 2.96). Now Forter's concept of signification trauma is exemplary for defining a process of traumatization that is essentially a matter of being afflicted with new ideas, where the core of trauma is precisely a kind of ambiguously involuntary mental creativity. As I have already hinted, I believe that cases of punctual trauma also involve abductive jumps of thought, but where threats of grievous personal harm are present, compensatory mental reactions are perhaps less recognizable as creative reinterpretations of world and self than are such reinterpretations when they are more subtly provoked. Clearly, the insult experienced by Sutpen at the door of the plantation falls short of the definition of the traumatic stressor specified for the diagnosis of PTSD. For a racist white man, to be directed to the service entrance by a black slave is interpreted as a symbolic, socially mediated putdown which, however stinging, still seems relatively less urgent than, say, the sight of a man pointing a gun at your head, or the lurch of the train leaving the tracks—the kinds of signifiers associated with punctual traumas. If Forter's structure of retrodetermination helps us to understand how such seemingly mild, "everyday," culturally specific slights can nonetheless give rise to momentous psychological consequences— the wholesale transformation of Sutpen's personality—the lesson is extended and productively refocused when we recognize that Forter's structure of retrodetermination in key respects is a recapitulation of Peirce's analysis of abductive thinking.

One of Peirce's most famous attempts to schematize abduction's "perfectly definite logical form," his formulation from the 1903 lectures at Harvard tracing the origin of the abductive thought from the observation of a surprising fact,[15] makes a good point of departure for the exploration of this relationship:

The surprising fact, C, is observed;
But if A were true, C would be a matter of course;
Hence, there is reason to suspect that A is true.

(CP 5.189)

Sutpen's experience at the plantation doorway is readily charted in terms of this formula. The surprising fact C is the servant's abrupt redirection of Sutpen from the front door to the service entrance. Hypothesis A is Sutpen's realization of the profoundly negative affective meaning of his own low social standing in the eyes of society, as personified by the plantation owner. The idea of humiliatingly low status is "new" in the sense that Sutpen previously has never thought of it. Certainly, this idea performs the function demanded of it by Peirce's formulation: if it is true that Sutpen is dirt in the eyes of society, his being told to go around to the back door is a matter of course.

Peirce emphasizes that abduction, unlike deduction and induction, is a weak kind of logical inference in the sense that it merely suggests that something may be so; the power of hypothesis A to render the surprising fact unsurprising warrants only the conclusion that there is reason to "suspect" that the hypothesis *may* be true.

Thus, in Peirce's full description of scientific inquiry, abduction makes up only the first phase, wherein hypotheses are generated and at most tentatively selected for further investigation. But here Forter's reinscription of the primal scene helps to suggest the nature of the mechanism by means of which abductive thought may exert a coercive persuasiveness in the context of trauma. In the immediate aftermath of Sutpen's realization, many different experiences illustrating and supporting this realization recur to his memory; episodes illustrative of the systematic operation of classist, sexist, and racist presuppositions in plantation culture throng to his mind.

In Forter's approach, these are the "primal scenes," events that have been registered as sensory impressions but until now have lain dormant. While these experiences have in the past seemed innocuous, in the immediate aftermath of the traumatic realization they seem to demand interpretation, and the hypothesis of humiliatingly low social status readily answers to this call, rendering them all collectively "a matter of course," just as it also explains the insult at the plantation door. Thus, these "primal scenes" become so many pieces of evidence for the new idea, the collective weight of which helps make it difficult or impossible for the young Sutpen to evade the recognition of shame and inferiority, however painful this must be. Equally unable to dismiss or embrace the disturbing new "truth," on the one hand, because it serves as an interpretive key to his own experiences, and on the other hand, because, in terms suggested by Ronnie Janoff-Bulman, it contradicts fundamental assumptions positing the goodness of self and world,[16] Sutpen enters the zone of the unspeakable. Because Sutpen's posttraumatic quandary is psychologically intractable during this period of crisis, it cannot (at first) be spoken. The toxic new data of traumatization must be shaped, tweaked, modified to be rendered somehow compatible with the need for minimal self-respect. Finally, paradoxically, fragments of Sutpen speak the unspeakable as the decision to become the incarnation of the Symbolic father, in so doing effecting the reemergence of a transformed Sutpen as a unitary self.

It is because the traumatic revelation at the plantation door has imposed itself so forcefully on Sutpen's mind—not like a tentative hypothesis at all, actually, but rather with an impact akin to that of an armed assault or train wreck—that the question which engrosses him in its immediate aftermath is, what should be done (now)? This is a question which accepts the destruction of the egalitarian assumptions that had guided Sutpen from early youth but holds out for a course of action that will somehow restore some sense of self-worth.

In semiotic terms, the course of action to be followed subsequent to the traumatic revelation of shame and inferiority aptly may be understood as one of the revelation's *interpretants*. An interpretant in Peirce's triadic sign theory is the effect that a sign has in the mind of an interpreter, one which is created by the action of a sign being determined by its object, but which is itself an equivalent sign that cannot be reduced to either the first sign or to the object. The dynamical interpretant is the direct effect actually produced by a sign upon an interpreter of it, and may be "energetic" (that is, behavioral) as well as conceptual or emotional. While "the new idea" of social inferiority is, apparently, inescapable for the traumatized Sutpen, the further question irresistibly opened up by the acceptance of this idea—what can I do about it?—clearly admits of more than one solution. During the period of psychic bifurcation, as we have seen, Sutpen's voices explicitly consider the feasibility of prompt retribution, the shooting of the plantation owner, only to reject this overly specific plan of revenge in favor of a strategy of emulation and rivalry: Sutpen vows to possess his own slaves and property. If the apprehension of inferiority and shame comprises the wedge-moment of traumatic abduction, the seemingly involuntary commitment to an affectively untenable explanatory hypothesis explicitly is followed by a choice between two ameliorative strategies: shoot the owner or compete with him on his own terms. But, then, what about the politically progressive option emphasized by Forter? How can Forter insist that Sutpen might have devoted himself to overcoming the hierarchical inequalities he has newly discovered, when an interpretant specifying a path of resistance is *not* actually produced in his mind at the time of crisis?[17]

The experiment of pursuing the critical articulation of trauma and Peircean abduction helps with this problem by suggesting that the pathway of political resistance is nonetheless in a sense included in Sutpen's abductive inference even if it is not explicitly mentioned. This is because the underlying mechanism of abductive thinking revealed by Peirce's 1903 theorem is the thought that we should consider the possibility that hypothesis A may be true if A makes surprising fact C seem to be "a matter of course." Applied to the existential problem of "how to be" that arises for Sutpen in the aftermath of the revelation of shameful inferiority, this logic would seem to dictate that the decision to devote one's life to the reformation of society meets the essential, minimal abductive requirement as well or better than do the options which are articulated in Faulkner's text. What goes together with the preservation of self-respect, making the maintenance of a sense of self-worth "a matter of course"? "Resist the system" is clearly better than "shoot the owner," and perhaps even competitive with "be the owner."

Providing a gloss for Forter's signification trauma, then, abduction theory helps us to see the moment of the unspeakable as one that is open to real possibilities of recuperation and growth. At the same time, this is a matter of seeing hope in a place where darkness reigns. Sutpen's career in Faulkner's novel on the face of it is not such as to encourage optimism for the fate of trauma victims. Thus, this essay concludes with a dawning sense of how much work there remains to be done. The project of theorizing moments of the unspeakable in literary texts and in everyday life in principle should be capable of doing justice to all imaginable vagaries of meaning, but a taxonomy of unspeakables that could be adequate to this challenge has not yet even begun to be worked out. What I hope I have secured thus far is simply this: a positive potentiality must be factored into any thorough-going attempt to parse the unspeakable in the context of trauma.

Notes

1. At this point, the body of work taking issue with "the currently dominant model of trauma" in literary studies (Forter 2007: 262) has grown sufficiently itself to require sorting out into subordinate categories. Responses that already seem classic include those of LaCapra and of Ruth Leys. LaCapra offers the paired critical terms "absence/loss" and "structural/ historical" to articulate conceptual points of resistance with respect to the transhistorical models of trauma implied by Caruth and Felman (2001: 43–85; 86–113). Ruth Leys' chapter sharply criticizing Caruth especially for eliding the distinction between victim and perpetrator remains a rallying point for many of those who most find fault with the dominant paradigm (2000: 266–297). Others who have interrogated the allegedly deleterious effects of a concept of trauma allied with the unspeakable include Debarati Sanyal (2002), Ann Cvetkovich (2003), and Amy Hungerford (2003). More recently, Michelle Balaev has criticized Caruth's position that trauma stands outside of representation as reductive and misleading (2008) and

has offered an alternative model emphasizing the importance of place (2012). Two other revisionist theorists include Naomi Mandel (2006) and a contributor to this collection Greg Forter (2007: 2011), discussed at length here.

   An important late-breaking development in revisionist trauma studies is the rise of postcolonial perspectives. The insistence on the importance of non-European contexts and sources has a complex, far-reaching impact on trauma theory, with postcolonial trauma theorists often appearing to be quite adversarial with respect to the dominant paradigm associated with the unspeakable. Thus, many of the contributors to the special issue of *Studies in the Novel* on "Postcolonial Trauma Novels" (2008) explicitly take issue with the event-based model of trauma associated with Caruth, arguing for a more localized, culturally sensitive and politically aware understanding of trauma in a way that seems broadly compatible with the approaches of Balaev, Mandel and Forter. However, Michael Rothberg's *Multidirectional Memory* (2009)—certainly an important text for the rise of postcolonial emphases in trauma studies—offers a nuanced defense specifically of Caruth (2009: 87–96). See also the essay of review Rothberg contributed to the special issue (2008: 224–234). I return to the discussion of postcolonial trauma studies and the critique of the event model in my section on Greg Forter's signification theory below.

2. More recently, Luckhurst traces a continuity between Caruth's concept of the trauma's deferred impact and Rothberg's idea of multidirectional memory, which conjunction of elements then becomes the theoretical basis of Luckhurst's own exploration of indirect literary representations of the Iraq war (2012: 274).

3. Interestingly, however, James Berger associates the unspeakable with what he calls "the counter-linguistic turn," a widely disseminated recent philosophical/critical/interdisciplinary development contradicting the central assertion of the famous "linguistic turn" which maintains "in broad terms" that "there is nothing other than language" (2005: 344). Berger thus would seem to ascribe to the unspeakable a suggestiveness diametrically opposed to the meaning ascribed to the unspeakable by Mandel.

4. That the dominant paradigm associated with Caruth and the unspeakable conceptualizes trauma with undue pessimism as a spreading contagion is one of the accusations commonly brought against it. See, for example, the conclusions of Forter's two essays on Faulkner (2007: 281–282; 2011: 136). There are important differences between being the victim of atrocity and being upset by reports of atrocity, assuredly; this, of course, is precisely my point. Still, that secondary trauma is real and potentially substantive cannot be denied.

5. Forter's chapter on Faulkner in *Gender, Race and Mourning in American Modernism* (2011: 96–136) is an expanded version of the essay he published in *Narrative* in 2007, "Freud, Faulkner, Caruth: Trauma and the Politics of Literary Form" (15, 259–285).

6. Roger Luckhurst remarks of Ruth Leys' attack on Caruth in *Trauma: A Genealogy* (2000): "After this mauling, it might be tempting to discard Caruth, were it not that the length of Leys' critique makes a strange kind of monument to its importance" (2008: 13).

7. In the earlier essay, however, Forter argues that, even within its own proper sphere, the punctual model leads to a transhistorical, structural understanding of trauma, turning "development into reprisal, change into recurrence, temporal movement into the static circularity of myth" (269).

8. "Retrodetermination" (21–22) is John Brenkman's translation of Freud's "Nachträglichkeit"—preferred by Forter over James Strachey's "deferred action" (2007: 264).

9. Nancy Van Styvendale's contribution to the special issue features a particularly direct critique of what she calls "the accident model" of trauma, which she contrasts to a "trans/historical" model attuned to the quandaries of contemporary Native North Americans that is "cumulative, collective, intergenerational, and intersubjective" (2008: 203). Many of the other contributors to Craps and Buelens' special issue take up the same issue, drawing upon Brown and Franz Fanon to provide alternatives.

10. Here I touch (very lightly) upon a major emphasis in Forter's book on modernism: his determination to push back against the valorization of melancholia over mourning in recent trauma studies, which valorization features a "critical discourse of recuperated melancholia, according to which 'surmounting' bereavement becomes a kind of specious denial of our predicament as linguistic beings" (19). Notwithstanding his sense that the positive role of melancholia has been overstated, Forter acknowledges the possibility that a moment of impacted melancholy (such as might be readily associated with the unspeakable) may make up a necessary moment of mourning, a possibility that Forter documents most specifically with reference to Alexander and Margarete Mitscherlich, *The Inability to Mourn* (1967) (Forter 2011: 17).

11. My recourse to semiotics, then, might be seen as potentially adding another layer to the still emergent interdisciplinarity of trauma studies, as exemplified most tellingly, perhaps, by the recent articulation of psychoanalysis and neurobiology around the idea of trauma in the work of Catherine Malabou (2012).

12. In brief, semiotics is distinguished from semiology by the triadic model of the sign insisted upon by Peirce, and consequently is associated with a complex system of triadic distinctions, including index, icon, and symbol. In part because Peirce's system explicitly recognizes in the index and icon the possibility of the natural sign, it may be preferred as an instrument for mapping the impact of the traumatic stressor, as compared to semiological conceptualizations focused primarily on language or other intentional, artificial devices.

13. Peirce interchangeably uses the terms hypothesis, abduction, retroduction, and presumption. In the context of my essay, the morphological

similarity between the words "retroduction" and "retrodetermination" appears to be not accidental, but suggestive of a substantive conceptual relationship between the two terms.
14. "Peirce began by viewing abduction as an 'evidencing process' and later switched to treating it as the stage of scientific inquiry which leads us to hypotheses" (Anderson 1986: 147).
15. Pragmatism and Abduction" is the last of seven lectures delivered at Harvard University from 26 March to 17 May 1903 (*CP* 5.180–212).
16. Although not itself explicitly semiotic, Ronnie Janoff-Bulman's groundbreaking treatise *Shattered Assumptions* (1992) provides a basis for the recoding of traumatization as abductive thinking.
17. To be fair, Forter does provide additional evidence suggesting the existence in Faulkner's text of traces of "the choice not made ... —of what one might think of as the revolutionary option— ... even within the ruthless instrumentalizations of the design [Sutpen] actually chooses" (117) when he cites a passage from the novel in which Sutpen expresses "the utopian wish that 'beating' the planter will redeem not only his own humiliation but that of all past and future boys like him, one of whom he imagines knocking and being admitted at his future self's front door" (117). In imagination Sutpen repeats his own original trauma, but with a saving difference: "[H]e would take that boy in, where he would never again need to stand on the outside of a white door and knock on it ..." (210).

Bibliography

Adorno, Theodor W. *Negative Dialectics*. Trans. E.B. Ashton. New York: Continuum, 1973.
Anderson, Douglas R. "The Evolution of Peirce's Concept of Abduction." *Transactions of the Charles S. Peirce Society* 22 (1986): 145–164.
Balaev, Michelle. "Trends in Literary Trauma Theory." *Mosaic* 41 (2008): 149–167.
Balaev, Michelle. *The Nature of Trauma in American Novels*. Evanston: Northwestern University Press, 2012.
Barthes, Roland. *Lemon*. Paris: Editions de Seuil, 1978.
Berger, James. "Falling Towers and Postmodern Wild Children: Oliver Sacks, Don DeLillo, and Turns against Language." *PMLA* 120 (2005): 341–161.
Brenkman, John. *Straight Male Modern: A Cultural Critique of Psychoanalysis*. New York: Routledge, 1996.
Brown, Laura. "Not Outside the Range: One Feminist Perspective on Psychic Trauma." In Cathy Caruth, ed. *Trauma: Explorations in Memory*. Baltimore: Johns Hopkins University Press, 1995, 100–113.
Caruth, Cathy (ed.). *Trauma: Explorations in Memory*. Baltimore: Johns Hopkins University Press, 1995.
Caruth, Cathy. *Unclaimed Experience*. Baltimore: Johns Hopkins University Press, 1996.

Craps, Stef and Gert Buelens (eds). "Introduction: Postcolonial Trauma Novels." *Studies in the Novel* 40 (2008): 1–12.

Craps, Stef and Gert Buelens. "Traumatic Mirrorings: Holocaust and Colonial Trauma." In Michael Chabon's, ed. *The Final Solution. Criticism* 53 (2011): 569–586.

Cvetkovich, Ann. *An Archive of Feelings: Trauma, Sexuality, and Lesbian Public Cultures.* Durham and London: Duke University Press, 2003.

Faulkner, William. *Absalom, Absalom! 1936.* New York: Vintage International, 1990.

Felman, Shoshona and Dori Laub. *Testimony: Crises of Witnessing in Literature, Psychoanalysis, and History.* New York: Routledge, 1992.

Forter, Greg. "Freud, Faulkner, Caruth: Trauma and the Politics of Literary Form." *Narrative* 15 (2007): 259–285.

Forter, Greg. *Gender, Race, and Mourning in American Modernism.* Cambridge UK: Cambridge University Press, 2011.

Garbus, Lisa. "The Unspeakable Stories of *Shoah* and *Beloved*." *College Literature* 26 (1999): 52–68.

Harper, Julie Rea. "PTSD: A Situated Look at the Semiotic Process and Role of Individual Umwelts in Human Existence/Function." *Semiotica* 157 (2005): 377–385.

Hartman, Geoffrey H. "On Traumatic Knowledge and Literary Studies." *New Literary History* 26 (1995): 537–563.

Herman, Judith L. *Trauma and Recovery.* New York: Basic Books, 1992.

Hirsch, Marianne. *Family Frames: Photography, Narrative, and Postmemory.* Cambridge, MA: Harvard University Press, 1997.

Houser, Nathan. "The Scent of Truth." *Semiotica* 153 (2005): 455–466.

Hungerford, Amy. *The Holocaust of Texts: Genocide, Literature, and Personification.* Chicago and London: University of Chicago Press, 2003.

Janoff-Bulman, Ronnie. *Shattered Assumptions: Towards a New Psychology of Trauma.* New York: Free Press, 1992.

Kapitan, Tomas. "Peirce and the Autonomy of Abductive Reasoning." *Erkenntnis* 37 (1992): 1–26.

Kapitan, Tomas. "Peirce and the Structure of Abductive Inference." In Nathan Houser, Don D. Roberts and James Van Evra, eds *Studies in the Logic of Charles Sanders Peirce.* Bloomington and Indianapolis: Indiana University Press, 1997, 477–496.

LaCapra, Dominick. *Writing History, Writing Trauma.* Baltimore: Johns Hopkins University Press, 2001.

Lanzmann, Claude. *Shoah: An Oral History of the Holocaust.* Trans. A. Whitelaw and D. Bryon. New York: Pantheon, 1985.

Lanzmann, Claude. "The Obscenity of Understanding: An Evening with Claude Lanzmann." *Caruth, Trauma* (1995): 200–220.

Leys, Ruth. *Trauma: A Genealogy.* Chicago: University of Chicago Press, 2000.

Luckhurst, Roger. "In War Times: Fictionalizing Iraq." *Contemporary Literature* 53 4 (2012): 714–737.

Luckhurst, Roger. *The Trauma Question.* London and New York: Routledge, 2008.

Magnani, Lorenzo. *Abduction, Reason and Science: Processes of Discovery and Explanation.* New York: Springer, 2001.

Malabou, Catharine. *The New Wounded: From Neurosis to Brain Damage.* (2007). Trans. Steven Bronx: University Press, 2012.

Mandel, Naomi. *Against the Unspeakable: Complicity, the Holocaust, and Slavery in America.* Charlottesville: University of Virginia Press, 2006.

McKaughan, Daniel J. "From Ugly Duckling to Swan: Abduction and the Pursuit of Scientific Theories." *Transactions of the Charles S. Peirce Society* 44 (2008): 446–448.

Mitscherlich, Alexander and Margarete. *The Inability to Mourn: Principles of Collective Behavior* (1967). Trans. Beverley R. Placek. New York: Grove, 1975.

Peirce, Charles S. *The Collected Papers of Charles Sanders Peirce.* Vols. I–VI ed. Charles Hartshorne and Paul Weiss. Cambridge, MA: Harvard University Press, 1931–1935. Vols. VII–VIII, ed. Arthur W. Burks (same publisher, 1958). The abbreviation followed by volume and paragraph numbers with a period between follows the standard *CP* reference form.

Psillos, Stathis. *Scientific Realism: How Science Tracks the Truth.* New York: Routledge, 1999.

Rothberg, Michael. *Traumatic Realism: The Demands of Holocaust Representation.* Minneapolis: University of Minnesota Press, 2000.

Rothberg, Michael. "Decolonizing Trauma Studies: A Response." *Studies in the Novel* 40 1–2 (2008): 225–234.

Rothberg, Michael. *Multidirectional Memory: Remembering the Holocaust in the Age of Decolonization.* Stanford: Stanford University Press, 2009.

Santaella, Lucia. "Abduction: The Logic of Guessing." *Semiotica* 153 (2005): 175–198.

Sanyal, Debarati. "A Soccer Match in Auschwitz: Passing Culpability in Holocaust Criticism." *Representations* 79 (2002): 1–27.

Thagard, Paul. "Abductive Inference: From Philosophical Analysis to Neural Mechanisms." In A. Feeney and E. Heit, eds *Inductive Reasoning: Experimental, Developmental, and Computational Approaches.* Cambridge, UK: Cambridge University Press, 2007, 226–247.

Van Styvendale, Nancy. "The Trans/historicity of Trauma in Jeannette Armstrong's *Slash* and Sherman Alexie's *Indian Killer.*" *Studies in the Novel* 40 (2008): 208–223.

Vickroy, Laura. *Trauma and Survival in Contemporary Fiction* Charlottesville VA: University of Virginia Press, 2002.

Whitehead, Anne. *Trauma Fiction.* Edinburgh: Edinburgh University Press, 2004.

3
Secondary Thinking and Trauma: Dostoevsky's *Notes from Underground*

Herman Rapaport

Secondary thinking is a concept advanced by the late André Green, who for several decades had been active as a major French theorist of psychoanalysis.[1] To his credit, Green, who for a time participated in Jacques Lacan's seminars, diplomatically negotiated the precarious spaces between the various Lacanian groups and more orthodox Freudian French analysts associated with the *Société psychanalytique de Paris*. In later years, he also had considerable presence in British spheres of psychoanalytical work, and eventually became a member of the prestigious British Psychoanalytic Society. In his book *Time in Psychoanalysis*, Green argued that secondary thinking accompanies the logic of the statement (*l'énoncé*) in relation to its enunciation (*l'énonciation*) at a level assumed by inference and mediated by the unconscious. "For each segment of discourse uttered, there are corresponding unexpressed thoughts which, while they seek to express themselves when they can, have a retroactive effect on the pathway already created; or, to be more exact, on one or other of the terms already uttered by this pathway, creating a retrospective process of linking, obtained retrogressively."[2] Secondary thinking therefore traverses explicit enunciation as an effect of what Green calls "retroactive reverberation" and "associative irradiation." Furthermore, secondary thinking concerns "multi-directional temporality" and "reticulated arborescence," which "stands in contrast to the order of words of the sentence interpreted in terms of the logic of consciousness."[3]

The general rubric under which all this is formulated is "time in treatment." However, one might find it difficult to read Green's account of secondary thinking and not be drawn to the possibility that what he is describing relates to the psychology of trauma in which traumatic associations, many of them not quite conscious, irradiate and reverberate by means of retroaction. Indeed, there is no reason to imagine that traumatic experience might not function as a process of secondary thinking, however intermittent and unexpressed in words, which does the work of linking the subject to "the signifying chain" (*l'énoncé*), thereby providing the subject with a "*social* identity," given that signification is socially mediated, and hence made recognizable by an other. Ultimately, in a context where one is being listened to (i.e., is given the power of redress), such identity speaks to one's place as a social subject who can account for himself or herself in social discourse by means of testimony (recounting, depiction, representation).

However, of interest in terms of secondary thinking is not so much this explicit, social representation of oneself as a trauma victim, but the experience of a fragmentary accompaniment of secondary thinking that isn't fully diegetic or mimetic and that doesn't necessarily lead to a coherent or even a very socialized type of subject. Typical of our perception of trauma victims is an awareness of a double narrative, that of normal lived experience, and that of an exceptional experience, perhaps even historically unrepresentable except in terms of fragments, that has moved from the foreground of the subject's existence into the background of an everyday life that has become "normalized" once more. For many trauma victims there is the sense that it would be best to simply forget or erase the exceptional experience of trauma so that its secondary thinking, in Green's sense, won't become a preoccupation, something that sets the stage for a return of the repressed, for example, in terms of dreams that the subject cannot self-consciously control. Secondary thinking, after all, is partly conducted as unconscious process. As Green puts it:

> Two temporalities are at work at the heart of conscious activity; one on the surface, following its course with the regularity that governs language, thus obeying the formation of linear linguistic sequences, according to a determined progression; the other, underlying the first, which seizes the opportunity of free association (none the less intelligible) to maintain a system of linking that is uncertain, changing, de-hierarchised, de-categorised, more or less actual-

ized, requiring [of the psycho-analyst] a different mode of listening (floating attention) guided by new referents organized in chains, according to the principle of pleasure/unpleasure or, beyond that, of the compulsion to repeat from the unconscious to the id which is in immediate contact with the preconscious.[4]

The two temporalities correspond to the primary and secondary modes of thinking and appear to be layered somewhat like a Baroque musical invention in which there are essentially two lines that counterpoint one another, the one temporally chasing the other, as if to catch up to it. In terms of this analogy, secondary thinking accompanies primary thinking which may be the more dominant until a moment when they switch roles in terms of importance, the secondary thinking becoming the more dominant line, even if it is the more freely associated, de-constituted, and uncertain of the discourses or "languages," should we suppose the unconscious is, as Lacan famously said, *like* a language. For trauma victims, the older temporality, which may have become latent for the sake of managing in a present that represents the newer temporality, repeats elements of the past that link up with the present, though with varying motives.

   Although secondary thinking isn't constantly making itself known, it is an unsaturated constant that accompanies primary thinking; that is, secondary thinking supplies a background of meaning that is unfulfilled and therefore under-saturated, even if its elements participate in what W.R. Bion called alpha function. This is the capacity to think constructively by means of thinking through mental content, though only to a limited extent, as secondary thinking also concerns what Bion called beta bits, or split off psychotic elements that don't link in order to form coherent and consistent thinking, let alone, thinking that corresponds well with what Freud called reality.[5] Drawing from Bion, Green imagines that secondary thinking can function as an attack on linking (mentally connecting with objects and persons), if not cognition in general, and he treats this in terms of gaps in the patient's discourse. "The more the analysand speaks, the more he says; the more he speaks without quite saying entirely what he has on his mind, the more he says and reveals that there are things he is not saying."[6] In this instance, secondary thinking shows through in terms of the absences, that is, of what is silent. "One should never lose sight of the relation between the positivity of what is said and the negative of what is silence, of what is repressed." Of course, this is familiar to readers of Freud. But what Green adds is that this interplay of presence and absence can provoke "untimely manifestations of another speech which escapes the dilemma of saying or not saying." And this speaks to the two temporalities mentioned above "at the heart of conscious activity," the one "on the surface," the other, "underlying the first, which seizes the opportunity of free association ... to maintain a system of linking that is uncertain, changing, de-hierarchized, [and] de-categorized."[7] As Green notes, this secondary underlying thinking "threatens to break the thread of the discourse" in analysis. This breaking of the thread may well occur when there is a retroactive effect, namely, what Green calls "the after-effect of the relation to speech and to silence" that is unsaturated and incomplete, hence raising questions about the meaning of what has been said or not said.[8] Green doesn't mention it, but the analyst's questioning sets the patient on the road to effective observation of how primary and secondary thoughts do and do not reinforce one another, since questioning is often directed at objectifying functions and relations, of establishing what Green calls "useful distance" between the observer and the observed. "What the analysand needs is nothing other than to reintegrate and re-appropriate meaning." [9]

Unbearable Speech

Readers of Fyodor Dostoevsky may recall that much of his literary writing involves characters who talk far too much in the service of ingratiating themselves to others while, simultaneously, exculpating themselves from blame, even though in so doing, they are led to confess something appalling about themselves. Their discourse is self-serving, narcissistic, tediously ingratiating, aggressive, and exhibitionistic. Such subjects, who deprecatingly identify themselves as buffoons and babblers, demand attention in the service of divulging a secret that requires time to reveal, given that the subject is reluctant to admit that at the core of what he is hiding lies an appallingly sinful act that is beyond forgiveness. Far from being unrepresentable, the act is inadmissible and only through the byways of considerable secondary thinking is, in Freud's terms, "refound." Actions are only identifiable insofar as the subject repeats them: in this case, verbally. However, it is a repetition that has to occur via the Freudian transference, which is to say, it is a repetition whose medium is that of testimony and confession before an Other who is, essentially, superior and yet unprepared and unable to take in and respond to the disclosure of the execrable. Jacques Derrida has written at length of what he calls "circum-fession" which is the process of circumnavigating the secret to be divulged. In André Green's terms, the circumnavigation is identified as a *tourbillion* or whirl. "The de-centered, rambling subject is undoubtedly in a whirl."[10] This is precisely how one perceives characters such as Dostoevsky's "underground man" who attempts to get close to us with his whirling thoughts about all sorts of slights and mishaps in day to day life, even while we are being swamped by stories and philosophical speculations whose purpose is to avoid psychic pain and escape what is mentally unbearable. In Bion's terms, what we see in Dostoevsky are attacks on linking that paradoxically are made in the desperate effort to connect with people generally.

In Dostoevsky, the reader is made to occupy the role of the Other to whom unbearable psychic pain is being transferred, often by witnessing its disclosure at second remove, and in ways that grossly abuse the relation between the confessor and the auditor.[11] In *The Brothers Karamazov*, Fyodor Pavlovich, a terrible reprobate, begins his confession to a church elder in the following way: "'Your reverence,' he exclaimed with a sort of instant pathos, 'you see before you a buffoon! Verily, a buffoon! Thus I introduce myself! It's an old habit, alas! And if I sometimes tell lies inappropriately, I do it even on purpose, on purpose to be pleasant and make people laugh. One ought to be pleasant, isn't that so?'"[12] Fyodor Pavlovich, whose sons will be the main actors in this novel, begins not by objectively stating his case, but by subjecting his audience to a labyrinth of secondary thoughts, already in process, that are supposed to take us into their confidence. The idea is to seduce others with one's supposed "humanity," to appeal to our common identity in order to form an inappropriate link between the damned and the saved, the wretched and the blessed. Here linkage is perverted.

Notes from Underground begins in very much the same way, though the man's interlocutors are imaginary:

> I am a sick man … I am a spiteful man. I am an unattractive man. I believe my liver is diseased. However I know nothing at all about

my disease, and do not know for certain what ails me. I don't consult a doctor for it and never have, though I have a respect for medicine and doctors. Besides, I am extremely superstitious, sufficiently so to respect medicine, anyway (I am well-educated enough not to be superstitious, but I am superstitious). No, I refuse to consult a doctor from spite. That you probably will not understand. Well, I understand it, though.[13]

The underground man's discourse sounds "live," but, in fact, Dostoevsky presents this discourse as a script. Its addressees are presumably the very sort of gentlemen with whom the underground man imagines himself conversing. The discourse is a solicitous, heightened, over-attentive consideration fueled by anxiety, not least, the fear of being cut off and abandoned. And yet, this sort of solicitous discourse is itself unbearable in a way that ensures the very abandonment or disgust that it so desperately attempts to forestall.

More importantly for us, this discourse is stitched together by secondary thinking of a free floating sort that criss-crosses everything the underground man says.[14] One can already see this at the very outset when the underground man offers contradictory thoughts on his being superstitious. These thoughts are not quite linked and approach the state of Bion's "beta bits": a scatter of thinking that leads to and away from some underlying traumatic experience. After all, the last thing this story turns out to be about is the man's liver, which, no doubt, is diseased on account of alcohol. And yet already in this opening there is a psychological theme or node that emerges—in Bion's terms, alpha function (sense making)—namely, the man's spite. "If I don't consult a doctor, it is from spite. My liver is bad—well, let it get worse!" We will hear quite a lot about spite in *Notes*, because it addresses the causeless cause of what the underground man attributes to modern man's most typical motivation. Anyone or anything can become an object for spite. Yet the man's relation to even this assertion of human motivation is negated and thereby contradicted: "I was lying when I said just now that I was a spiteful official. I was lying from spite ... in reality I could never become spiteful." And, "it was not only that I could not become spiteful, I did not know how to become anything: neither spiteful nor kind, neither a rascal nor an honest man, neither a hero nor an insect."[15] This sort of discourse, which is shot through with disavowals, that is, negations, of the most awkward sorts, is perhaps typical of Green's "rambling subject," one that in Dostoevsky's story careens between highly elevated and degraded oppositions, the subject as a glorious and significant somebody in society versus the subject as a non-entity who is even to be considered subhuman.

One senses throughout the text that almost everything the underground man says has to be retracted, effaced, such that the discourse is being split up into opposing positions that are affirmed despite their being mutually contradictory. This splitting refers to what in his earlier writings Freud called *dissociation*. In later works, when this was revised, Freud offered the term *Spaltung*, which had to do with a splitting of the ego, that is, the introduction of more than one discursive point of view that was being held simultaneously. For the fetishist this meant that the mother does and doesn't have a phallus and that, therefore, the fetishist is trapped within a contradiction in which disavowal is paramount. Melanie Klein, founder of the British School, developed Freud's view that one can also split an object into "good" and "bad," something she ascribed, in particular, to the maternal breast. In *Notes from Underground*, the underground man's apprehension of woman is deeply conflicted in terms of this split between good and bad. Klein, for her part, understood the splitting of the ego in terms of a splitting off of the self into dissociated bits that had the equivalence of good and bad objects, though the fragmentation of the self, in the context of psychosis, also could give rise to feelings of self-liquidation. For André Green, secondary thinking is an effect of splitting insofar as it concerns a discourse characterized chiefly by avoidance, fragmentation, negation, and retroaction (repetition). Here too the ego is being split, though as we have seen, emphasis falls upon conscious versus preconscious and unconscious processes, and temporalization.

The literary critic, Roland Barthes, also looked at splitting when he argued that literary texts are based on what he called a "symbolic code," which he modeled on Lacan's concept of the symbolic order, which has to do with how signification is predicated on an unconscious internalization of binaries in the social order that are related to kinship, leadership, and so on. In Dostoevsky's story, we repeatedly encounter the opposition between high and low, dignity and wretchedness, honor and shamefulness, success and failure, a set of binaries that are socially determined and that follow the logic of splitting in

Klein's work. As it happens, this opposition isn't offset in Dostoevsky's Russia by that vast middling group of people we term "average," given that in Dostoevsky's world, the "average" social subject doesn't seem to exist. That is, "average man" (Ortega y Gasset's so-called "mass man," a mix of success and failure, honor and shamefulness) isn't yet an established norm whereby one's sense of hopefulness and hopelessness as a social subject is ameliorated into the compromised identity of the mediocre "middle class" individual. By contrast, the underground man, who lives in a pitiless hierarchical society, cannot tell whether he's vastly superior or inferior to everyone else, because he has no normative measure of success in what appears to be a terrifyingly exploitative world of extremes in which success and failure appear to be entirely arbitrary and illogical. In this world all social subjects are unsynthesized contradictions (an illogical mix of good and evil) who have been driven past their breaking points. This has a direct effect on the underground man's discourse which is never able to decide the success/failure opposition. In other words, "symbolic code" is vexed in Dostoevsky.

No doubt, for Dostoevsky the figure of the prostitute is perhaps the most exemplary personification of splitting (half saint, half sinner). She is the figure of Mother Russia, beautiful and soiled, good and bad. And yet, as corrupt as she is, she is still the "good object." Notice, for example, the following dialogue from part four of *Crime and Punishment* in which Sonya, who is a fallen woman, and Raskalnikov are speaking at a fever pitch:

> "I don't understand ..." Sonya whispered.
>
> You'll understand later ... Haven't you done the same thing? You, too, have stepped over ... were able to step over. You laid hands on yourself, you destroyed a life ... *your own* (it's all the same!). You might have lived by the spirit and reason, but you'll end up on the Haymarket ... But you can't endure it, and if you remain alone, you'll lose your mind, like me. You're nearly crazy already; so we must go together, on the same path! Let's go![16]

The Haymarket is where whores end up de ad. In the passage above Raskalnikov is desperately trying to rescue Sonya, though, in fact, she will be his salvation, the point being that they will transcend what is "bad" within them by means of their love for one another. But this is what cannot happen in *Notes*. There redemption by the woman of ill fame is refused just at the moment it appears possible.

This speaks to the crisis in the story, whose traumatic content is simple to tell. The underground man, a relatively destitute petty bureaucrat, psychologically abuses a rather young and impressionable woman, who has become a prostitute. She is perhaps the only woman in the world that could genuinely love him, but leaves, most likely out of disgust, and vanishes into the city's streets, never to be seen again. Only a few moments after she has walked out does he realize the horror of what he has done, given that only then does he recognize his love for her and that only through her might a wretch such as himself be redeemed. After the fact, the underground man is psychologically fated to repeat this traumatic break over and over, though retroactively. That is, he repeats it *before* it happens. This occurs by way of an endless small talk that differs itself from and defers the inevitable monstrosity of what he has done to himself. In fact, this small talk concerns events in which the horror of the woman's walking out is prefigured in terms of numerous slights and humiliations that have made up the content of the man's life. Moreover, the rejection of the woman was all a consequence of secondary thinking, too, most of which concerns the man's capacity for discursive splitting, his ability to simultaneously look at everything as good *and* bad in a way that is unhelpfully contradictory. All of this takes the place of what should have been primary thinking: proper understanding of his relation to Liza, who religiously represents a divine grace that the man couldn't perceive until it had been withdrawn. So pathological is this secondary thinking that it even accompanies the man in the very moment of his revelation:

> Where had she gone? And why was I running after her? Why? To fall down before her, to sob with remorse, to kiss her feet, to entreat her forgiveness! I longed for that, my whole breast was being rent to pieces, and never, never shall I recall that minute with indifference. But—what for? I thought. Should I not begin to hate her, perhaps, even to-morrow, just because I had kissed her feet today? Should I give her happiness? Had I not recognized that day, for the hundredth time, what I was worth? Should I not torture her? I stood in the snow, gazing into the troubled darkness and pondered this.[17]

Many years later, the underground man will admit, "all this is somehow a very evil memory. I have many evil memories now."[18] This contrasts with *Crime and Punishment* in which Raskolnikov, who has committed sins far worse than the underground man, puts together the wreckage of his life and of life generally in Russia in a revolutionary mental framework that exceeds the petty morality of an exploitative social order—hence his ability to comprehend Sonya. In *Notes* the nameless underground man is, to the contrary, quite incapable of mentally resolving the exploitative contradictions that constitute him and others as social subjects. If the notes have some integrative or "alpha function" (Bion), they nevertheless document the prevalence of secondary thinking.[19]

Obsessional Neurosis

Of course, the evil memories are what give rise to the secondary thinking and to the endless circumlocutions and contradictory explanations that are at once self-incriminating and self-justifying. These secondary thinking processes, in fact, have to take place insofar as the underground man has an obsessive psychology; that is, he is incapable of not thinking about what he has done and is drawn obsessively to the very evil memories he would rather not possess. Addressing obsessional neurotics, Jacques Lacan once remarked that the function of the obsessive's ego is *to dispossess the subject of himself.* "If the obsessional mortifies himself, it is because more than any other neurotic, he binds himself to his ego, which bears within itself dispossession and imaginary death."[20] Notice, with respect to Lacan's formulation, that the man in Dostoevsky's novella is the "underground" man, the man living an imaginary death, and that the entirety of his discourse is a self-mortification bound to his ego: "I am a sick man ... I am a spiteful man ..." Moreover, the man's ego is typical of that of the obsessive's ego: it is too conscious, too aware, even to the point of mental illness. "I swear, gentlemen, that to be too conscious is an illness—a real thorough-going illness." And, "every sort of consciousness, in fact, is a disease."[21] We are being told this because the man has come to realize that he is being persecuted by his thinking. Rather than arguing "I think, therefore I am," as Cartesians do, the underground man takes the obsessive's option of "I think, therefore I mortify myself."

Lacan rightly saw that the ego of the obsessive is, in fact, the ego of the Other, the one who is the obsessive's master and whom the obsessive is out to kill. If the underground man is out to kill by endlessly mortifying himself, as opposed to killing others as in the case of, say, Raskalnikov in *Crime and Punishment*, the object of his aggression too is the Other as omnipotent sadist, that is, society generally. The obsessive's strategy is clever, Lacan points out, because he mortifies himself in order to *preempt* the pleasure of the sadist and, in that way, takes away the master's power. Obsessive behavior of this sort amounts to the usurpation of the Other's role, but in reverse—as the obsessive subject is himself the object of sadistic treatment. That the obsessive subject takes pleasure in being this persecuted object speaks to how masochism functions as a ruse to arrogate for oneself the sadist's mastery by depriving the sadist of it, the point being that within this standard Freudian model, elaborated by Lacan, there is a disjunction in which the aggressivity of self-mortification, which in Dostoevsky's story is expressed in terms of discourse, is detached from its aim: to get back at society generally. Hence all the talk about spite.

This detour into the Freudian psychology of obsessive behavior modifies somewhat Green's emphasis upon decentering in that obsessive behavior, for all its circumlocution, is quite fixated and therefore noticeable in terms of its repetitiousness. Foundational, too, is the fact that the obsessive compulsive subject is responding to trauma, which in the case of the underground man has to do not only with the loss of Liza, but much earlier with his being rejected to the point of feeling that he has been socially erased. Note that with respect to the earlier trauma even his servant doesn't recognize him in any meaningful way, and that throughout his musings we sense a splitting wherein everything he says affirmatively is retracted, erased, wiped out, as if to repeat what has been done to him in some vague distant past before the story has begun. That is, in the distant past he has been expelled to the underground—or what amounts to "social death"—whereas in what is still his future he will expel Liza with the consequence that this expulsion will repeat his own and thereby expose the original trauma by way of its unforeseen reoccurrence. Whereas the underground represents a condition of expulsion from a world in which the man still lives and moves around that requires him to fantasize relations to others (since they cannot exist otherwise) the expulsion of the woman represents a condition of self-destruction that isn't imaginary and in which the man is suddenly present as a social subject who is being recognized and taken very seriously by an other. As Slavoj Žižek might put it, the encounter with Liza is the man's Hegelian moment in which he is recognized and mediated (judged) by an Other. But, of course, it is precisely this that the obsessive compulsive cannot bear, given that it is experienced as an attack upon his narcissism—his obsession with *himself*. And yet, through all his secondary thinking, he does *claim* this experience.

It is notable that whereas we are not told, precisely, about what we might call the traumatic ground-zero of the man's social death, he does tell us in detail about its repetitions, including that of the catastrophic loss of Liza, deferred until the end. Indeed, he defends against that traumatic loss of the woman—of what he comes to understand as the preeminently "good object"—by regressing to a stage before that episode happened, a stage in which all sorts of humiliations are paraded in front of us with a sort of masochistic delight. This, of course, is one of the temporal functions of all his secondary thinking: to demote the most shocking catastrophe to one of a series of ridiculous events. But that defensive strategy requires the obsessive to keep talking of the trauma, to keep claiming it by circling around it, because this gives pleasure or at least some relief, even if the trauma itself remains unsupportably painful.

Masochism

Especially in Part I, Section 4 of *Notes from Underground*, we can see a very explicit instance of secondary thinking in which somatic pain functions as a substitute for and example of psychic pain. In particular, we will be told about a toothache, which is both excruciatingly painful and yet somehow also pleasurable. Speaking to his imaginary interlocutors, the underground man adopts what he imagines to be their point of view: "'Ha, ha, ha! You will be finding enjoyment in toothache next,' you cry with a laugh. 'Well? Even in toothache there is enjoyment,' I answer." Structurally we are witnessing a neurotic psychology of obsession that affirms pleasure in trauma. The section begins with "I had a toothache for a whole month and I know there is [pleasure in it]" but transitions into observations of "an educated man ... suffering from toothache." We are told that the educated man's

> moans become nasty, disgustingly malignant, and go on for whole days and nights ... he is only lacerating and harassing himself and others for nothing [...] his whole family listens to him with loathing ... and inwardly understand that he might moan differently, more simply, without trills and flourishes, and that he is only amusing himself like that from ill-humor, from malignancy. Well, in all these recognitions and disgraces it is that there lies a voluptuous pleasure.[22]

The reader doesn't have to be a literary critic to see that the underground man is really talking about his own discourse, that this is an allegory about his own speaking, which to him is a response to something like a toothache, only much worse. Through the split off persona of the imaginary family man with the toothache, the underground man interpolates himself, when he ascribes to the educated sufferer "a voluptuous pleasure" that delights in its imposture, in its lack of self-respect. Speaking of himself, the underground man says, "my jests, gentlemen, are of course in bad taste, jerky, involved, lacking self-confidence. But of course that is because I do not respect myself." Generalizing to all educated men, the question is posed: "Can a man of perception respect himself at all?"[23] Here, as throughout the monologue, the underground man sees himself from both within and without, as himself and as another, hence splitting the discourse in order to split off bits of himself for self-mortifying dissection. What we see here, and elsewhere, is a break up of the ego into so many "bad objects" for the reader's delectation, hence inscribing us into his nasty game. This break up has gone so far as to literally segment the physical body into distinct bits, the teeth being isolated as a particularly painful part of the body when infected. This is an experience that the underground man attempts to make pleasurable by means of perversion: the advancement of a secondary line of reasoning that reverses or inverts the experience of somatic trauma by using it as a means to obtain pleasure by way of what the man calls malignancy or, as Nietzsche might have said, *ressentiment* (spite), which is something one activates along some secondary psychological route or byway that will facilitate pleasure.

The Infinity of Minor Paths

As we can see, the splitting of the self and the splitting of the discourse are related. As if to deny the relation, in Section 9 the underground man will defend himself against being thought mad (dissociated, contradictory, incoherent) by arguing that men *in general* are "predestined to strive consciously for an object and to engage in engineering—that is, incessantly and eternally to make new roads, *wherever they may lead.*" These new roads, of course, are the secondary routes of thinking that are the product of ceaseless "engineering" whose result is inevitably to go off "on a tangent." One cannot help but make roads, whether they go anywhere in particular or not. Lacan famously spoke to this activity of road building by pointing out that metaphorically normalcy is characterized by people taking to the highway (*la grande-route*) as opposed to a series of minor roads that go every which way. "If I take the highway as an example, it's because, as Monsieur de la Palice would say, it's a path of communication."[24] For Lacan it's the Roman road that serves as the model because "wherever it went, it left traces that are practically irremovable. Roman imprints, with everything that developed around them, are essential—as are, moreover, interhuman relationships of law, the mode of transmitting the written thing, as well as the mode of promoting the human appearance, statues." The highway, as Lacan puts it, has the "the function of the signifier," by which he means that it affords one an identity by means of establishing a coherent cultural environment in which everything has significance in terms of where and what it is. It is not by accident that the highway is the route (the life course, the way) that "everyone" is supposed to take, though there will be those who leave the highway and are forced "to combine minor paths," those who will encounter "separate modes of grouping meaning." To take the secondary roads, by-ways, and trails would be "to have a choice between different components of the network"; therefore, "we can take this route, or that route, for various reasons—for the sake of convenience, in order to roam, or simply because of a mistake at a crossroads." This, in Lacan's view, is what typifies the mentally ill patient, who can't abide the highway and who tends to get lost in a tangle of secondary routes.[25]

In the context of André Green's work, this is not atypical of secondary thinking in the sense of what Lacan calls "the infinity of minor paths."[26] No doubt, the underground man appears to be quite aware of this infinity and the madness to which it points, though in the passage from *Notes* above he is engaged in denying that he is any different from anyone else. And yet he immediately negates himself by playing the role of his accusers. That is, he splits. He plays the part of the Other:

> You thirst for life and try to settle the problems of life by a logical tangle. And how persistent, how insolent are your sallies, and at the same time what a scare you are in! You talk nonsense and are pleased with it; you say impudent things and are in continual alarm and apologizing for them.[27]

It is at about this point that we are alerted to the fact that the monologue we're reading is just a written document that stages a confession in front of others more or less theatrically, so that, true to the pathology of the obsessive neurotic, we hear that "Of course, I myself have made up all the things you say."[28] Typical of obsessive compulsive behavior, he is casting and playing all the parts himself. He splits up the world and its actors as he sees fit. Unlike the psychotic, who undergoes self-annihilation, the obsessive compulsive individual stays firmly in control as "director" and "playwright," despite his getting lost in the by-ways and off-shoots of reticulated discourse.

Repetition Compulsion

As it happens, the revelation of the underground man's unbearable trauma is the third act in a series of episodes that occur in the social world, not underground. These three acts comprise the second half of *Notes* (Part II). Act one begins with something that is extremely secondary, which is to say, minor and ridiculous, namely, an attempt to get into a brawl at a tavern out of envy for someone who was getting a sound thrashing by being thrown out of a window. Key to this episode is the underground man's masochistic aggression, which Dostoevsky sets up in order for the catastrophic last episode to make sense. That is, Dostoevsky begins by providing an explicit exposition of the man's pathology that repeatedly causes his downfalls. Much to the underground man's disappointment in the tavern, nothing happens, because "an officer put me in my place from the first moment." Why? Because the underground man is a coward, a "spindly little fellow" who is confronted by a man "over six foot." The underground man's humiliation leads him to fabricate obsessively an elaborate set of phantasies about the officer whom he sees on the street from time to time. This leads to an extreme ambivalence concerning admiration and resentment of the officer and imaginary scenarios in which the underground man will stage some sort of encounter on the street in which the officer is made to step aside so that the underground man can pass by. One day, the underground man absurdly stumbles in front of the officer and falls down at his feet. "He calmly stepped over me."[29]

Act two is substantially longer and concerns the underground man's reunion with his old schoolfellows, which enables Dostoevsky to give us some background about the underground man's humiliating past, though not the ground zero of his trauma. That the underground man gets us sidetracked in this episode speaks to retroaction, both in terms of his past and in terms of what is to come, which temporally has already occurred. In other words, the dinner with the schoolfellows has what Green calls "multi-directional temporality" and articulates a "reticulated arborescence." The episode with the schoolfellows starts out badly because the underground man is too poor to afford the dinner and drinks. But even worse, he cannot help but shamefully and pointlessly insult everyone when the reunion does take place and, in the end, having spoiled the reunion for everyone, degrades himself in front of his acquaintance Simonov by begging him for money. "Simonov pulled out the money and almost flung it at me. 'Take it, if you have no sense of shame!'"[30]

The reunion episode is yet another instance of repetition compulsion. It is a grotesque display of groveling, self-deprecation, feeling slighted, behaving arrogantly, and playing the bully almost all at once. That no one takes the underground man seriously as a threat makes him all the more frustrated and out of sorts, because it speaks to his irrelevance as a social being. Indeed, the reunion is typical of the endlessly digressive and dead ended sorts of discussions that the underground man has with himself in that the conversation among the schoolfellows suddenly shifts from one topic to the next without much logic. And, to top it off, everyone becomes rather drunk, and, as the episode progresses, everyone's sense of reality starts to disintegrate, something that enables us to transition to act three in which the underground man encounters Liza.

This crucial third act has a dreamlike prelude (this is one of Dostoevsky's masterful Freudian anticipations) in which the underground man suddenly notices that he has been left behind at the place where they were all having dinner. Was he sleeping? or unconscious? Hastily, the man goes into the street and gets into a carriage, having guessed the place to which everyone probably went. "There was a perfect whirl in my head" Thinking of one of the schoolfellows, Zverkov, whom the underground man especially resents, he day-dreams of beating him and his female friend, Olympia. "That damned Olympia! She laughed at my looks on one occasion and refused me. I'll pull Olympia's hair, pull Zverkov's ears! No better one ear, and pull him by it round the room. Maybe they will all begin beating me and will kick me out."[31] One can see how quickly the discourse frays into secondary side shoots. Retroactively this discourse takes us back to the prior episode with the officer; in fact, Zverkov and the officer seem closely identified if only because the underground man wants a violent confrontation with someone, anyone, who is his envied superior, if only to be beaten into masochistic satisfaction, which would at least be some sort of recognition of his existence. These thoughts are then followed by all kinds of secondary thoughts about being arrested, sent to Siberia, and so on. "At last we arrived. I jumped out, almost unconscious, ran up the steps and began knocking and kicking at the door." Typical of dreams in which one misses an appointment, the underground man arrives too late. Everyone has already gone. But being tired, he walks through what is a shop by day and a house of ill repute at night. Entering a drawing room, out of nowhere he is met by a "madam ... who had seen me before."[32] Seeing her he feels saved from the fate of his ridiculous brawling phantasies, since he knows he's too cowardly to really act them out:

> They were not here and ... everything had vanished and changed! I looked round, I could not grasp it yet. I looked mechanically at the girl who had come in: and had a glimpse of a fresh, young, rather pale face, with straight, dark eyebrows, and with grave, as it were wondering, eyes, that attracted me at once. I should have hated her if she had been smiling. I began looking at her more

intently and, as it were, with effort. I had not fully collected my thoughts.[33]

The ellipsis indicates an instance of "fading" which has the effect of a swoon. The girl, who later will identify herself as Liza, also appears as if out of nowhere. That is, she is just "there." And immediately the man begins to identify with her. He likes it that she's no beauty, that she doesn't smile, that she has a grave expression. "Something loathsome stirred within me. I went straight up to her at once." Catching a glimpse of himself in the mirror, he sees the revolting image of himself: "pale, angry, abject, with disheveled hair." And he concludes: "I am glad that I shall seem repulsive to her; I like that."[34] Disgusting as this sounds, it prepares the way for him to be accepted as the "bad object" that he is.

The Action of the Signifier

Lacanians are sensitive to the insight that the ego supports the Other with its discourse, but that there is something about the Other that the ego cannot sustain, a dimension of the Other that is not correlative to the ego and not accountable to it.[35] Discourse is what Lacan calls "the action of the Signifier" that makes a demand of the Other. That demand, it turns out, is always going to be made in a state of some ignorance, because one is making a demand of someone who is, in part, definitively an unknown. When Lacan speaks of love and hate, he points out that these are demands necessarily made in ignorance. Just as the underground man hates an officer who is, in fact, a complete stranger and of whom the underground man is completely ignorant, so he will similarly put a demand to Liza who is just as much an unknown. However, whereas the underground man's demands have been frustrated and brushed aside in the past as nuisances, Liza will answer (or return) the underground man's demand in a way that will both situate his desire and deprive him of its object. In psychoanalytical terms, she doesn't merely humiliate him; she castrates him. This is why one can speak of the last act in and of itself as traumatic.

In the recounting of Liza we get the report of what must have been a *real* conversation, not an imagined one. Liza, clearly, must have perceived a demand for love that shines through what could be called beratement. This beratement is the action of the Signifier whose effect is to bring Liza and the underground man into a personal relationship by means of which the demand can be made credible:

> "Why, do you think that you are on the right path?"
>
> "I don't think anything."
>
> "That's what's wrong, that you don't think. Realize it while there is still time. There still is time. You are still young, good looking; you might love, be married, be happy ..."
>
> "Not all married women are happy," she snapped out in the rude abrupt tone she had used at first.
>
> "Not all, of course, but anyway it is much better than the life here. Infinitely better. Besides, with love one can live even without happiness. Even in sorrow life is sweet ..."[36]

The Signifier that he is casting out before her is that of love, and he has secondary and tertiary reasons for doing so, because of a need to manipulate and dominate which requires elaboration by taking all those by-ways that Lacan had identified with those who go off *la grand-route*. Hence we get a whole discourse on marriage. "Indeed, I knew a woman like that: she seemed to say that because she loved him, she would torment him and make him feel it ... There are some women who are jealous ... Love is a holy mystery," and so on.[37] Quite far into all these speculations, Liza says with a pause in the middle, "Why you ... speak like a book."[38] This is one of those silences that would interest André Green. In fact, the underground man knows quite well that his discourse sounds artificial because, in large part, it is merely playacting and, as such, is a psychological defense, given his wariness of anyone who is really real. Therefore, when after engaging in tirades of what will happen to Liza if she continues to sell herself in brothels, he notes, "But now, having attained my effect, I was suddenly panic-stricken."[39] Whereas for the underground man the discourse is something of a game, for her it's not, because in all this talk she is hearing a persistent demand for love, however displaced and disguised in all the secondary thinking he can muster.

The encounter with Liza in the makeshift house of ill repute is followed up four days later by her coming to see the underground man in his shabby flat. He has given her his address, which later he regrets out of shame for his impoverished state. What he reveals to us in his notes is something that looks like a mental collapse that is precipitated in earnest when Liza arrives at his door. This reflects panic at the thought of being in the presence of a genuine Other, someone who for the man is now really real and not an object of phantasy—that is to say, someone who psychologically can have power over him. It all begins rather badly with Apollon the servant. In a state of complete panic, the underground man implores Apollon to go to a restaurant to get some tea and rusks. The underground man is so wound up that he even gives Apollon his wages then and there. "If you won't go, you'll make me a miserable man! You don't know what this woman is … This is—everything!" Apollon doesn't move, at least, not at once. "'I will kill him,' I shouted suddenly, striking the table with my fist so that the ink spurted out the inkstand."[40] The frenzy and the stupidity of it all reveals the man's relationship with Apollon, which is that the underground man feels persecuted by his servant, who is a source of frustration. "He is my torturer." Having "acted out" something in front of Liza that shamefully reveals his relationship with others, he suddenly busts into tears. "It was an hysterical attack. How ashamed I felt …" That sort of experience of shame, as we've seen before, is immediately compensated for by spiteful anger and hatred which the underground man predictably aims at Liza, as she's seen as the cause for the upset. "I was fully conscious of my spiteful stupidity and yet at the same time I could not restrain myself."[41] He is so angry, so hurt, and so humiliated precisely because this is such a familiar repetition of something that is compulsively set up to happen despite the fact that the consequence, each time, will be psychically painful to the man to an excruciating degree.

Liza, who is entirely unaware of this dynamic, broaches her own wish to escape entrapment as a prostitute. What she wants is to be rescued. But unable to extricate himself from his humiliation and the anger he has toward its supposed cause, Liza, he ignores her demand and spitefully and perversely *retracts* everything kind that he had said to Liza four days before in bed. As opposed to being compassionate and caring, despite all the secondary thinking, he now claims that he was cynically manipulating her in order to have a good laugh. "So you may as well know that I was laughing at you then. And I am laughing at you now."[42] Then, most cruelly, he logically reconstructs the events of four days ago by centering everything around his wounded narcissism, which, oddly enough, is a faithful representation of his behavior generally, but, in this case, a gross distortion of what really happened:

> I had been insulted just before, at dinner, by the fellows who came that evening before me. I came to you, meaning to thrash one of them, an officer; but I didn't succeed, I didn't find him; I had to avenge the insult on some one to get back my own again; you turned up, I vented my spleen on you and laughed at you. I had been humiliated, so I wanted to humiliate; I had been treated like a rag, so I wanted to show my power ... That's what it was, and you imagined I had come there on purpose to save you. Yes? You imagined that? You imagined that?[43]

This entire account is, in fact, a disavowal and negation of what really occurred, which is that the usual pattern of frustrated spite in the face of self-induced humiliation got derailed because of an unexpected interruption and intrusion: the sudden discovery in an inebriated state that the schoolfellows were absent followed by the surprising dreamlike appearance of Liza. In the revised account, Liza is viewed as a substitute object for the schoolfellows, in particular, Zverkov, but that's not at all what she was at the time. Rather, it is what she would have been had the underground man been entirely self-aware of what he was doing. What really occurred is that the underground man experienced something that didn't go to plan, *a chance occurrence* that disrupted his familiar pattern of behavior. In other words, what happened was *an attack on linking*. That is to say, the girl's appearance was an attack on and breach of the man's repetition compulsion that occurred at a moment when he couldn't defend against it. However, when she comes to the man's house four days later, he self-consciously deploys his all too familiar defensive mechanism by excessively repeating his compulsion to spitefully and aggressively debase himself in order to "kill the Master," as Lacan would put it. That Liza is master was revealed to the servant when he was told "you don't know what this woman is," namely, the beloved Other, the one who is superior. That her status of "good object" is being negated and retracted so vehemently by the underground man only establishes it all the more credibly. Of course, his retraction of everything that passed between them on their first encounter is itself a sort of secondary revision that transposes love (the good) into hate (the bad). The unadulterated good, of course, is unfamiliar and alien to the man. As such it underscores the approach of an Other who not only shatters the man's familiar assessment of others, but the approach of an other who *is* Other, and who cannot be entirely known and controlled, which for an obsessive neurotic is unmanageable. By expressing himself hatefully, the man mounts an attack on linking up with the woman for the sake of ensuring a reinforcement of the man's repetition compulsion. To put it simply, he loves his pathology more than he could ever love the woman. Therefore he even deprecates any capacity for love that he might imagine. "With me loving meant tyrannizing and showing my moral superiority." Not without self-insight, the underground man knows that he cannot abide the inalienable freedom that is constitutive of an Other, if not what the man calls "real life" which "oppressed me with its novelty."[44]

Apparently, the man leaves Liza to sit behind a screen by herself, and in time she picks up her things and leaves. Out of spite, the man puts money into her hand, in order to humiliate her. Only after she leaves does he notice that she has thrown the five ruble note upon his table. He quickly "flew like a madman to dress," and then runs after her.[45] Even if she could not have gotten too far away, she has vanished into the cold night. "Never had I endured such suffering and remorse." And yet, this shattering traumatic moment is everywhere accompanied by the side-routes of secondary thoughts. "Should I not begin to hate her, perhaps, even tomorrow ...," "tomorrow I should have defiled her soul," "the feeling of insult will elevate and purify her," and so on.[46] The man feels "ill from misery" and yet has everywhere cocooned himself in defensive alibis that negate the horror of what he has done to himself, which was to turn out the only person in his life who might have been able to love him. Such alibis, which are the foot soldiers of an attack on linking to the real world, comprise a network of secondary thoughts that oppressively lead to and away from how an obsessive compulsive neurotic figures trauma, as an unbearability that is nevertheless obsessively sustained and shouldered.

Conclusion

This paper has presupposed a notion of trauma that is quite different from what has characterized understandings of trauma in the 1980s and 1990s as developed in books by Cathy Caruth and others who had been arguing for the unrepresentability of trauma. As Robert Jay Lifton had put it in the context of Holocaust studies, "one moves forward into a situation that one has little capacity to imagine."[47] Of course, that fits the death camp experiences that Lifton was studying, but it doesn't necessarily correspond so well to obsessive compulsive trauma, given the work of repetition compulsion, primary narcissism, masochism, splitting, and secondary thinking. Whereas trauma in Lifton's studies is without doubt entirely unbearable, unimaginable, and unrepresentable, in Dostoevsky's *Notes* we have been able to see a brilliant literary elaboration of trauma that is incessantly being represented: worked and reworked discursively, though not necessarily *worked through* or resolved. W.R. Bion spoke to this, when he wrote in "Attacks on Linking" that "we are confronted not so much with a static situation that permits leisurely study, but with a catastrophe that remains at one and the same moment actively vital and yet incapable of resolution and quiescence."[48] That vitality has to do, precisely, with representations that are not absolutely localizable to some unspeakable gap or rupture in the historical past, but that are being incessantly elaborated in the background of one's thoughts as an accompaniment made up, at times, as a rather complex networking of accounts, some more broken off than others, which are the product of associative irradiation.

Did Lacan, in the mid 1950s, anticipate associative irradiation in *Seminar III* when he spoke of an "infinity of minor paths"? Lacan recognized madness as an actively vital exploration of paths that lead one quite far away from the main routes on which humanity commonly makes its way. These are the routes of the underground person whose abandonment of the main route is an attack on linking, a disconnection with society and the social. Additionally, for Lacan the taking of secondary routes signifies a repudiation to acknowledge or abide by a limit, that of the path in common, something that in the case of psychosis leads to a discourse that no longer has, as its main function, that of addressing an other who is perceived as an equivalent partner, as someone who is like oneself. By contrast, however, the obsessive compulsive is always communicating with an other who is supposedly like himself along endless secondary routes when he knows full well that this other isn't equivalent at all, but a rapacious, sadistic Other whose enjoyment is annihilating. In *Seminar XXI: The Non Dupes Err [1973–1974]*, Lacan asked how men and women fall in love and answered: "by chance."[49] For the obsessive compulsive it is this "by chance" that constitutes traumatic experience, because chance and danger are one and the same existential threat. Therefore, it's precisely *not* by means of chance that the obsessive compulsive person manages his life. This occurs not only because structures, however far flung and labyrinthine in their secondary thinking, provide security, but because there is the traumatic, happenstantial potential of suddenly finding oneself by chance in the presence of an Other whose demand (irrational, rapacious, desiring, unfulfillable) cannot be borne. To both appease and frustrate that rapacious demand is precisely what the obsessive person is attempting to accomplish, something that is experienced in terms of a pleasure that motivates a steady stream of secondary thinking that cannot help but surface and at times take over the obsessive subject's behavior, hence subverting him. However, this is the price the underground man in Dostoevsky's text has to pay for subverting the Other, as well. What this tells us is that in the case of obsessive compulsive behavior trauma and subversion are linked via a seemingly endless network of secondary routes of thought.

This construction of trauma differs from that of Cathy Caruth's formulations insofar as she has argued, not without good reason, for an understanding of trauma in which memory and forgetting are paradoxically intertwined, such that remembering trauma can be figured in terms of its erasure, or, in some cases, in terms of its misrecognition. In other words, her account of trauma concerns the inability to confront and hence retrieve the past, even as one dwells upon it by means of what the Freudians call repetition compulsion. In Caruth's studies the experience remains "unclaimed," despite efforts to appropriate and reappropriate it.[50] As we have seen, secondary thinking, by contrast, however much it leads away from trauma also manages to claim that experience, and perhaps all too well. There's nothing the underground man doesn't confront. Apparently, there's no experience ugly enough or humiliating enough that he will not claim as his. Indeed, it's his ability to claim that experience over and over again through both primary and secondary thinking that makes him incurable for the simple reason that he takes so much pleasure in meticulously mounting and remounting the traumatic dramas of his demise. This is not to say that there isn't considerable aversion, avoidance, and circumlocution at work in the underground man's thought processes, only that, at the end of the day, he doesn't leave his experiences unclaimed.

Notes

1. André Green, whose family was Jewish, was born in Egypt and emigrated to Paris in 1946. He refused to take sides between the Lacanians and the more orthodox Freudians, with whom he worked in the Société Psychanalytique de Paris, and established various study groups that brought Lacan's thinking in relation with that of other analysts and non-analysts, including Jacques Derrida. He participated in Lacan's seminars and gave a long paper on the psychoanalytical understanding of phantasy in Lacan's seminar on the phantasm in 1964. In the 2000s he traveled quite a bit to London in order to lecture to British analysts, where his ideas became very influential and authoritative. A review of his theories can be found in his book *Key Ideas for a Contemporary Psychoanalysis* (London: Routledge, 2005) that was published in translation in association with The Institute for Psychoanalysis, London.
2. André Green, *Time in Psychoanalysis* (London: Free Association Books, 2002), p. 54.
3. Ibid., p. 53.
4. Ibid., p. 55.
5. Bion discusses alpha function and beta bits in *Learning from Experience* in *Seven Servants* (New York: Jason Aronson, 1977). *Seven Servants* collects four short books, *Learning from Experience, Elements of Psycho-Analysis, Transformations, and Attention and Interpretation*.
6. *Time in Psychoanalysis*, p. 54.
7. Ibid., p. 55.
8. Ibid., p. 56.
9. Ibid., p. 57. Bion is in general agreement, which is why he developed his own psychological epistemology in order to better understand resistances or pathologies with respect to sabotaging integration of this sort. In Bion's symbolic vocabulary –*K* represents attacks on meaning and knowledge in the service of conscious and unconscious aggression. Secondary thinking can, in various respects, be equated with –*K*, particularly when that thinking splits off and fragments psychic content, despite that content being repeated in ways that are structurally apparent.
10. *Time in Psychoanalysis*, p. 58.
11. Other readers have noticed this dynamic, of course. See Peter Brooks, *Troubling Confessions: Speaking Guilt in Law and Literature* (Chicago: University of Chicago Press, 2000). "[Such] monologues implicate the

words and anticipated reactions of their listeners so that the listener, or reader, cannot escape scot-free from having listened to them," p. 32.
12. *The Brothers Karamazov*, trans. R. Prevear and L. Volokhonsky (New York: FSG, 1990), p. 40.
13. *Notes from Underground*, trans. Constance Garnett (New York: Barnes and Noble, 2003), p. 209. *Notes* was first published in the original Russian in 1864. Some may consider the Garnett translation to be outdated, but it retains a passionate intensity that later translations lack. Moreover, it's serviceable given that I am not doing any close linguistic analysis, which, in any case, would require considerable familiarity with Russian.
14. My consideration of the underground man differs quite markedly from M. Bakhtin's, which I think goes a bit too far in maintaining that this man "dissolves in himself all possible fixed features of his person, making them all the object of his own introspection ..." The problem, in my view, is that this homogenizes the discourse to such a point that one wouldn't be able to differentiate primary from secondary thinking. This flattening of the discourse from a psychoanalytical perspective is repeated when Bakhtin argues that there isn't a monologic word in the story, that, in fact, everything is dialogical in that everything the underground man says is mediated by an other. Of course this is true, but there is a psychological explanation for this that exceeds dialogism as a rhetorical principle. And, too, dialogism functions to occlude what Green calls secondary thinking. See Mikhail Bakhtin, *Problems of Dostoevsky's Poetics*, ed. and trans. Caryl Emerson (St Paul: University of Minnesota Press, 1984), p. 51 and on dialogism, pp. 228–229.
15. *Notes*, p. 210.
16. *Crime and Punishment*, trans. R. Pevear and L. Volokhonsky (New York: Random House, 1993), p. 329.
17. *Notes*, p. 312.
18. Ibid., p. 313.
19. In *Troubling Confessions*, Peter Brooks cites J.M. Coetzee, who has intuited the secondary thinking in *Notes* without having conceptualized it. "Behind each true, final position lurks another position truer and more final," Coetzee writes in the absence of realizing that he is dealing with what is a very canny depiction of a psychological neurosis. What Coetzee notices is both an "endless generation of the text of the self" and that as a "hungerer after truth," the underground man produces a "sterile, deferring truth, endlessly coming to no end." Quoted in Brooks, p. 292. Indeed, Brooks himself sees this tendency in confessional discourse to occlude truth as "a problem for law enforcement," which is to say, he reads Dostoevsky in utilitarian terms from the perspective of law and justice. What concerns Brooks is why it is one cannot wring the truth out of people even when they themselves are eager to confess at length. For him, truth is the concern rather than trauma.
20. Jacques Lacan, *Seminar II*, trans. S. Tomaselli (New York: Norton, 1988), p. 268.
21. *Notes*, pp. 211, 212.

22. Ibid., pp. 218, 219.
23. Ibid., pp. 219.
24. Jacques Lacan, *Seminar III: The Psychoses*, trans. Russell Grigg (New York: Norton, 1993), p. 290.
25. Quotes from *Seminar III*, 292–294.
26. Ibid.
27. *Notes*, pp. 236–237.
28. Ibid.
29. *Notes*, p. 253.
30. Ibid., p. 274.
31. Ibid., p. 275.
32. Ibid., pp. 277, 278.
33. Ibid.
34. Ibid.
35. This insight has its source in Jean-Paul Sartre's *Being and Nothingness* where he speaks of concrete relations with others. Sartre's point is that the Other possesses a freedom that the sadist cannot ever possess, no matter what tortures are applied. Well known is that much of Lacan's thinking is predicated on his reading of Sartre.
36. Ibid., p. 282.
37. Ibid., p. 286.
38. Ibid., p. 288.
39. Ibid., p. 292.
40. Ibid., pp. 304, 305.
41. Ibid., pp. 305, 306.
42. Ibid., p. 306.
43. Ibid.
44. Ibid., p. 310.
45. There seems to be an absence or gap in the narrative that suggests the underground man may have had sex with Liza on their second encounter, which would account for his giving her money. She is depicted sitting behind a screen in the man's room, which suggests they may have been intimate. Alternatively, the man may have screened her off for the sake of privacy and in order that she not see the squalor in which he has been living. In this we can see a rather complex sort of secondary speculation that is nascent. That the man has to "dress" in order to go out, adds to one's sense that intimacy took place.
46. Ibid., p. 312.
47. Cathy Caruth, "Interview with Robert J. Lifton," in Cathy Caruth, ed. *Trauma: Explorations in Memory.* (Baltimore: Johns Hopkins University Press, 1995), p. 137.
48. "Attacks on Linking" in W.R. Bion, *Second Thoughts* (New Jersey: Jason Aronson, 1993), p. 101.
49. *Seminar XXI* is still unpublished, though transcripts have been in circulation. Lacan's remark is well known among Lacanians.
50. Cathy Caruth, *Unclaimed Experience: Trauma, Narrative, and History* (Baltimore: Johns Hopkins University Press, 1996).

Bibliography

Bakhtin, Mikhail. *Problems of Dostoevsky's Poetics*. ed. and trans. Caryl Emerson. St Paul: University of Minnesota Press, 1984.

Bion, W.R. *Learning from Experience*. In *Seven Servants*. New York: Jason Aronson, 1977.

Bion, W.R. *Second Thoughts*. New Jersey: Jason Aronson, 1993.

Brooks, Peter. *Troubling Confessions: Speaking Guilt in Law and Literature*. Chicago: University of Chicago Press, 2000.

Caruth, Cathy. "Interview with Robert J. Lifton." In Cathy Caruth, ed. *Trauma: Explorations in Memory*. Baltimore: Johns Hopkins University Press, 1995.

Caruth, Cathy. *Unclaimed Experience: Trauma, Narrative, and History*. Baltimore: Johns Hopkins University Press, 1996.

Dostoevsky, Fyodor. *The Brothers Karamazov*. Trans. R. Prevear and L. Volokhonsky. New York: FSG, 1990.

Dostoevsky, Fyodor. *Notes from Underground*. Trans. Constance Garnett. New York: Barnes and Noble, 2003.

Green, André. *Time in Psychoanalysis*. London: Free Association Books, 2002.

Green, André. *Key Ideas for a Contemporary Psychoanalysis*. London: Routledge, 2005.

Lacan, Jacques. *Seminar II: The Ego in Freud's Theory and the Technique in Psychoanalysis*. Trans. S. Tomaselli. New York: Norton, 1988.

Lacan, Jacques. *Seminar III: The Psychoses*. Trans. Russell Grigg. New York: Norton, 1993.

4
Colonial Trauma, Utopian Carnality, Modernist Form: Toni Morrison's *Beloved* and Arundhati Roy's *The God of Small Things*

Greg Forter

In the Introduction to his *Postcolonial Narrative and the Work of Mourning*, Sam Durrant makes a powerful case for the salience of trauma to the study of colonialism. Durrant asks us to attend anew to the moment in Fanon's *Black Skin, White Masks* when a child points at the author and says, "'Dirty Nigger!' Or simply, 'Look, a Negro!'" This textual moment, he argues, "memorializes a traumatic event" that

> interpolates Fanon not as an individual but as a member of a race ... apart, other, nonhuman. The experiences of racism that he [Fanon] goes on to recount do not add up to a narrative precisely because they cannot be integrated into a life history; they are repetitions of an "originary" event that bars him from having a life history and from the temporality of the human. (2004: 14)

Durrant is in part making an incontrovertible point: that the potential for traumatization is a constitutive feature of colonial (race) relations, inasmuch as these are always and everywhere relations of domination. By locating the analysis of trauma at the heart of a founding postcolonial text, moreover, he emphasizes the power of this analytic to reveal the effects of colonial domination on individual and collective identities, and perhaps even to ameliorate the legacy of those injuries in the present. In this way his project joins the work of Leela Gandhi, Ranjana Khanna, Vijay Mishra,

Christine van Boheemen-Saaf, and others, each of whom offers a model of colonialism in which the organizing facts are trauma and its consequences for colonized peoples.

The brief quotation from Durrant is also enough to begin to specify how a "traumatic" analysis understands such consequences. Colonial trauma entails in these works some combination of the following: a profound psychic disorientation; the deformation or eclipse of memory; an exile from chronological sequence and into the compulsive repetition of past injuries; and a form of writing that must, if it is to keep faith with this experience, mime and transmit to readers a break in linear, conventionally narrative representation. Underlying these entailments is a specifically psychoanalytic understanding of "trauma." That term refers, in these accounts, to an event so overwhelming and inassimilable that the self responds by absenting itself from direct experience of the event. The trauma therefore lives on (in the subject) only in this lacuna where the self "was not." From there it erupts unbidden into consciousness not in the form of narratable story, but as intrusive, belatedly experienced, and achronological memorial shards (flashbacks, nightmares, image-traces, and so forth), which can remain "true" to the traumatizing event only insofar as they are not sublated into conventional linear narration.[1]

The challenge of transposing this psychic account into the social domain accompanies all efforts to think about trauma in colonial contexts. What, for example, is the collective equivalent within colonialism of the self-absenting or dissociation so central to the etiology of trauma? And what is the relation between the forms of amnesia that result from such self-absenting and those that are rather the effects of an enforced rupture with previous social forms—the disruptions of the Middle Passage, for example, or the imposition of European value-systems upon those subject to the "civilizing mission"? Questions like these admit of no easy answers. Their difficulty gives rise to what seem to me two main strands of work on postcolonialism and trauma, which I shall call the therapeutic and the anti-therapeutic strands.[2] Each of these is prone to an equally distinctive kind of problem that issues from the way it conceives the relation between psychic and social domains—more particularly, the way it *analogizes* the social with the psychic. Let me begin by approaching the strands singly, with an eye to both their roots in analogy and the problem peculiar to each, before turning to the two novels in my title and showing how they offer egress from the impasses of postcolonial trauma theory.

The therapeutic strand is perhaps the more familiar of the two. It is the one to which David Lloyd calls attention in his influential essay, "Colonial Trauma/Postcolonial Recovery?" (Lloyd cites Leela Gandhi in particular.) Centrally at issue in that text is the danger of an analogy between the individual and the social by which once-colonized peoples are encouraged to "work through" their attachment to past injuries in the name of an untroubled adherence to modernity. Here the model of trauma relies on a normative conception of recovery that at once replicates an aspect of colonialism and collaborates with postcolonial nationalism. For just as, in colonial societies, "The social forms of the colonized become 'survivals' of a ... precolonial past" that the colonizers disparage as pathology—and just as this leaves "No space ... for the unfolding of the capacities of the colonized that are out of kilter with modernity"—so, too, does postcolonial nationalism "reproduce the effects of colonial modernity by selecting and canonizing elements of the colonized culture that can be refunctioned within the terms of the modern state." The latter process "relegate[s] those elements that are incommensurable with modernity to the position of a backwardness that is symptomatic of a refusal to be cured" (2000: 219). To "recover" from colonial trauma is then to accept the cure of identifying one's interests with those of the modern nation-state. The emphasis on postcolonial recovery compels a species of historical forgetting, a renouncing of the "archaic" potentialities that hegemonic modernity's narrative of development requires its subjects to snuff out.

It's this forgetful attachment to the modern that Lloyd urges his readers to resist:

> In the shadow of nationalism, as of colonialism, there lurk, we might say, melancholy survivals. For those of us who would persist in critiquing and opposing the ubiquitous and seemingly endless violence that is constitutive of modernity, it is crucial to discern in these "melancholy survivals" complex forms of *living on* that do not simply preserve belated and dysfunctional practices, but [foster] potentialities for producing and reproducing a life that lies athwart modernity. (219)

The aim of postcolonial thought should thus be to retrieve and encourage these "complex forms of living on"; it should seek to render socially feasible the lives that "lie … athwart modernity," rather than encourage the analogy-therapy by which the health of communities is made to align with the norms of hegemonic modernity.

The anti-therapeutic strand of criticism takes a resistance to this alignment as its starting point. Lloyd's essay is in many respects representative of that initiative; the works I have in mind display a basic agreement with his arguments (i.e., Khanna, Durrant, Mishra). Yet Lloyd's essay is remarkable partly because it avoids the central pitfall of work in the anti-therapeutic vein, a pitfall best described as a tendency to ontologize the social.[3] I mean by this that work in this strand conceives of trauma as so thoroughly embedded in sociality *per se* that it's difficult to see how we might overcome it. An analogy between the psychic and the social now models "the social" on the traumatized psyche—on the psyche as *constitutively* traumatized—in a manner that scarcely admits of amelioration. It's as if this work responds to the therapeutic model with a crippling double move: first, a commendable shift of emphasis to the constraints imposed on working-through by the extra-psychic domain, but second, a conceptualization of that domain *as always already traumatizing*, as a realm whose collective, social character is indistinguishable from the pathogens that "constitute" it as social. The result is that the social body takes on the symptoms of a melancholic illness that no amount of transformative agency will be enough to cure.

We can see this process at work in the very best of the recent works in the field, Durrant's *Postcolonial Narrative and the Work of Mourning.* The book is distinguished by its conceptual rigor and sophistication on one hand, the attentiveness of its close analyses on the other. Working together, these strengths generate compelling accounts of how Toni Morrison, Wilson Harris, and J.M. Coetzee engage traumatic histories in their texts to arrive at different modalities of "working through" (or declining to do so). That each author confronts an historically specific articulation of colonial domination is central to the book's appeal. Yet in Durrant's hands, such differences are often flattened out by a theory that views domination as explicable only through recourse to the extra-historical. His analysis grounds colonialism in an "originary" forgetting of the humanity of the racial other, an event which can never be known or narrated because it remains radically extrinsic to history and representation. Durrant thus refers to this Forgetting as "primary repression"; it "founds the European subject" and is a "foreclosure" that "constitutes the *prehistory* of [that] subject" (2004: 5). By this latter, he clearly means not that the Forgetting is an event or historical process that separates, say, the (modern) European subject from some premodern past, but that it is a *non*-historicizable Event that exists nowhere "in" history but is that history's very condition. The historical domain is thus the effect of a "prehistorical" exclusion from which the movement of History is itself born.

Nevertheless, Durrant persists in giving the "Forgotten" an expressly social content: "Narrative histories that seek to recover ... a black subject must ignore that the term ... 'black man' is ... the figure of an exclusion. They [such histories] 'chronologize a time that is not chronological' and thus function as a mode of insulation against the achronological traumatic temporality of racism" (6).[4] If "black man" is indeed the "figure of an exclusion," this is because Durrant's analysis has made him a metaphor for the primordial, foundational foreclosure from which the historical is said to emerge. The achronology of colonial trauma becomes thereby an effect of how history emerges from a founding *racial* exclusion.

> Fanon's image of the body in pain ... functions to indicate a breach in time; it memorializes a traumatic event without placing it in a chronology. It does not retrieve an encounter with the white man's gaze that occurred at a particular place and time but rather marks an experience that is unhistoricizable both because it repeats itself infinitely, in Fanon's life and in the life of other black men ... and because the experience is in and of itself an experience of the breakdown of chronology, a confirmation that the black man is indeed, to paraphrase Hegel, outside history. (16)

The result of this recourse to prehistory is that the "story" of colonial trauma becomes implacably anti-historical and radically non-representational: it is the Real that precedes yet is produced by and haunts the historical order itself. "[T]he black man is indeed ... outside history" because his humanity is the object less of an historical denial than of a foreclosure that founds (yet troubles) the movement of History. What thus begins as a laudable skepticism toward the project of "historicism"—toward those forms of historiography that homogenize time in the name of putting the (colonial) past securely to rest—ends as ahistorical mythology in which colonial domination is inaugurated by the exclusion of a Real that the analysis names "race," and in which race exists "in" history only as that which punctures and ruptures the sequence of historical time.

I leave entirely aside the fact that this view grants a dubious causality to racism in the genesis of colonialism and slavery: as many historians have now shown, the racialization of dominion was in fact the secondary result of a set of labor demands and crises precipitated by colonial capitalism's expansion in the seventeenth and eighteenth centuries (e.g., Morgan; Saxton). More important for my current purpose is that, as in the case of the therapeutic model, the difficulty in Durrant's account hinges on a faulty analogy between the psychic and the social. The analysis surreptitiously analogizes historical reality with human subjectivity: the model of history as produced by a founding exclusion of what will henceforth count as "Real" derives from Lacan's account of the production of human subjects from just such a process. The analogy matters from a political standpoint because of the transhistorical and intractable character of the category of the Real. It is, in short, hard to see how social change can come about if racial exclusion is the indigestible kernel of a Real whose foreclosure founds human history. It's difficult to see how one might remember the trauma of colonialism and challenge its lingering effects if the trauma is, as Durrant at times contends, *impossible* to remember or represent without betraying its Real unrepresentability (16). And it's hard to square those places in Durrant's text where he exhibits a fine sensitivity to the value of "working through" with his theoretical commitment to the proposition of "infinite" and "inconsolable" grief—to the ethical necessity of never "assigning a limit" to the work of mourning (10, 115).[5]

* * *

I'm suggesting that approaches to colonial trauma cluster around opposing politico-affective poles. The therapeutic approach tends toward an over-optimism about "recovery" that's based in a covert acceptance of the health of postcolonial modernity; the anti-therapeutic model exhibits an excessive pessimism based in a tendency to conflate the historical (and thus remediable) *un*health of colonialism with the inaugural and irremediable "injuries" of subject-formation.[6] These difficulties issue in each case from a flawed analogy between psychic and social worlds. The therapeutic view extrapolates from the psychic domain a notion of cure that fails to question the norms upon which such a cure is based; the anti-therapeutic response extrapolates history from a view of subjectivity as constituted by a traumatic rupture with what will henceforth disrupt the self from within—a negativity that, on this account, neither the subject nor the social order can ever hope to surmount. In both cases, the recourse to analogy disturbs the effort to redress the injuries inflicted by colonial regimes. For this latter requires a procedure about which Adorno's remarks concerning Holocaust remembrance remain especially insightful: "We will not have come to terms with the past until the causes of what happened then are no longer active," he writes. "Only because the causes live on does the spell of the past remain to this very day unbroken" (1959: 29). Implicit in this statement is a view of "working through" based less in analogy than in a dialectic of psycho/social causation. The injuries of eliminationist anti-semitism, slavery, and colonialism are *caused* by specific social formations, which are of course themselves the products of human mind and labor; to "come to terms" with such injuries is then to mobilize contemporary minds and bodies in the name of eradicating the social conditions that caused them in the first place. Such a view leaves open the possibility of non-historical or subjectively originary forms of "trauma"—inaugural injuries that are insusceptible to ameliorative action. Yet by resisting the analogical temptation, it retains a distinction between such injuries and those that are historically induced and thus in need of *social* remediation. Adorno's vision grasps as well that efforts to "come to terms with the past" through purely psychic healing, or through a healing that readily assumes the "health" of the present order, are dangerously naïve. His comments exhibit sufficient skepticism toward a conciliatory, meretricious "cure" to exempt him from the criticisms leveled by thinkers suspicious of therapeutic recovery—even as he remains committed to the possibilities of a social working-through.

It's in the context of these latter comments that I wish to locate my discussion of Morrison's *Beloved* (1987) and Roy's *The God of Small Things* (1997). As with Adorno, these works link the social and the psychic dialectically rather than analogically. Their ways of conceiving that link have important consequences both for *what* the books represent and for *how* they represent it. A commitment to the problem of causation, for example—to exploring how trauma is produced and reproduced, induced and transmitted, through the institutions of colonialism and its postcolonial avatars—leads them to insist on the irreducible particularity of suffering. Colonial trauma is comprehensible here only by attending to specific bodies and psyches that occupy specific social locations, and by depicting historically explicable instances of colonial violence. The "unrepresentable" character of trauma is thus due not to its being "originary" and hence, beyond history and representation. Rather, it has to do with the enforced rupture with precolonial pasts and the prohibitions against remembrance enforced by particular regimes of power. This means that such pasts are *in principle* recoverable, representable, narratable. Yet each of the novels is concerned to delineate the difficulties and ethical challenges of remembrance. Each insists on the complicity between conventional narrative and hegemonic modernity, at least for the telling of *these* stories. And each thus intuits that, within the current social and representational order, to "give voice" to the silenced requires the violation of that representational order, an effort to shatter linguistic forms that conspire in the illusions of total understanding.

It's out of this intuition that the books' formal innovations arise. Those forms are efforts to speak the "unspeakable" of an *historically-induced* repression or silence whose content can only emerge in the interstices of what can currently "be said." Modernist techniques, in other words, are here forms deployed for the purposes both of approximating the disruptions of traumatized consciousness and of retrieving what that consciousness has been forced (through social violence) to forget. Such a retrieval can never be complete under current social conditions; the victims of history can *fully* "speak" only with the birth of new social forms. Nevertheless, these books attempt through their formal innovations to provide the residual lineaments of those stories. They seek as well, in doing so, to give us glimpses of what a future social restitution might look like. Their disruptions to conventional narration open up new kinds of "negative space" in which each work envisions a world—evanescent, provisory, infinitely fragile—where the causes of social injustice and trauma have truly "ceased to be active." These utopian elaborations are shown to *fail*, as we shall see. But part of the books' radicality for our moment consists in their willingness to take the risk of envisioning these alternate worlds, against a consensus that views such efforts as always and everywhere symptoms of a politically dangerous nostalgia.

I

Let us begin with Morrison's *Beloved*.[7] The violence of Atlantic world slavery and the slave trade is registered here primarily in terms of the traumas they inflict on the black woman's body.[8] The novel imagines these afflictions most fully, within its central narrative strand, in the scenes where two of Schoolteacher's pupils first hold Sethe down and steal her milk, then help Schoolteacher to whip her for telling Mrs. Garner about the pupils' violation. The first of these acts has an especially complex resonance in the novel at large. On one hand, it literalizes the violence intrinsic to a system of wet-nursing in which "the little whitebabies got it [the milk] first and [the black ones] got what was left. Or none" (Morrison 1987: 236). The stealing of milk stages, in this sense, the threat of a draining of the maternal breast so total that it cannot sustain the black child's life. On the other hand, this literal and expressly mortal threat subtends a less biological but equally devastating danger. This is a danger that follows from the metaphorical meaning of mother's milk. It has to do with the way such milk is never reducible to its vital function, but carries within it a set of meanings about the extent and depth of the mother's devotion. Milk, in short, at this second level, is nothing less than a metaphor for maternal love. To be forced to withhold it from one's child while giving it to a white child is to be made to communicate to the black child a secondariness and relative unloveableness. The scene in which the pupils steal Sethe's milk is thus one that allegorizes the violence by which slavery compromised not just black women's efforts to "realize" their life-sustaining capacities but also their ability to transmit to their children the very substance of love.

This truncation is "traumatic" partly because of the process by which it induces a violent negation of the mother's self-worth. Chattel slavery renders concrete a white belief in black people's sub-humanity (whether or not the slaveholder consciously believes this), which Sethe confronts when she overhears Schoolteacher telling a pupil to list "her human characteristics on the left; her animal ones on the right" (228). The momentousness of this remark—Sethe immediately recoils from it—coupled with Sethe's incomprehension of it—she asks Mrs. Garner what the word "characteristics" means (229–230)—suggests that it transmits to her a latent, traumatogenic significance, an uncomprehended but devastating "meaning" that will lie dormant within her until a second event retrospectively determines its effects.[9] This second event is that in which Sethe is "milked" by Schoolteacher's pupils. Later she remembers the event thus: "I'll tell Beloved about that; she'll understand. She my daughter. The one I managed to have milk for and get it to her even after they stole it; after they handled me like I was the cow, no, the goat, back behind the stable because it was too nasty to stay in with the horses" (236–237). If Schoolteacher's remark contains the potential for an *internal* self-negation, the scene of "milking" realizes that potential by forcing Sethe to occupy the position of a degraded animality (neither horse nor cow, but goat). It's this, I suggest, that shatters her with the knowledge that "anybody white could take your whole self for anything that came to mind. Not just work, kill, or maim you, but dirty you. Dirty you so bad you couldn't like yourself anymore. Dirty you so bad you forgot who you were and couldn't think it up" (295). The violence of this animalizing degradation "fulfills" the traumatizing potential of Schoolteacher's remark, activating an implanted self-debasement by way of that draining of milk that metaphorizes the thwarted transmission of maternal love.

The novel in this way begins to trace out an exceedingly complex psychosocial scenario. It suggests that slavery works in part by coercing black women into being mothers (i.e., raping and impregnating them) while blocking their efforts to "realize" a mother's affection. This blockage in turn produces a traumatizing subhumanization that poisons the mother's regard for herself—a "dirtying" that negates her self-worth and makes it impossible for her "to like [her]self anymore." The clear implication of such a depiction is that slavery traumatizes *women* by way of a kind of surplus violence. It not only robs them of self-ownership, coerces their labor, and physically brutalizes them—all of which it does to men—but *also* soils and degrades their self-conception by compelling them to be mothers while thwarting their efforts at maternal love. *Beloved* devotes itself in part to exploring the consequences of this thwarting. One of these consequences—perhaps the most central—is what I would call

Sethe's compensatory idealization of her children. "[T]hough she and others lived through and got over [the dirtying]," Morrison writes,

> she could never let it happen to her own. The best thing she was, was her children. Whites might dirty *her*, all right, but not her best thing, her beautiful, magical best thing—the part of her that was clean. ... [N]o one, nobody on earth, would list her daughter's characteristics on the animal side of the paper. (295–296)

Here, the experience of self as soiled and of the barriers to love as formidable gives rise to a split-off projection of *all* value (cleanliness, beauty, "best-ness") into the child, and to a fierce determination to protect that child from the mother's fate. It's this compensatory idealization that Paul D denounces as Sethe's "too thick" love when he finds that she killed Beloved in an effort to keep her "safe" (193). The novel itself demurs, of course, from Paul D's scathing judgment. It shows that Sethe's love is "too" thick only in the sense that the institution of slavery diminishes the effectiveness of the black mother's devotion to the point where her daughter's likely fate is a repetition of her own soiling; hence slavery *requires* an "excess" of love in the form of a violence that robs the slaveholder of the opportunity to perform that soiling. Sethe's rejoinder to Paul D—"Too thick? ... Love is or it ain't. Thin love ain't love at all" (194)—captures this view with precision. It affirms the value of *infanticidal love* as one kind of ethical response to a system that thwarts black women's conventionally maternal, ordinarily protective love. "Too thick" love is, in this sense, nothing less than the tragic yet ethically efficacious residue of slavery's brutal effort at curtailment.

The question of the appropriateness of "thick" love in the Postbellum period is one to which I return below. Here I wish to emphasize that the psychosocial dynamic I'm describing, by which slavery has highly particular and traumatizing effects on black female subjects, has in *Beloved* an historical dimension as well. The harrowing stream-of-consciousness chapters in Book Two make this connection with force. In these chapters, especially the ones devoted to Beloved's voice, Morrison gestures toward the Middle Passage and—through it—the enslavement and expropriation of Africans as the historical events out of which emerged the conditions of its "present." She does so in terms that might seem at first to endorse the anti-therapeutic arguments discussed in my introduction. Beloved appears here, for example, as a kind of spectral figuration of the collective slave dead; she inhabits a timeless, derealized topography "beyond" discernible historical sequence, seeming in fact to (have) exist(ed) at once on the ships of the Middle Passage, in the posthumous waters from which she emerges in the story proper, in and as Sethe's daughter before she kills her, and in a future that appears indistinguishable from each one of these moments. This timeless time is the medium in which the wounds of slavery and Middle Passage are reenacted without cease: "there *will never be a time*," Beloved laments, "when I am not crouching and watching others who [crouch]" (248; emphasis added). The "I" of this statement could clearly be read as an anti-temporal figure of disruption, the specter "in" historical time of a properly non-historical wound that can, accordingly, *never* be fully represented or surmounted.

Plausible as this reading may sound, it seems to me to miss the novel's striking account of historical causation. The timeless time of slavery's specters is here the *effect* of a dominative history that has not yet given way to a "now" in which those specters might find repose. The founding events are not "prehistorical"—not a Forgetting that initiates human history by way of an exclusion which haunts that history with a constitutive (ineradicable) specter. Those events are, instead, the eminently historical acts associated with racial capitalism and slavery. Beloved herself makes this point evocatively: "Three times I lost her: once with the flowers because of the noisy cloud of [gun]smoke; once when she went into the sea instead of smiling at me; once under the bridge when I went in to join her and she came toward me but did not smile" (253–254). These three moments allegorize the movement from capture and enslavement in Africa, through the horrors of Middle Passage, and on to the brutalities and—especially—the enforced separations of slavery in the New World. Morrison embeds this allegory in Beloved's associative ruminations in order to stress how the specters produced by this history become "available" only in techniques that violate the logic of realism and its homogenous temporality. For historical specters—once produced—do indeed exist outside such homogenous/historicist time, haunting all three moments with the lamentations of unmourned dead. They await a proper reckoning with the social conditions from which they emerged and that continue in modified form to shape the postcolonial present. But this is only another way of saying that the specters of slavery are, precisely, ghosts of an historical violence, one to which we *can* but *have not yet been able to* do justice.

The allegory embedded in *Beloved*'s lament accretes historical significance as the novel unfolds. That significance once more takes the form of a gendered legacy of violence. The brutality of Sethe's "milking," for example, is only the latest in a series of traumas inflicted on women in the course of the history sketched by *Beloved*'s lamentation. Sethe herself is the daughter of a woman who embodies especially the first two moments—a woman stolen from Africa and transported across the Atlantic to the New World, and a woman raped repeatedly along the way. *Beloved* stresses that this woman threw overboard the white-fathered babies to which she gave birth on the journey, but "kept" Sethe and let her live because her father was an African. It thus reveals the conditions by which a certain maternality gets historically reproduced: Sethe's infanticidal love belongs to the history of black women's response to the forms of motherhood forced upon them by the institutions of slavery and the slave trade. Those institutions made infanticide *less repugnant* than other options. They circumscribed for women a minimal arena of choice, the space for a kind of refusal—as when the mother "throws away" the children fathered by white rape—or alternately, an affirmation—as when she "keeps" the one fathered by a black man and gives that child the father's name. Sethe's infanticide is in this way related to her mother's acts *historically*: it is an act of agency performed in the context of a dominative history by *this particular person* at *this particular* moment in time and in *this* geographical location. The act is "like" Sethe's mother's in being a maternal violence made ethically defensible by the gendered brutality of chattel slavery. Yet it's unlike those acts in that Sethe is not "on" the Middle Passage, and the daughter she kills is not the product of white rape. She (Sethe) is a runaway slave whose children were fathered by a black man; she's living in the suburbs of Cincinnati, Ohio, at a moment (1855) when the 1850 Fugitive Slave Law is fully in effect; and she's therefore placed in the intolerable position of having to express her love through a violence that can alone, within these parameters, keep her daughter safe from harm.

This emphasis on historical specificity is absolutely central to *Beloved*'s vision. It shapes not only the book's view of history but its treatment of how characters respond to the history of which they're a part. It is especially evident in the novel's account of the conditions under which a traumatic past can be "worked through": how can those subject to a legacy of trauma come to feel the present as *different* from a past whose crimes have yet to be socially reckoned? Is it possible to keep faith with past traumas, and with the dis-remembered dead, without repeating or extending that past in a new (if still imperfect) "present"? These questions take on special urgency in relation to the problem of temporal futurity; for the problem of honoring without succumbing to the past is intimately bound to the question of whether trauma's victims can make for themselves a future that does not reprise the past. *Beloved* addresses these conditions most fully in the contrasting set of meanings it assigns to Paul D and Beloved, and hence it is to that contrast that I wish now to turn.

II

Perhaps the best way to map the tension is to say that, for Sethe, Paul D represents the possibility of a future that extends yet differs from the present while Beloved portends a foreclosure of that future in the name of exclusive devotion to the past. Paul D begins his tenure at 124 by chasing Beloved's ghost from the house while "stoking" Sethe's "mind" with "the notion of a future" (51); Beloved responds by physically incarnating herself, reasserting the claims of the past against this temporal reorientation. One effect of her incarnation is Sethe's reprieve from the demands of memory: Beloved's return leads her to think of "everything she won't have to remember" anymore (214–217). The reason for this is that a past which inhabits the present is no longer past at all; it not only *need* not but *can*not be recalled—cannot be separated out in time sufficiently to be an "object" of memory—because it insists on materially cohabiting (with) the here and now. The novel clearly means to suggest that this cohabitation is preferable to Paul D's effort at banishment. And yet *Beloved* does not propose that the cohabiting should be "without end"; it does not suggest that the incarnation of past as present is either a condition that should be made permanent or one that can't be surmounted, insisting instead on the mortal dangers of making the specter permanent.

These mortal threats have been the subject of such a rich body of criticism (e.g., Wyatt 1993; Morgenstern 1996) that we need only touch upon them here. They include the devouring, identificatory love by which Beloved seeks to "join" (Morrison 1987: 251) with Sethe to the point of the latter's extinction—"Beloved ate up her life, took it, swelled up with it, grew taller on it. And the older woman yielded it up without a murmur" (295)—as well as the fact that Sethe seems less "to want forgiveness" "for the handsaw" than to "want ... it refused" (295, 297). Such a dynamic asks to be read as an enactment of the dangers inhering in unmetabolized or unworked-through trauma; the impasse between mother and daughter suggests that the specter's embodiment is a kind of historical malady rather than an instantiation of the non-historicizable "truth" undergirding historical experience. Beloved's demand for exclusive attention bespeaks the intrusion in the present of a past so indigestible and all-consuming that its demands can only be met by way of a total maternal self-sacrifice (death). That past consists less of a prehistorical Forgetting than of a history of the gendered traumas inflicted by that variant of colonial modernity called plantation slavery. *Beloved* does not, therefore, recommend that one submit to the specter's "ineradicable" presence, but rather explores how that specter might find repose through rituals of collective restitution.[10]

The novel's closing Book is in part an account of this restitutive ambition. That Book describes a chastened version of Paul D's effort at temporal reordering; it once more banishes Beloved from the present, but does so on the other side of an encounter that has acknowledged the need to "relive" the past as a moment in working it through (see Freud 1914). The second banishment is initiated by Denver: having recognized the mortal danger posed by Beloved to her mother, she leaves the yard of 124 to seek out help from a world she has not even entered for years. This movement marks a tentative affirmation of the historical specificity foreclosed by the traumatic experience of time. It affirms that the world of 1873 is *not* that of 1855—that the present differs from the past, however much it also resembles it; and that despite Sethe's claims to the contrary, there are no "places in which things so bad happened [to Sethe] that when you [Denver] went near them it would happen again" (Morrison 1987: 287). Denver's gesture stirs a *collective* (social) action as well: the black women of the town band together to "sing" Beloved out of the present and thereby save Sethe's life.[11] The ameliorative, exorcizing aim of this action is clear from what ensues. Sethe remains so gripped by past trauma that she mistakes the ex-abolitionist Edward Bodwin for the overseer Schoolteacher; she attempts to stab Bodwin with an ice-pick while overcome by a flashback reprising the moment when Schoolteacher came to reclaim her and her children from freedom. If the women's singing seeks in part to relegate Beloved to the past, therefore, it aims as well to insist on the distinction between these men—between the *past* embodiment of a murderous racial violence and a man in the novel's present who, though not without his racist blind spots, "kept Sethe from the gallows" after the infanticide and has "never turned [black people] down" (312).

But let us be very clear about this. *Beloved* does not pretend that Ohio in the aftermath of Reconstruction was an interracial paradise. It does not suggest that the (gendered) traumas of slavery had been worked through by 1873 (or, for that matter, by 1987). The "second" banishment of Beloved produces in Sethe less the release of reclaimed capacities than a new kind of melancholic illness. In a repetition of Baby Suggs's final act, she takes to her bed and seems on the verge of fulfilling the self-obliterative urge that prevailed during her entanglement with Beloved. ("Now [Paul D] knows what he is reminded of," Morrison writes, "and he shouts at her, 'Don't you die on me! This is Baby Suggs' bed! Is that what you planning?'" [320].) The novel's point here seems to be that even the collective confrontation with the past metaphorized by the black women's singing is not enough to work through trauma in the absence of a reckoning by the larger social order. Such a reckoning is the minimal condition for altering the material and psychic arrangements that sustain both racial and gender domination. Because the reckoning has yet to take place, the novel can only gesture toward what a worked-through relation to slavery's injuries might turn out to look like.

The contours of that gesture are nonetheless worth tracing. They can be grasped by recalling that the central trauma of slavery in this book is the gendered one of a violence that, by forcing black women to be mothers and then compromising their maternal love, "dirties" black female subjects in a way that makes them unloveable (to themselves). A working-through of slavery's trauma must therefore entail the making of a world in which black women can reclaim and revitalize their capacity for self-love. This is, I suggest, precisely the world Baby Suggs tries to build upon gaining her freedom and settling in Ohio. She proselytizes in the name of that world as a materialist prophet of Eros, inviting the black community to participate in a ritual of polymorphous (self-)love. "Here," Baby says—meaning on this earth—

> we flesh; flesh that weeps, laughs; flesh that dances on bare feet in grass. Love it. Love it hard. Yonder they do not love your flesh. They despise it. They don't love your eyes; they'd just as soon pick em out. No more do they love the skin on your back. Yonder they flay it. And O my people they do not love your hands. Those they only use, tie, bind, chop off and leave empty. Love your hands! Love them. Raise them up and kiss them. ... Touch others with them ... stroke them on your face. ... *You* got to love it, *you*. And no, they ain't in love with your mouth. ... *You* got to love it. ... The dark, dark liver—love it, love it, and the beat and beating heart, love that too. (103–104)

The body becomes here the medium for a sociality of reciprocal touching, which is based, in turn, on a reclamation of the capacity for self-love. That self-love is emphatically corporeal: Baby Suggs tells her "congregation" "that the only grace they could have was the grace they could imagine. That if they could not see it, they would not have it" (103). The singling out of those parts of the body reviled and degraded by white racism becomes then the prelude to authorizing that body's incremental, libidinal reinvestment. This reinvestment is at once personal—"*You* got to love it, *you*"—and collective; it is precisely a *ritual* of love in which each person's affirmation of flesh is consecrated and rendered "real" through the flesh's *collective* affirmation (in song and dance, for example: 104). If the bodily love asserted in this manner is ungendered rather than particular to women, this is only *Beloved*'s way of stressing that Baby Suggs's utopian intimations recover the potential for an ecstatic carnality that "transcends" the limits of gender—not by reference to some supra-carnal reality, but in and through the material insistence of the black body.

I'm suggesting that this Erotic reclamation is Morrison's way of imagining a ritual that confronts the injuries of slavery while gesturing toward a social order "on the other side" of that confrontation. The basis for this "other" order is a bodily love that counters at once the *racist* denigration of the black body, the *capitalist* transmutation of the slave body into money, and the *gendered* norms that sullied black women's bodies and made them unloveable to themselves. But this is a ritual that also fails, as Morrison goes on to show; in the course of the novel, Baby Suggs renounces her calling and retreats to her solitary bed, where she does no more than "think about color" for the years remaining till her death. This retreat takes place in response to Sethe's act of infanticidal love, which shatters Baby with the recognition that no amount of reclaimed (self-)love can stop whites armed with the law from "coming into her yard" (211)—and hence, from proving that the ritual of Eros is insufficient by itself to undo love's deformation by slavery. That ritual comes to represent, in this sense, less an actualization of community in the present than the figure for a yet-to-be-realized, future convocation.

Two points follow directly from this proleptic repositioning of Eros. First, the repositioning means that, in 1873, a pallid echo of Erotic affirmation and a qualified opening onto futurity are the closest one can come to working through the traumas of slavery. Paul D's professions of love for Sethe in the penultimate chapter may mark his repentance for telling her earlier (when she describes what happened to Beloved) that she has "two feet, not four" (194); he may promise a future relatively cleansed and unhaunted by the past when he tells her, "me and you, we got more yesterday than anybody. We need some kind of tomorrow" (322); and he may, finally, provide a basis for that future when he counters Sethe's compensatory idealization by saying "You your best thing, Sethe. You are" (322). But none of this indicates that love has succeeded in conquering slavery's injuries in the present, or guarantees that it will do so in the future. The novel ends with Sethe still in bed, reprising Baby Suggs's retreat; she responds to Paul D's "You your best thing" with a question rather than an affirmation: "Me?" she asks; "Me?" The question is Morrison's way of signaling that, if the injuries of slavery are eminently historical and therefore capable of being worked-through, that working through requires a set of "good enough" environmental provisions that the U.S. offered neither in 1873 nor in 1987 (nor today, for that matter). Hence the sweeping of ghosts from the present and the incarnation of a future that does not merely reprise the past—these remain at novel's end uncertain possibilities. They are, quite simply, questions ("Me? Me?"), which it remains for us to answer through our response to *Beloved*'s inducements.

My second point has to do with the complexity of the novel's form. I mentioned earlier that *Beloved* depicts the temporal roaming of slavery's specters in its stream-of-consciousness section, as a way of indicating that the specters resist a strictly historicist ordering. Here I wish to point to how the book's very forms propose an ordering that, while not historicist or thoroughly homogenizing, is nonetheless *integrative*. This is an ordering that conjures coherence as the emblem for a future in which *historical* ghosts have been worked through and sufficiently laid to rest. (I stress again that this says nothing about those "ghosts" which may belong to our being-in-language, but which we would do well not to conflate with historical specters.) It is an ordering for which the novel provides its own internal depiction. Toward the end of *Beloved*, Paul D remembers the words that a slave named Sixo once spoke about his beloved: "She is a friend of my mind. She gather me, man. The pieces I am, she gather them and give them back to me in all the right order" (321). The motivation for recalling these words is that they give Paul D a model for responding to Sethe's devastation in the wake of losing Beloved a second time; they enable him, that is, to have the conversation just described—in which he tells Sethe she's her own "best thing"—and to propose a future comprised of their mutually related yet independent "stories" ("He wants to put his story next to hers" [322]). This gesture of reparation provides the harmony of restored internal *order*; yet it does not prejudge the *nature* of that reorganization. The "right order" refers merely to that reflection or "giving back" of the self's "parts" that *feels right* to the one receiving it. This means that, temporally speaking, the order need not be chronological; it need not conform to the kind of narration that moves sequentially through time. The passage can therefore be read as describing an intersubjective restoration of self that integrates without compelling a specifically chronological sequence.

To think of Sixo's words as a meditation on the novel's form is to say that *Beloved*, too, provides an order that declines chronological sequence; it, too, displays or enacts a formal "integration" that defies the logic of historicist temporality. The defiance serves a relatively straightforward function, as I've said already: it is a way of depicting the inner experience of traumatic disruption (rather than its surmounting); it reflects at the level of form the characters' fragmented inner experiences, and thereby gestures toward things that our national narrative has sought to elide. The book's overriding coherence, however, has less a mimetic than a proleptic significance. It promises a *future* integration on the far side of trauma's working through; it suggests what an harmonious coherence might look like *after* the ghosts of the past have been confronted and laid to rest. This is why we must remember that however much Sixo's beloved reflects him back to himself as "whole," that wholeness is in fact shattered by the representatives of chattel slavery. (Schoolteacher captures and burns him to death.) The love she offers will only be capable of *social* realization in a materially transformed future, just as the Eros of Baby Suggs's preaching requires the prior production of those "good enough" environmental conditions which make the polymorphosis of love not just imaginable but socially viable.

The integrative aspect of *Beloved*'s form models one way of figuring such future coherence. If this formal aim conflicts with that of depicting the disorganizing effects of trauma, this is only a way of saying that the novel thinks *dialectically* about the relations between disruption and its (future) overcoming. It at once enacts the broken form of traumatized memory *and* provides a remedial order that fixes Beloved in the memory of readers to counter the characters' "forgetting [of] her" (323)—and fixes her there through a narrative coherence that keeps her from "erupting into her separate parts" (323). It is, finally, in this double sense that Morrison's is a story "not to be passed on" (324). The statement on the one hand asks that the broken memory embodied in the book's forms *not* be transmitted to future generations. (It's a story whose depicted and enacted disturbances must not be perpetuated.) On the other hand, the statement asks that the story not be "passed on" in quite a different sense: it projects an anticipatory, yet-to-be-realized "wholeness" that even our skepticism toward meretricious recovery ought not lead us to decline (as in "I think I'll pass on that"); and it insists that this wholeness can only be reached by passing "through" the historical injuries that the book remains committed to depicting.

III

Though set in twentieth-century India rather than the nineteenth-century U.S., *The God of Small Things* shares a number of

Beloved's main concerns. It focuses on colonial trauma as an expressly gendered phenomenon, stresses how descendants of the colonized are haunted by ghosts of the dis-remembered dead, and points toward a social working-through that's neither meretricious nor *de facto* interminable. I explore each of these similarities below. Here, however, I wish to stress that beneath and animating the resemblances I've named is a rather more surprising one. Like *Beloved, The God of Small Things* links the experience of colonial trauma to the problem of Erotic attachment. The catastrophes that the book explores "began thousands of years ago," Roy writes, "in the days when the Love Laws were made. The laws that lay down who should be loved, and how ... And how much" (Roy 1998: 33). The novel's emphasis on these "Laws" is meant to supplement rather than abrogate an historical understanding. *Beloved's* account of how maternal love is deformed by the institutions of slavery is here expanded into an inquiry about the normative conscription and regulation of love relations in colonialism more generally. This move entails suggesting that domination of *all* kinds is propped upon a libidinal set of compulsions and taboos.[12] Prior to and informing each historical instance of dominion on the subcontinent—from "before Christianity arrived in a boat and seeped into Kerala like tea from a teabag" through the Dutch, Portuguese, and British colonial regimes and beyond (33)—is a group of "Laws" that determine at once the appropriateness of love objects ("who should be loved"), the form of love appropriate to each object ("how" they should be loved, i.e., with filial, brotherly, or sexual love, etc.), and the degree of intensity with which one is required or permitted to love a given object (i.e., "how much"). *The God of Small Things* is especially concerned with the forms these compulsory affects and taboos took under British rule. These extended while transforming a set of earlier, precolonial patterns of power in relation to Eros, and they were in turn extended yet transformed in the postcolonial world comprising the book's present.

   This pattern is nowhere clearer than in the colonial production of "Anglophilia" among upper-caste Indians. "We are a *family* of Anglophiles," says Chacko, the brother of Ammu and uncle of her twins Rahel and Estha. "[O]ur minds have been invaded by a war. A war that captures our dreams and re-dreams them. A war that has made us adore our conquerors and despise ourselves" (51–52). These formulations point to colonialism's infiltration and redirection of indigenous, precolonial affections. The British could rule India, Chacko suggests, not just because they forcibly came to control such material and institutional domains as legislative bodies, agricultural production, transportation networks, legal systems, land rights, and so forth, but also because they "conquered" Indians' minds and colonized their "dreams." Their rule indeed relied as much on winning this "War of Dreams" as it did on physical coercion (52). The result of that victory on those it vanquished was at least threefold. First, it entailed a negation of Indian self-worth—a "despising" of "ourselves"—akin to the one we saw with respect to African Americans in *Beloved*. To drive this point home, Chacko has the twins look up the word "despise" in the dictionary; they find that it means "*To look down upon; to view with contempt; to scorn or disdain*," and Chacko tells them that in their case the word connotes "all of these things" (52). Second, the corollary to this self-contempt is that—unlike slavery in *Beloved*—colonialism here incites love and desire for one's "conquerors," i.e., for the British. This incitement is the very motor of Indian Anglophilia ("love of things British"); its concrete and catastrophic significance is clear from the fact that Chacko has married (and divorced) an English woman, Margaret, and that all of the novel's disasters follow from this marriage-divorce and its effects on the daughter (Sophie) who is its issue.

Third and most complex is the way that *God of Small Things* imagines this process to have expressly traumatic results. The violent (and hence, traumatogenic) character of the process is inscribed in the term "War of Dreams," with its implication that what is at stake must be won through brutal force. But even more, the dynamic produces a version of the temporal derangement so characteristic of traumatized consciousness and so central to Morrison's text. The conquest of dreams gives rise, for example, to a deformation of Indian *futurity*: "dreams" refers to the realm of desires, with their insistently forward-projecting arc, so that to have dreams "re-dreamt" by the colonists is to be made to desire a future that conforms to the colonists' vision of it. The future Indians make for themselves will entail a compulsive reprisal and incarnation of the British self-understandings that have displaced the Indians' own dreams. At the same time, defeat in the War of Dreams here means an alienation from one's *past* that brings with it the entire problematic of spectral haunting discussed above. Chacko at one point tells the twins that Indians are trapped outside their own history and unable to retrace their steps. ... He explained to them that history was like an old house at night. With all the lamps lit. And ancestors whispering inside.

"To understand history," Chacko said, "we have to go inside and listen to what they're saying. And look at the books and the pictures on the wall. And smell the smells."

Estha and Rahel had no doubt that the house Chacko meant was the house on the other side of the river, in the middle of the abandoned rubber estate. ... Kari Saipu's house. The Black Sahib. The Englishman who had "gone native." Who spoke Malayalam and wore mundus. Ayemenem's own Kurtz. Ayemenem his private Heart of Darkness. He had shot himself through the head ten years ago, when his young lover's parents had taken the boy away from him and sent him to school. ... The house had lain empty for years. Very few people had seen it. But the twins could picture it.

The History House. ...

"But we can't go in," Chacko explained, "because we've been locked out. And when we look in through the windows, all we see are shadows. And when we try to listen, all we hear is a whispering. And we cannot understand the whispering, because our minds have been invaded by a war." (51–52)

If the Indian people *are* a people by way of their commerce with dead ancestors, then to be "locked out" of the ancestors' house is to be exiled from the source of collective identity. The passage is emphatic about the cause of this alienation. Indians cannot "hear" or "see" or "smell" their ancestors "*because* our minds have been invaded by a war"—that is to say, because the War of Dreams has "made us adore our conquerors and despise ourselves." The root of Indians' alienation from history is thus the Erotic dynamic I've described; that exile follows directly from the specific forms that colonialism gave to the Love Laws' compulsory proscriptions and prescriptions. That alienation produces, in turn, that experience of existential insignificance so common to colonial structures of "belatedness": severed from the precolonial past and yearning toward a future Britishness that will be deferred indefinitely, the characters find that "We belong nowhere. We sail unanchored on troubled seas. We may never be allowed ashore. Our sorrows will never be sad enough. Our joys never happy enough. ... Our lives never important enough. To matter" (52).

By linking this exile from history to the story of Kari Saipu, Roy both highlights the place of Eros in domination on the subcontinent and proposes that this conjuncture generates a specific kind of haunting. The doubly transgressive character of his object-love—interracial, homosexual—violates the Love Laws' (post)colonial forms. The suicide that fells him indicates that the cost of transgressing against those laws is a potentially lethal retribution (here enacted by Kari Saipu himself). This retributive violence haunts the History House in the form of a ghost that has displaced the beneficent past that Chacko imagines. History, in other words, *is* now the specter of a violence that disrupts ancestral transmission with the retributive image of what has befallen, and will befall, those who run afoul of colonial and postcolonial Love Laws.

It follows from this that the History House resembles yet differs in striking ways from the house at 124 Bluestone in *Beloved*. In both cases, the house embodies the gothic excess of a past that has not been laid to rest. Both are *haunted* houses, in other words, because of the violence that each has witnessed, and because the historical causes of that violence have yet to be confronted. In both cases too the violence follows upon the configurations of Eros within a particular regime of power. But while *Beloved* encourages a recognition of the *difference* between slavery and the post-emancipation world (a difference asserted by the second banishing of Beloved from 124), *God of Small Things* aims to reveal the continuity of the colonial past with the postcolonial present—and hence, the links between the History House and the wider social world. The specter that's so materially present as to threaten Sethe's life in *Beloved* is here *in*adequately present to most of the novel's characters. The ghost of Kari Saipu haunts those characters *without their being aware of it*; the disasters in the present indeed reprise the past *because* of this unconsciousness. The novel therefore aims to show the effects of an inability to constitute the specter as a living reality, stressing that the past repeats itself when a collectivity fails to incarnate it as a "moment" in the process of social working-through.

This danger is especially visible in two areas. First, the failure to confront what Kari Saipu represents leads to a disastrous repetition of his story in the scene at Abbilash Talkies. This is the theater where Estha, Rahel, Ammu, and the twins' baby grandaunt, Baby Kochamma, go to watch *The Sound of Music* on the day prior to Sophie Mol's arrival, and Estha is molested in the lobby by the "Orangedrink Lemondrink man"

(98). His violation reprises Kari Saipu's story not so much in its details as in its larger, Erotic-political significance. As in the case of the Black Sahib, the sexual act is here both homosexual and pedophilic (Kari Saipu's lover is "a boy"). As in that case, too—and despite the fact that both characters are now Indian—Estha's violation turns out to have a *racial* and a *colonial* dimension. Upon reentering the auditorium, he finds himself transfixed by the image of Baron von Trapp on screen.

> Arrogant. Hardhearted. ... A captain with seven children. Clean children, like a packet of peppermints. He pretended not to love them, but he did. He loved them. He loved her (Julie Andrews), she loved him, they loved the children, the children loved them. They all loved each other. They were clean, white children, and their beds were soft with Ei. Der. Downs.

This image of familial love generates a longing that leads Estha to ask:

> Oh Baron von Trapp, Baron Von Trapp, could you love the little fellow ... in the smelly auditorium? He's just held the Orangedrink Lemondrink Man's soo-soo in his hand, but could you love him still? And his twin sister with her fountain [of hair] in a Love-in-Tokyo? ... Could you love her too?

The Baron has "questions of his own," however:

> *Are they clean white children?*
> No. (*But Sophie Mol is.*) ...
> *Have they, either or both, ever held a stranger's soo-soo?*
> N ... Nyes (*But Sophie Mol hasn't.*)
> "Then I'm sorry," Baron von Clapp-Trapp said. "It's out of the question. I cannot love them. I cannot be their Baba. Oh no."
> Baron von Clapp-Trapp couldn't. (100–102)

The scene allegorizes the process by which the Erotic conscriptions of colonial relations are installed *as trauma* in the Indian subject. Estha's molestation indeed acquires its traumatic significance from watching the film. *The Sound of Music* retroactively determines the content of his violation, just as the stealing of Sethe's milk determines the traumatic meaning of Schoolteacher's earlier remark to her. The trauma's content concerns, in this case, the conjuncture of race and lovability; Estha is assailed with the conviction that his molestation dirties him by repeating or echoing his Indianness, thereby rendering him unloveable in the eyes of the only "Baba" who matters—a white one. This unloveability unspools itself by way of extended *comparison*: what Estha and Rahel are not (white, loveable, sexually untainted), Sophie Mol is. The unloveability signals in turn the alienation inscribed at the heart of dreams re-dreamt by one's conquerors: *The Sound of Music* at once solicits and repulses Estha's Erotic investments; he can't *not* want to find his place within its representations, even as the novel reveals that the film's Erotic-familial regime is covertly white and—hence—foreclosed to him.

The scene's reprisal of the Black Sahib's story suggests that the violation Estha suffers *follows from* the failure of India to materialize and confront the specter of colonial Eros. If Kari Saipu's ghost exposes the continuities between the colonial and postcolonial eras, that ghost is in the narrative present confined to the History House grounds, immobilized there and impaled to a tree by Vellya Paapen's sickle (189). This confinement enables a sustained disavowal of the links between past and present. It defends against the possibility of actually engaging the specter, artificially delimiting its reach and so *un*haunting the larger social space in which the novel's main actions take place. It is, in other words, because the ghost is spatially isolated that such places as the Abbilash Talkies are "free" to repeat the past in the present without confronting or working it through.

The second area where this dynamic plays out is in the realm of gender. The novel deftly lays out the links between colonial Anglophilia and the perpetuation of male violence. Ammu's father, Pappachi, for example—an Imperial Entomologist at the Pusa Institute in Delhi—is both a lover of all things British and the embodiment of patriarchal brutality. "[E]very single day [of his life] Pappachi wore a well-pressed three-piece suit and his gold pocket watch." The picture he keeps of himself on his dressing-table reveals

> a photogenic man, dapper and carefully groomed. ... His light-brown eyes were polite yet maleficent, as though he was making an effort to be civil to the photographer while plotting to murder his wife. ... He had an elongated dimple on his chin,

which only served to underline the threat of a lurking manic violence. A sort of contained cruelty. He wore khaki jodhpurs though he had never ridden a horse in his life. His riding boots reflected the photographer's studio lights. An ivory-handled riding crop lay neatly across his lap. (48–50)

The sartorial details in particular suggest that Ammu is right to call Pappachi "an incurable British CCP" or "shit-wiper" (50). It is in describing their father, indeed, that Chacko embarks on the explication of Anglophilia discussed earlier. But the passage also links those details to a "lurking" violence that turns out to be more than merely potential. After Pappachi retires and moves with his wife to Ayemenem, Mammachi starts a pickle-making business that her husband

> greatly resented. He slouched about the [pickle] compound in his immaculately tailored suits, weaving sullen circles around mounds of red chilies and freshly powdered yellow turmeric, watching Mammachi supervise the buying, the weighing, the salt-ing and drying, of limes and tender mangoes. Every night he beat her with a brass flower vase. The beatings weren't new. What was new was only the frequency with which they took place. (46–47)

This violence relates to Pappachi's Anglophilia in a clearly *causal* manner. Roy proposes that the thwarting of his identificatory love of Englishness in the public world leads him to brutalize his wife and child in the home. As with Estha's violation, moreover, the perpetuation of this violence in the present results from a failure to constitute and con-front the ghosts produced in the past. The failure takes the form here less of the ghost's geographical containment than of an acknowledgement of the specter that—by misnaming it—obscures its significance. This misnaming has to do with what Roy calls "Pappachi's Moth." The great professional disappointment in Pappachi's life concerns a species he discovered but was prevented (for bureaucratic reasons) from claiming or christening with his name.

> In the years to come, *even though he had been ill-humored long before he discovered the moth*, Pappachi's Moth was held responsible for his black moods and sudden bouts of temper. Its pernicious ghost—gray,

furry and with unusually dense dorsal tufts—haunted every house that he ever lived in. It tormented him and his children and his children's children. (48; emphasis added)

While the novel does indeed suggest that Pappachi's children (Chacko and Ammu) and children's children (Estha and Rahel) are "tormented" by his legacy, the professional disappointment is emphatically *not* that torment's cause. The torment rather follows from the dynamic I have described: an Anglophilic cultivation of British gentlemanliness comes up against the barrier of race, to which Pappachi responds by beating his wife (and child) in frustration at that barrier's insurmountability. This is why the novel stresses that "he had been ill-humored long before he discovered the moth." The ghost of Pappachi's Moth is just a fable the family tells itself to keep at bay a reckoning with the historical ghost of his patriarchal cruelty.

It would be possible to show in detail that Chacko is the pivotal figure in the transmission of this ghost to the present generation, despite his deep investment in not knowing he is its bearer. In the interest of space, let me point only to what Roy calls the "contradiction between Chacko's Marxist mind and feudal libido" (160). The part of him that plays "*Comrade! Comrade!*" with his employees in the pickle factory—telling them that he's violating their labor rights and encouraging them to organize—conflicts with the part that behaves like "a [feudal] landlord forcing his attentions on women who depended on him for their livelihood" (63). The personal contradiction is fully commensurate with the configuration of Love Laws on the postcolonial subcontinent: Chacko's family conspires in it by dignifying his feudal libido with "the enigmatic, secretly thrilling notion of Men's Needs" (160). Mammachi goes so far as to build a separate entrance to Chacko's rooms, "so that the objects of his 'Needs'"—the female employees he seduces—"wouldn't have to go traipsing *through* the house. She secretly slipped them money to keep them happy. ... The arrangement suited Mammachi, because in her mind, a fee *clarified* things. Disjuncted sex from love. Needs from Feelings" (160–161). The fee, in other words, secures that sexual double standard by which men's needs acquire the status of an openly acknowledged secret, while the objects of those needs are placed in the category of the instrumentalized-but-not-loved. Those objects become mere adjuncts to the material working-out of male narcissism; they are the equivalent in the sexual domain of Chacko's proprietary possessions—"*my* Factory, *my* pineapples, *my* pickles" (56); "My pickles, my jam, my curry powders" (116)—just as those possessions are tokens of a (feckless) entrepreneurial spirit that transforms Mammachi's small-scale but profitable business with "no name" into a debt-capitalized, fully industrial, yet money-losing proposition called "Paradise Pickles & Preserves" (55–56).

It might seem that this dimension of Chacko has at least the benefit of having sublimated Pappachi's physical brutality. In transforming Mammachi into the "Sleeping Partner" of her own enterprise (55), in jokingly admitting that the business and landholdings are indeed *his*, no matter how diligently Ammu works, because legally she is a daughter and therefore has no "Locusts Stand I" (56), in embracing even his Anglophilia with a typically melancholy irony, Chacko seems a relatively benign and even charming sort of chauvinist. Yet to leave it there would be to diminish the transpersonal force and effectiveness of his father's legacy. If the precipitating act in what Roy calls "the Terror" is Ammu's sleeping with Velutha—a Touchable coupling with an Untouchable, the unloveable recast as loveable—the catastrophes that follow are at once lethal in their violence and irrevocably bound to the transgenerational dynamics of gender. Baby Kochamma responds to the story of the affair by saying *How could she stand the smell? Haven't you noticed? They have a particular smell, these Paravans"* (243). "With that olfactory observation," Roy continues,

> the Terror unspooled. … Mammachi's rage at [Velutha's father, who informs the two older women of the affair] was re-directed into a cold contempt for her daughter and what she had done. … Her tolerance of "Men's Needs," as far as her son was concerned, became the fuel for her unmanageable fury at her daughter.

> She thought of her naked, coupling in the mud with a man who was nothing but a filthy *coolie*. She imagined it in vivid detail. … His mouth on hers. His black hips jerking between her parted legs. … His particular Paravan smell. *Like animals*, Mammachi thought and nearly vomited. *Like a dog with a bitch on heat.* … She had defiled generations of breeding … and brought the family to its knees. (244)

Here the Terror "unspools" unambiguously as a misogynist reaction to caste "pollution." The indulgence toward male sexual prerogatives that dignifies Chacko's liaisons as Men's Needs becomes the propellant for Mammachi's "unmanageable fury" at Ammu. There is, in other words, a *dynamic* relation between these two responses. The exemption that allows Touchable men to "Disjunct ... sex from love [and] Needs from Feelings" is buttressed by the remorselessness with which Touchable women are denied a comparable exemption. Those women bear the "surplus" burden of being safeguards against pollution: they are what keeps matter "in its place," to borrow and revise a phrase from Mary Douglas (35–36). Their bodies secure through sexual propriety the border of Touchability against the unclean (i.e., the smelly), thereby consecrating the social distinctions between clean and dirty, inside and outside, the beloved and the abject, animalized, and defiled.

I'm suggesting we read the events called "the Terror" as an explosively social reenactment of the father's violence toward Ammu and Mammachi—inasmuch as that violence was *always* social rather than narrowly personal, and inasmuch as it has yet to be grappled with or socially reckoned. What "haunts" his children (and children's children) is less the ghost of Pappachi's Moth than the specter of a patriarchal brutality based not in India's "atavistic" kin relations but in the Touchable family as (re)made by the Raj's incitements to and proscriptions on desire. Chacko's charming incompetence or powerlessness and his ostensible repudiation of hierarchy are symptoms of his refusal to confront the specter of a paternal legacy that this refusal in fact keeps alive. The echo of that legacy can be heard even in the asthmatic fit that kills Ammu. The "rattle in her throat that sound[s] like [the shouting of] a faraway man," who grips her in his "steely fist" and finally refuses to let go (151, 154)—who is this man if not the internalized (encrypted) ghost of the violence that haunts familial and social relations in this book? It is the same man invoked when the novel refers to the violence that kills Velutha as "Man's sublimated urge to destroy what he could neither subdue nor deify"—or, more pointedly, as a further expression of "Men's Needs" (292). Mammachi's term for Chacko's libido is here refitted to describe the act of "inoculating a community against an outbreak" (293), expanding the social significance of the violence inscribed in that libido's expression.

IV

It remains now to trace the temporal "shape" of traumatic experience in this book, and to link that shape to the novel's form. The fullest depiction of psychic trauma concerns—surprisingly—neither Ammu nor Velutha. It does not concern the generation that transgresses against the Love Laws in 1969 at all, but rather members of the next generation—that is, Rahel and (especially) Estha. Such a representational choice suggests that a disavowed historical specter wreaks its damage *especially* on those who are as yet "innocent" of history, at least in the sense of not being old enough to be accountable for its injustices. The damage in fact takes the form of the twins' precocious initiation into those injustices. They're seduced into collaborating in Velutha's death and his erasure from history. They agree, that is, to betray him by confirming the account of the Terror concocted by Baby Kochamma and endorsed by the police, namely, that Sophie Mol died when Velutha kidnapped all three children in revenge for being fired after attempting to rape Ammu.

At stake in this confirmation is a specifically narrative form of complicity. Estha and Rahel are conscripted into a *story* about Velutha's guilt and asked to complete that tale by choosing for it an appropriate ending. Roy emphasizes the narrative character of this procedure by noting that, as Baby Kochamma enlists them in her account, the twins sit rapt, "Fascinated by the story she [Baby Kochamma] was telling them. *Then what happened?*" (300). The suggestion here is that Estha and Rahel are interpellated into a story so enthralling that even as participants who know it to be false, they cannot but be gripped by a desire to know—and help shape—its outcome. The damage they do and suffer results from this conscription into narrative desire. The twins are neither physically forced nor tricked into betraying Velutha. "They both knew that they had been given a choice," Roy writes. "And how quick they had been in the choosing!" (302). Neither forced nor tricked, then, but seduced; and seduced not merely as passive listeners, but as imaginative—collaborative—co-authors. The narrative shape of the story Baby Kochamma tells requires that they furnish it with an ending; the apparent choice is constrained, however, by the historically specific configuration of Love Laws in which the choice is couched: "which ending do we prefer?" means also, whom do the Love Laws *require us to love more*—the woman who is "[our] Ammu *and* [our] Baba" and who "love[s us] Double" (155), or the Untouchable, ostensibly polluting, olfactorily offensive Velutha? The "rapidity" of the choice is Roy's way of marking how these laws compel pre-adolescent psyches toward specific narrative conclusions. It is as if, phenomenologically speaking, the choice of an ending is no choice at all, as if the postcolonial order in India proposes to let you write your own story while shaping your affective life so deeply that a given (normative) resolution is all-but guaranteed in advance.

The results of this narrative conscription are deeply—and precisely—traumatizing. Because they are co-authors in the official story of Velutha's crimes, the twins find themselves unable to "claim the tragic hood of victimhood." They cannot "purchase" a therapist's assurance that they are "the Sinned Against" rather than the "Sinners," that as children they "had no control" and are thus "the *victims*, not the perpetrators." They cannot do this because they know that "there were many perpetrators that day but only one victim," and that is the one named "Velutha" (182). Hence they're unable to name an agent of violence who *is not also them*. The trauma they suffer consists, indeed, in the breakdown of a critical distinction: anger must here be aimed at the self because the self is *in fact* guilty—they made the choice that broke faith with Velutha and consolidated the official version of events. To direct their "fury" at historical injustice is therefore also to rage at themselves. Trauma becomes exceedingly difficult to "work through" in this scenario. It is the already-internalized effect of the twins' complicity in a specific kind of story—a story that's both "about" homogeneity (the preservation of caste and gendered borders) and formally homogenizing in its drive toward linear, unerring conclusion.

It's as a response to this narrative compulsion that I suggest we read the book's form. Roy's technique is (like Morrison's) "modernist" in its achronological inclinations; its deep hostility toward linear narration gives rise to a fragmentary, temporally reshuffled, and associative narrative design. The aim of such a technique is partly the one encountered in *Beloved*: to capture the temporal dislocations that characterize the traumatized consciousness of its central characters. As in *Beloved*, too, however, the temporal disorder has an additional, properly utopian purpose. It aims to resist and offer an alternate ending to that secured by Estha's "yes." This purpose is perhaps most evident in how the book itself concludes. For Roy ends not with the present-day effects of Estha and Rahel's trauma (in 1993), but with the event from which it issued (in 1969); she ends, that is, not with the extraordinary if regressive act of incest by which the twins attempt to recapture a presocial, pretraumatic oneness—as if the only way "out" of their trauma is "back" to a time when they felt themselves one. Instead, the novel concludes with Velutha and Ammu's adult transgression—a sexual act that belongs in the past but that the novel has till now withheld from narrative view. Such a choice has the effect of conjuring Eros as alternate conclusion to the novel's events (see here Outka, 45). The temporal inversion works, in other words, to counter the end-result of the Terror with an ending that might *in principle* provide some other way of living the body and organizing human relations around it.

Nowhere is this possibility more palpable than in *The God of Small Things'* final word: "tomorrow." That is the word with which the lovers promise each day to return and renew their transgression. "Tomorrow," Roy writes—*Naaley* (tomorrow): it is a tantalizing word on which to end. It points to a moment that never *arrives*, that derives its meaning from a present whose future has not yet been realized or incarnated. And yet this word, within this novel, describes a *past* reprised each day for a dilatory, ecstatic fortnight. The word describes a *past* inasmuch as the act it promises to renew comes "before" all the novel's main events; but "tomorrow" is also and by definition a forward-pointing word, one that here, as the text's final word, gestures beyond the text to a moment that only the reader can actualize. The novel might in this sense be said to offer the image of a past fulfillment as template for a utopian future that we alone can realize. It invites us to renew and fulfill the promise that Ammu and Velutha reiterate each night until their destruction; it asks us, in other words, *not* to replicate the traumatizing betrayal that so cripples Estha and Rahel. To avoid this betrayal requires resisting the conventional, chronological "closure" that the twins are seduced into enforcing. It's to substitute for that ending an image that recovers our bodies' polymorphous pleasure from a fictive time "before" the Love Laws, while projecting that image in the form of a future that is to-be-realized beyond Roy's text. This is, of course, another way of saying that the inverted form of this novel's ending enacts a utopian recovery that echoes *Beloved*'s Erotic prolepses. If modernist forms continue to *matter* to postcolonial approaches to trauma, it's partly because they orchestrate this encounter with an ecstatic past that until now may have resided only in our utopian tomorrows, but that this ending invites us to retrieve—and thereby to render "tomorrow" today.

Notes

1. This model derives from Freud's late texts, especially as refracted by Caruth's *Unclaimed Experience*.
2. These are not the only current approaches, nor the only kinds of problems attendant on them. I am trying, rather, to isolate the most persistent tendencies in recent work. For other approaches and problems, see Visser's useful essay and the special edition of *Studies in the Novel*, ed. Craps and Buelens.
3. Lloyd's essay aims at liberating capacities that have taken melancholic form only *because* of colonialism and postcolonial nationalism—and that might, therefore, take non-melancholic form with a transformation in social conditions.
4. The interpolated quotation is from Lyotard, who is also the source of Durrant's theorization of Forgetting.
5. Here the Lacanian underpinning of Durrant's project combines with the late Derrida's emphasis on the spectral residue of lives that *must* haunt the present because to mourn them is to betray history's victims by "forgetting" them.
6. Van Boheemen-Saaf's book employs both models but does not successfully integrate them.
7. The critical literature on this novel is voluminous. See esp. Durrant, chap. 3; Spargo; Flanagan; Morgenstern.
8. In the interest of concision, I leave entirely aside the novel's powerful exploration of slavery's effects on black masculinity—especially as embodied in Paul D.
9. This is to say that the logic here is that of Freud's *Nachträglichkeit*. He means by this term a temporal dialectic by which some kinds of trauma emerge from the gap separating two distinct events, the first of which is incomprehensible as such but becomes at once comprehensible and traumatic by way of the second event.
10. Durrant's analysis also stresses the value of working-through for *Beloved*'s characters. He associates this process with a "cultural memory" that traffics in representations and culminates in the "recovery of an African American subject." He opposes this, however, to what he calls "racial memory," which is a product of primordial Forgetting and whose object is unrepresentable because "Real in the Lacanian sense" (84). This form of remembrance is for Durrant closely allied with *Beloved*'s own grief-work (as distinct from its characters'). It marks the novel's inability "to retrieve [slavery's] anonymous victims from historical limbo" and signals Morrison's affirmation of a melancholic inability to remember (20–21; 87ff). My readings (below) of *Beloved*'s ending and its form are intended to counter this latter move.
11. This action marks an historically-inflected version of the moment Leader describes (following Lacan) as the performance of a "second" or "symbolic" death: we must (symbolically) kill the dead "again" by way of commemorative rites and rituals, in order to secure the porous border

between the living and the dead (116, 119–120). The political stakes of this process are raised considerably in cases of historically-induced loss.
12. Discussions of the politics of Eros in the novel have often been heated. See esp. Ahmad and Bose. Outka's essay offers a measured recasting of the debate.

Bibliography

Adorno, Theodor. "What Does Coming to Terms with the Past Mean?" 1959. *Bitburg in Moral and Political Perspective*. Ed. Geoffrey Hartman. Bloomington: Indiana University Press, 1986. 114–129.

Ahmad, Aijaz. "Reading Arundhati Roy *Politically*." *Arundhati Roy's* The God of Small Things. Ed. Alex Tickell. New York: Routledge, 2007. 110–119.

Boheemen-Saaf, Christine van. *Joyce, Derrida, Lacan, and the Trauma of History: Reading, Narrative, and Postcolonialism*. Cambridge: Cambridge University Press, 1999.

Bose, Brinda. "In Desire and In Death: Eroticism as Politics in Arundhati Roy's *The God of Small Things*." *Arundhati Roy's* The God of Small Things. Ed. Alex Tickell. New York: Routledge, 2007. 120–131.

Caruth, Cathy. *Unclaimed Experience: Trauma, Narrative, and History*. Baltimore: Johns Hopkins University Press, 1996.

Craps, Stef, and Gert Buelens, eds. "Postcolonial Trauma Novels." Special issue of *Studies in the Novel* 40.1–2 (2008).

Douglas, Mary. *Purity and Danger: An Analysis of the Concepts of Pollution and Taboo*. New York: Praeger, 1966.

Durrant, Sam. *Postcolonial Narrative and the Work of Mourning: J.M. Coetzee, Wilson Harris, and Toni Morrison*. Albany: State University of New York Press, 2004.

Flanagan, Joseph. "The Seduction of History: Trauma, Re-Memory, and the Ethics of the Real." *CLIO: A Journal of Literature, History, and the Philosophy of History* 31.4 (2002): 387–402.

Freud, Sigmund. "Remembering, Repeating, and Working-Through." 1914. *The Standard Edition of the Complete Psychological Works of Sigmund Freud*. Trans. James Strachey. 24 vols. New York: Norton, 1955–1973. Vol. 12. 145–156.

Gandhi, Leela. *Postcolonial Theory: A Critical Introduction*. New York: Columbia University Press, 1998.

Khanna, Ranjana. *Dark Continents: Psychoanalysis and Colonialism*. Durham: Duke University Press, 2003.

Leader, Darian. *The New Black: Mourning, Melancholia, and Depression*. London: Penguin, 2008.

Lloyd, David. "Colonial Trauma/Postcolonial Recovery?" *Interventions* 2.2 (2000): 212–228.

Mishra, Vijay. *The Literature of the Indian Diaspora: Theorizing the Diasporic Imaginary*. New York: Routledge, 2007.

Morgan, Edmund S. *American Slavery, American Freedom: The Ordeal of Colonial Virginia*. New York: Norton, 1975.

Morgenstern, Naomi. "Mother's Milk and Sister's Blood: Trauma and the Neoslave Narrative." *Differences: A Journal of Feminist Cultural Studies* 8.2 (1996): 101–126.

Morrison, Toni. *Beloved*. 1987. New York: Vintage, 2004.

Outka, Elizabeth. "Trauma and Temporal Hybridity in Arundhati Roy's *The God of Small Things*." *Contemporary Literature* 52.1 (2011): 21–53.

Roy, Arundhati. *The God of Small Things*. New York: HarperCollins, 1998.

Saxton, Alexander. *The Rise and Fall of the White Republic: Class Politics and Mass Culture in Nineteenth-Century America*. New York: Verso, 2003.

Spargo, R. Clifton. "Trauma and the Specters of Enslavement in Morrison's *Beloved*." *Mosaic: A Journal for the Interdisciplinary Study of Literature* 35.1 (2002): 113–131.

Visser, Irene. "Trauma Theory and Postcolonial Literary Studies." *Journal of Postcolonial Writing* 47.3 (2011): 270–282.

Wyatt, Jean. "Giving Body to the Word: The Maternal Symbolic in Toni Morrison's *Beloved*." *PMLA* 108.3 (1993): 474–488.

5
Trauma and Power in Postcolonial Literary Studies

Irene Visser

When, in 1995, Geoffrey Hartman presented trauma theory in his influential article "On Traumatic Knowledge and Literary Studies" as offering a welcome "change of perspective" to literary studies, not only at the level of theory but also "of exegesis in the service of insights about human functioning" (544), he correctly predicted the huge impact that trauma theory would have on literary criticism. Part of the widespread impact of trauma theory has however been its critique by theorists and critics in the field who have pointed out many controversies, contradictions, and limitations in the theory originally conceptualized by Hartman, Cathy Caruth, and others of the Yale School. In postcolonial literary studies in particular, criticism of the dominant trauma paradigm has been a constant since trauma theory first appeared in this field. In 2008 several publications pointed out the limits of trauma theory for postcolonial studies, such as its depoliticizing and dehistoricizing tendencies. Roger Luckhurst remarked in *The Trauma Question* (2008) that in overlooking political concerns, trauma theory "shockingly fails to address atrocity, genocide and war" (213). In a special issue of *Studies in the Novel* (2008), devoted to a project to effectuate a "rapprochement" between trauma theory and postcolonial literary theory, trauma theory was presented in the introduction as having strengths for postcolonial literary studies to incorporate, but also weaknesses to be reconfigured. However, while the editors Craps and Buelens emphasized possibilities, the separate articles in the journal tended to emphasize the obstacles to this "rapprochement," signaling the need for further debate about the complex relationship between trauma theory and postcolonial literary studies, particularly in the field of non-western cultures. In the journal's concluding article, Michael Rothberg expressed serious doubts as to whether in its present form "trauma provides the best framework for thinking about the legacies of violence in the colonized/postcolonial world" (Rothberg 2008: 226).

Increasingly the consensus in postcolonial literary studies has been that trauma theory has not entirely fulfilled its initial promise of offering insightful exegetical tools for the literary analysis of human functioning. A number of publications of 2011 examined the theory only to conclude that the constraints of trauma theory necessitate expansion and redirection of the theory in order to adequately understand the problems of trauma during and after colonization and to situate these traumatic experiences in specific societal and historic perspectives (Baxter; Collins; Herrero and Baelo-Allue; Visser). Due to the substantial range of national literatures in postcolonial literary studies and their many specific cultural contexts, a necessary advance in postcolonial trauma studies would be to make the theory more comprehensive, yet also to allow more specificity than the present dominant trauma theory in literary studies.

An important consideration is that indigenous narrative traditions and modes of representing trauma often include emphases on rituals and ceremony which fall outside the framework of trauma theory. The critique that spirituality is not conceptualized adequately in trauma theory has been frequently made. Anne Whitehead, in an article on trauma in Wole Soyinka's fiction, questions the practice of mislaying a Western construct such as trauma theory onto the very different experiences of wounding and suffering narrated in African postcolonial literature, observing that "Soyinka forces us to encounter a response to trauma that asserts the relevance of localized modes of belief, ritual, and understanding, thereby undermining the centrality of western knowledge and expertise" (27). Merlinda Bobis presents a convincing case for the inclusion of spirituality and oral modes of literary expression in postcolonial theories of trauma by illuminating how orality and rituals function as catalysts in processes of mourning and grieving in the aftermath of traumatic events. In the Philippine perspective, Bobis argues, trauma is closely connected with the recuperative influence of narrative, and with the healing forces of the spiritual and the magical (62). Other recent critical essays also point out the complex interrelatedness of trauma, power, and recovery in postcolonial literature, indicating that social activism and political protest may be integral to the aftermath of the trauma of colonization and decolonization. In this respect, resistance and resilience are to be seen not merely as responses of individuals but more importantly, as part of a communal process of living and working through trauma. This resonates with Chinua Achebe's remark in a recent essay, published in 2010, that while colonialism "was essentially a denial of human worth and dignity" it is important to understand that "the great thing about being human is our ability to face adversity down by refusing to be defined by it, refusing to be no more than its agent or its victim" (22–23).

What recent postcolonial literary engagements with trauma demonstrate, then, is that trauma theory as formulated by Hartman, Caruth and associates in the 1990s has lost ground as a theoretical model in postcolonial criticism due to its inherent limitations. In his book *Postcolonial Witnessing: Trauma Out of Bounds* (2012), Stef Craps reinforces the notion often expressed in postcolonial studies that literary trauma criticism is still too reliant on the earliest founding texts of the mid-1990s, whose hegemony should be overturned. There is, then, in postcolonial literary studies currently a clear call for a new model for reading, understanding, and interpreting trauma that would enable more differentiated, and more culturally and historically specific notations, and would also provide ways of reading collective trauma.

The disciplines often marked as being capable of providing this new model are sociology and anthropology, which have a greater theoretical openness to the collectivity of trauma due to their strong traditions in theorizing general societal responses. Indeed, as Erikson states, in sociology it is "well-travelled conceptual ground" to theorize trauma as collective (229). In their introduction to *The Splintered Glass: Facets of Trauma in the Post-Colony and Beyond* (2011) editors Dolores Herrero and Sonia Baelo-Allue argue for a change towards a sociological orientation in response to the general discontent with contemporary trauma theory based on deconstructionist and psychoanalytical orientations, pointing at useful contributions to trauma theory made in works by sociologists such as Jeffrey Alexander. Katherine Baxter, too, argues that a sociological framework for a theory of trauma may answer the present need to rethink and resolve the continuing tension between the desire for specificity and comprehensiveness in postcolonial literary studies. Drawing on the work of sociologist Kai Erikson, Baxter presents an interesting case study of the analysis of trauma in Marinovich and Silva's memoir *The Bang-Bang Club*. Baxter finds that using sociological theory provides a way of avoiding the prescriptiveness of the currently dominant trauma theory in literary studies whose focus on individual trauma "potentially closes off other modes of presenting trauma" (19). Craps, in his critique of what he terms "Caruthian theory," argues that if trauma studies are to "have any hope of redeeming its promise of ethical effectiveness," the social and historic relations must be taken into account, and that traumatic histories of subordinate groups should be situated against the histories of socially dominant groups (Craps 2012: 53).

It seems therefore worthwhile to consider theories developed in sociology and anthropology for their conceptualizations of collective responses to trauma. Unlike what is currently the dominant idea in trauma theory, social fracture, alienation, and a weakening of social cohesion, are not the only, nor perhaps even primary characteristics of trauma. In fact, while trauma may cause divisiveness, it can also lead to a stronger sense of belonging and can in fact *create* community. Erikson, one of the first to theorize collectivity and trauma, states that when feelings of hurt move to the centre of people's being and make them feel "marked, maybe cursed, maybe even dead," this sense of difference can draw people to others similarly marked, and in this way can serve as a source of community "just as a common language or a common cultural background can" (231).

The variety of traumatic experiences poses a challenge to a framework for trauma theory in postcolonial literary studies. Trauma has both centripetal and centrifugal tendencies; it is not by definition coherent in cause and effect. It can negatively affect individuals and communities, forcing open fault lines that "once ran silently through the structure of the larger community, dividing it into divisive fragments" (236). Yet trauma can also positively affect individuals and communities by consolidating a sense of belonging, of kinship and mutual trust. These two tendencies, however opposite in effect, are widely observed and can occur "either alone or in combination," as Erikson remarks (237). Trauma, then, is a very complex phenomenon. It is not only to be understood as acute and event-based, but can also be chronic and non-event based; it can be debilitating and disruptive to individuals and communities, but it can also create a stronger social cohesion and a renewed sense of identity:

> Literature reflects and constructs that complexity. As the site for the narratives that abound after an overwhelming social event, as anthropologist Victor Turner remarks, literature's function is to "explain that event, extol, ethicize it, excuse it, repudiate it, name it as a significant marker of collective life-experience, as a model for future behavior" (Turner 1987: 33).

Literature thus performs a major part in what sociologist Jeffrey C. Alexander terms the "trauma process," the process that gives narrative shape and meaning to "harmful or overwhelming phenomena which are believed to have deeply harmed collective identity" (Alexander 2004: 10). Collective trauma, in Alexander's definition, is not the traumatic event or its latent presence, but the result of a sociocultural act of constructing a traumatic experience through narrative. "Events are not inherently traumatic," Alexander states, but, rather, trauma is "a socially mediated attribution" to events, usually after an event but also as events unfold, or even before they occur (8). This approximates Freud's early notion of trauma as *Nachträglichkeit* (belatedness) or retrodetermination, which posits that repressed infantile erotic experiences or fantasies are not necessarily painful in themselves but only retrospectively become traumatic, namely when the child (in puberty) can reconstitute and "understand" the erotic experience, which only then becomes traumatic. Alexander similarly argues that collective trauma is to be defined as the remembering or constructing of an event which in itself need not be painful. Referring to sociological evidence, Alexander states that even events that have not actually occurred but are only imaginary can be "deeply traumatizing," as for example Hitler's "grotesque assertion" that Jews were responsible for Germany's losing World War I (8).

What Alexander's striking example of Hitler's construction of national trauma also illustrates is that collective identity is a crucial factor in the trauma process. Since a community's sense of stability and continuity is closely predicated on its sense of self, an event (or even imaginary event) that undermines this sense of a stable identity will have a profound impact. As processes that dislodge cultural meanings and social patterns, colonialism and decolonization deeply affect a community's sense of self, and are remembered and re-constructed by communities in narratives of loss and wounding. It is the function of narratives to provide expression to collective responses to the profoundly destructive acts of colonialism, material as well as immaterial, such as the suppression or profanation of sacred indigenous rituals and values. Colonialism's traumatic aftermath continues until the present day; a condition, as Achille Mbembe explains, known as the post-colony: "the effective continuation of the authority structures of the colony in the post-imperial nation despite 'flag independence'" (Mbembe 2010: 7). Postcolonial literature is a major contributor to the trauma process the sociocultural construction of trauma in the postcolony. In postcolonial literary criticism, then, an important advance would be the mapping out of lines of relationality between trauma and power and ideology in social groups. To adequately engage with literature, as several critics have argued, trauma theory must be open to power structures, as a necessary and new perspective.

As a very complex phenomenon, trauma defies the construction of a single theoretical framework to address and interpret its multifarious complexities in postcolonial literary studies. I would suggest that what is currently useful is to introduce not only new interdisciplinary concepts but also theoretical instruments to expand the present analytic repertoire. In this article I present such an instrument, taken from the work of social anthropologist Mary Douglas. Douglas's theory of cultural groups offers a reliable and flexible model for the research of cultural thought styles in relation to power structures. This theory and its grid-group diagram has been tried and tested in many disciplines since the 1970s. In her overview of its history of application in her book *Natural Symbols*, Douglas mentions fields as diverse as geology, economics, environmental studies, political sciences, theology, and applied philosophy (xxvi–xxix). Douglas's grid-group model is based on four distinct cultural types or "thought styles" which are differentiated by their relation to power, hierarchy, and authority. In this chapter I adapt the theory to use it as an instrument to read trauma in relation to power structures in postcolonial narratives. The traumas of the colonial legacy are shaped by collective and individual experiences with repressive authority structures, and it is precisely the relations between preferred thought styles and hegemonic authority structures that the grid-group model illuminates. In postcolonial literary criticism, power would be situated in the domain of the postcolony, but the model also allows for other power structures, such as patriarchy, tribal models of authority, or political systems of governance after decolonization or, as in South Africa, the democratic government installed after apartheid.

Douglas's cultural theory, then, enables both a comprehensive interpretation as well as a specific focus on individual trauma in literary criticism. It answers the current need in postcolonial trauma studies, as formulated by Craps, to expand our reading of trauma "from sudden, unexpected catastrophic events that happen to people in socially dominant positions to encompass ongoing, everyday forms of violence and oppression affecting subordinate groups" (Craps 2008: 54). Douglas's theory enables conceptualizations of trauma as experienced by social groups differentiated by social positions from dominance to subalterity, and connected by distinct allegiances to power. It has as its central tenet that any society or community has in embryo four cultural types, each in a distinctly different manner oriented towards power and authority (Douglas 175). In stating this, I am aware that to propose to use a model of only four types of thought styles for the analysis of power relations may invite an immediate resistance, if not charges of determinism and reductionism. In fact, these charges have been raised and adequately addressed in the three decades of interdisciplinary application of this model. Douglas's own response to these charges have been expressed most concisely and directly in her essay "Four Cultures: The Evolution of a Parsimonious Model" (1999). In this article she grants that while the grid-group theory of cultural types is, indeed, a parsimonious model which distinguishes only four intrasocietal cultural types, nevertheless four types and two dimensions have proven to be "theoretically sufficient" and it has been conclusively proven that the model has "theoretical muscularity" (411, 413).

Moreover, as Douglas writes in her preface to the 2010 reprint of her book *Natural Symbols*, the model harbors no assumption of fixity and leaves interpretive space for historic specificity as well as cultural diversity; it is not only a model to support "the collaborative effort to think about life and human values" but also "a tool that systematically questions the thinker's own starting point" (xix, xxix). In an article purposely examining the usefulness and reliability of the theory, D. Douglas Caulkins notes that precisely the applicability of the theoretical model in so many cross-cultural research areas refutes the charges of reductionism, and concludes that the theory underlying the model has been "both stimulating and fruitful" to "an interdisciplinary variety of scholars" over many years, with an ongoing activity of "spirited e-mail exchanges among the European network of grid/group theorists" (Caulkins 1999: 115).

In order to present the theory as offering an interpretive tool for literary analysis it will be necessary first to clarify the general theoretical assumptions underlying the model. After this, the model itself will be explained in some detail with use of literary examples taken primarily from *Ways of Dying* (1995), Zakes Mda's ground-breaking and widely discussed novel on the turbulent and violent days of the early 1990s post-apartheid years in South Africa. *Ways of Dying* takes a central place in the body of literatures that include the literature of the Holocaust and the literature of colonial and postcolonial conditions, in Rothberg's definition, which "bear witness to forms of extreme and everyday violence perpetrated in the name of racial ideologies and imperial political projects" and which "grapple necessarily with the burden of history" (Rothberg 2008: 14). The novel's representation of many atrocities (in an astounding variety of ways of dying) and collective and individual trauma in relation to various repressive authority structures make it very suitable for demonstrating, even in the limited scope of this article, the versatility and flexibility of the grid-group model, as well as the interpretive insights and innovative questions that it opens up for further research.

Douglas's grid-group diagram or cultural map explores four "cultural types," which may be understood as four thought styles or distinct types of preferences, each anchored in a different relation to power and hierarchy. These four thought styles are cross-cultural and cross-temporal, comprising the basic relations between groups and individuals in any society or community, on the premise that individuals are social beings who live together and collectively shape each other's ideas, fears, hopes, and values, and act on these collective beliefs in what Douglas claims in *Implicit Meanings* are standard ways (5–7).

The four thought types in *Thought Styles* are four main styles of relationality to power, and their relation to power structures individuals' life choices, preferences, and life style (Douglas 43). It belongs to the domain of literature to imaginatively construct and represent these four basic thought styles of societal groups in characterization, plots, and settings, through a variety of differences in outlook, in nuances, contradictions, and ambiguities. Postcolonial literature, almost by definition, dramatizes the trauma of colonization, as the disruptive and overwhelming invasion of a society's physical, moral, and conceptual realms, and reflects on its aftermath, engaging with cultural value systems and individual orientations towards power and oppression. Hegemonic authority and power are central determinants in this diagram, which makes it a useful tool for the analysis of trauma in postcolonial texts which, as Rothberg states, reflect how "colonial and other racist societies intensively police relations among social groups and seek to produce various kinds of segregation" but also "how traumas associated with racism create a psychically and socially relational intimacy across groups" (Rothberg 2008: 15). Douglas's four cultures or thought styles are grouped in a diagram divided into four quadrants, A, B, C, and D. I have drawn a simple diagram in Figure 5.1 to demonstrate this (mine reflects Douglas's more complex diagram found in *Thought Styles* on page 43):

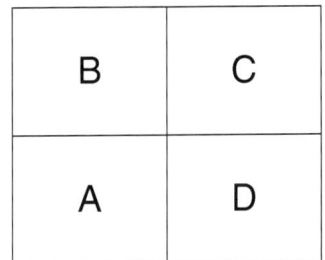

Figure 5.1

The thought style in quadrant A is the cultural type which favors materialism and individualism and seeks to benefit from connections with power and hierarchy; it is thus characterized by an active and competitive individualism and loyalty to power and hierarchy. In *Ways of Dying* there are several characters that embody this thought style, most prominent among them the millionaire entrepreneur Nefolovhodwe, who lives in isolation in a splendid mansion in the city, having cut off all communication with his relatives and former friends. Nefolovhodwe supports the government, hoping to make alliances with people in power. His coffin business profits hugely from the many ways of dying during these transitional years of the apartheid regime, and Nefolovhodwe, while in the midst of death and bereavement, seems personally unaffected by the trauma of loss and dislocation, and by the secondary trauma of witnessing deaths and suffering. This imperviousness to traumatization is worth noting, and I will return to Nefoldovhodwe and similar A-type characters in the subsequent discussion.

The B thought style is anchored in individualism, too, but is characterized by resistance to oppressive authority structures, which is expressed by withdrawal from society. Isolation is here the strategy to resist "the oppressive controls of the other forms of social life" (Douglas 1996: 42). The B thought style clearly accords with the condition of melancholy, reduced vitality and emotional numbness that trauma victims often experience. Whereas trauma is by definition a condition in which unconscious processes impact on a person's health and well-being while the precise nature, or even cause, of the trauma remains unknown or "unsayable," the many symptoms of trauma are overt and debilitating. In *Ways of Dying* the two protagonists Toloki and Noria are both severely traumatized and, at the start of the novel, are both exponents of the B thought style, seeking isolation as their preferred mode of resistance to the dominant power structures that have caused and condoned the traumatic events in their lives. Toloki, scarred by childhood abuse and by the many atrocities he has been witness to (secondary traumatization), desires to live like a monk, in isolation from the world of social intercourse and physical desires. Noria, who like Toloki is in her early thirties, has also chosen sexual abstention and withdrawal from society, traumatized by the violent ways of dying of her young sons. As Courau and Murray state, the novel's focus here is on the widespread "ritual enactments of the memory and loss of relatives," which in the early 1990s was "a source of continuity and form of relation for the larger black community" (Courau and Murray 2009: 91). The lives of Toloki and Noria, each in their way, provide testimonies to the traumatic aftermath of the violence and injustice of the apartheid years.

The C thought style of the diagram is oriented toward the conservative value system of the social group's authorities; its dominant characteristic is complete loyalty to power and hierarchy. In *Ways of Dying* this sector is powerfully present as a repressive backdrop to the various narratives: it is the thought style not only of the government, the police, the right-wing supremacists, the Boers, and Battalion 77, but also of the tribal chief and his reign of terror, and, significantly, the ANC, here called the people's political movement. The people's political movement has become a repressive authority, as is evident from instances when it ruthlessly enforces submission to its own authority. This happens most poignantly when party officials refuse to support Noria and deny her a fair hearing after the murder of her child Vutha by the Young Tigers. Prioritizing power over equality and justice, the people's political movement party has moved away from its initial egalitarian principles (D, see below) and has become complicit in the traumatization of individuals and communities.

The D thought style is, like B, that of resistance to dominant power structures. The difference is that this is a type that seeks consolidation in an organization or group, designated by the term "dissident enclave," and is, furthermore, averse to materialism and political opportunism. The dissident enclaves of the D quadrant are generally small groups that are organized by shared ethical, egalitarian, or ecological concerns (Douglas 1970: 44). In *Ways of Dying*, the women's organization in the settlement, described as "two hands that wash each other" (69) demonstrates the D thought style, displaying egalitarian principles in "trying to improve conditions for everyone at the settlement" (118).

The narrative arc of this novel is primarily the development of the relationship between Noria and Toloki, which may be analyzed as a movement from thought style B towards D, and which here constitutes a movement towards social connectedness, creativity and recovery from trauma. In terms of the diagram, when at the end of the novel Noria and Toloki have become part of the dissident enclave, this is the closure of their movement along the B–D diagonal. Steps on the way to health can be indicated on this diagonal, with perhaps the most significant of all being the protagonists' discovery of the mysterious powers of the imagination, in a scene where they paste pictures from back issues of *Home and Gardens* on the walls of Noria's shack, creating an environment of enchantment and tranquility in the midst of the violence of the squatter camp. This episode, which has gained "iconic status" in South African literature (Courau and Murray 2009: 98), centrally situates part of the process of healing in the liminal, dreamlike state of the creative imagination. Proceeding on the B–D diagonal (concretely, Toloki moves to the settlement and shares Noria's shack) the two protagonists eventually form a creative partnership through a slow process of "working through," aided by the narration of traumatic memories, which results in greater social confidence and sexual and emotional sensitivity. At the end of this novel, both Toloki and Noria show that by working constructively and collectively towards improving conditions for the entire community, their change of life styles (from B to D) has been recuperative. This prompts a tentative conclusion that a B–D movement in trauma engagement is a necessary and positive movement towards health and recuperation.

In Mda's novel, the enclavist culture of the settlement provides what according to sociologist and trauma theorist Kai Erikson victims of collective trauma need: "a human context and a kind of emotional solvent in which the work of recovery can begin" (Erikson 1994: 232). In Ewald Mengel and Michela Borzaga's recent collection of essays on the complex relationality of trauma, memory, and narrative in South African literature, contributors underscore that Caruthian trauma theory is not adequate to the analysis of trauma in the "postcolony" situation of South Africa and its recent historical condition of apartheid which caused the collective traumatization of several generations. This trauma, as they argue, is not an unclaimed nor unclaimable experience, but rather is reclaimed in narrative, both orally and in writing, as ways of coming to terms, however haltingly and incompletely, with the aftermath of apartheid and its atrocities. In their introduction to this volume, editors Mengel and Borzaga object specifically to what they term the "melancholic vocabulary" of theorists like Caruth, Laub, and Hartman, which is marked by "notions of absence, holes, deferral, crises of meaning, unknowing and dissociation" and which precludes "any possibility for healing for individuals or entire nations" (Mengel and Borzaga 2012: xiii). To this I would add that it can be maintained that the experiences underlying the characters' trauma can be fully understood, or claimed; the precise nature of the psychic wounding may remain inexpressible (in Caruth's eponymous phrase, as "unclaimed experience") but the characters find ways of coming to terms with the past and moving on with their lives in new and creative ways.

Not only the B–D diagonal discussed so far, but also the A–C diagonal of the cultural map diagram is a significant plot movement in *Ways of Dying*, which I have drawn below in Figure 5.2 (mine is based upon Douglas's more complex diagram on page 45 of *Thought Styles*). Both diagonals indicate dynamics between opposite quadrants, as follows:

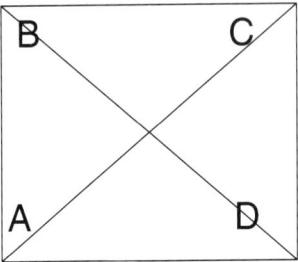

Figure 5.2

It is interesting to consider the engagement with trauma along the A–C diagonal. This diagonal indicates an increasing approximation towards the C thought style that prefers authority and hierarchy, and, like the B–D diagonal, demonstrates a movement away from isolation and individualism toward a group or communal system. In literary analysis, these diagonals are of signal importance, indicating how characters' choices and preferences oscillate, as, indeed, movement between the cultural sectors, as Douglas states in *Thought Styles*, is "theoretically easy" (1996: 45). It is in these movements that characters develop and conflicts unfold. In trauma theory, traumatization is defined as leading to stasis and melancholia, a condition which is intrinsically impossible to access or to fully understand. Indeed, following Caruth's thinking, trauma critics generally reject the notion of a resolution to trauma following the narrativization of traumatic memory. In Caruth's view, expressing trauma through narrative is to be seen as a loss; "the loss, precisely, of the event's essential incomprehensibility, the force of its affront to understanding"; and, even, as the betrayal of "the truth of the traumatic past, which cannot be represented" (1991: 154). However, in Mda's novel the many poignant narratives of loss, bereavement and almost inassimilable wounding (e.g., the death by "necklace" of Noria's child) follow a narrative movement towards resilience and resolution. In the book's final pages, on the cusp of a New Year, the smell of burning rubber is no longer mingled with the "sickly stench of roasting human flesh" but is just "pure wholesome rubber" (Mda 1995: 212).

This clearly presents an alternative to the currently dominant idea in trauma theory that social fracture, alienation and a weakening of social cohesion are the defining characteristics of individual and collective trauma. It opens up conceptualizations of trauma processes that can be strengthening and recuperative, in accordance with Erikson's findings that trauma can be a source of community (Erikson 1994: 231). Douglas's model presents an analytical tool with which to demonstrate not only these centripetal and centrifugal movements, but also, I would suggest, the defining influence of power and authority structures as determining gradations of social and interpersonal involvement in these movements.

The relation to authority and hierarchy as a central element in the investigation of postcolonial literary trauma can usefully be demonstrated by an exploration of the A–C diagonal in *Ways of Dying*. We now return to the character of Nefolovhodwe, the successful businessman who seems unaffected by many experiences that in others would be deemed traumatic. The only indications that Nefolovhodwe is troubled are his recurring dreams and his worries about his flea circus; these nightmares may be seen as trauma symptoms, but in the novel they are explained to us as the promptings of spirits who want him to perform an act of reconciliation with Toloki and the settlement enclave. This ethical gesture, once completed, brings peace of mind (as well as restored health to the fleas), but it does not entail a change in thought style. In terms of the diagram, Nefolovhodwe continues his movement along the A–C diagonal very successfully, and at the end of the novel is happy to be "invited to dinners by white people who held the reins of government" (Mda 1995: 206). We can conclude from this that the materialist and individualist thought style appears to provide a shield against secondary traumatization, that of living amidst death and ways of dying.

This conclusion is supported by a similar dynamic along the A–C diagonal that is observable in Mda's later novel *The Heart of Redness* (2000). The setting here is democratic South Africa, but it is also the trauma of history, a long-standing tribal conflict deriving from the historic event known as the Xhosa cattle killing, which is part of the legacy of nineteenth-century colonialism. In this novel Xoliswa Ximiya is a character that adheres to the materialist, individualist (A) thought style. Having just been appointed school principal in Qolorha-by-Sea, she seeks a position closer to power and authority (C), and at the end of the novel succeeds in obtaining a well-paid government position in Pretoria (Mda 2000: 262). Like Nefolovodhwe, Xoliswa Ximiya successfully completes the movement on the A–C diagonal, and like him, she is relatively unaffected by the trauma that for so long has caused conflict and suffering to others. Like Nefolovodhwe, too, she appears to be immune to the effects of transmission, the transfer of trauma through the generations, or the secondary traumatization that bystanders and witnesses of trauma experience, even though she also experiences symptoms of trauma. In her case these are scars that appear on her body. These "scars of history" are to be understood as the physical markers appearing in her ancestral bloodline, of the traumatic past of her people. Xoliswa Ximiya's response to the appearance of the scars is to ignore and deny them; rather than to address the trauma of history, she resolves to have the scars surgically removed by specialists in Pretoria (Mda 2000: 261).

From these examples we may draw the further, tentative conclusion that in the A quadrant of thought styles collective trauma is not a factor to be negotiated so much as ignored, denied, and avoided. Despite the very real suffering and even "ways of dying" witnessed closely by Nefolovodhwe and Xoliswa Ximiya, as A-type individualist entrepreneurs they succeed in disengaging from trauma, and apparently function perfectly efficiently afterwards. This is to be attributed to their primary orientation toward authority and power, as the defining aspect of their thought style, which underlies the close alliance of A with C that eventually prompts these characters to move increasingly closer to the location of the culture of power. This accords with Jeffrey Alexander's discussion of social groups and their commitment or non-commitment to solidarity in the aftermath of traumatic events. Alexander states that it is by refusing to participate in the socio-cultural act of constructing trauma through narrative (which he calls "the trauma process" or the process of trauma creation) that "social groups restrict solidarity, leaving others to suffer alone" (Alexander 2004: 1).

Conversely, when social groups commit to solidarity with other groups, Alexander argues, sharing their suffering, they "expand their circle of belonging" and thereby achieve "a moral stance" (1). This can be demonstrated clearly from analyzing plot movements with the use of the grid-group diagram: the movement along the B–D diagonal that Noria and Toloki display is that of a closer approximation with the dissident enclave; a dynamic that brings individuals closer to a connection with a social community (D) and a communal resistance to the dominant power structures. Whereas the A–C movement is restrictive, a-moral and undermines the trauma process in Alexander's terms, the B–D movement is expansive and connective, and aids the trauma process. Various critics have interpreted this movement as an allegorical representation of the transition from apartheid to democracy; Courau and Murray view it as "the community's dynamic towards survival" (93). This movement B–D is also a major structural element in *The Heart of Redness*, where protagonists Camagu and Qukezwa move from initial positions of social isolates (B) to eventual membership of an egalitarian cultural community (D). The fact that the characters on the B–D diagonal are all protagonists allows the conclusion that the B–D diagonal is a determining plot movement in Mda's oeuvre, and that social activism and egalitarian and ecological ideology are defining elements in his work, more defining than are power structures, ideologies, and hierarchies in themselves.

It is a remarkable finding that on the A–C diagonal, trauma symptoms are a much weaker incentive to action, and that in fact characters here prefer to ignore and avoid them. This suggests that the A–C diagonal dynamic in postcolonial trauma novels may be the place to investigate and theorize ambiguities of complicity and guilt. This is a relatively unexplored area of research, which has been delineated as needing critical attention. Writing about African literature after decolonization, Achille Mbembe points out the complexity of the "entanglement of desire, seduction and subjugation; not only oppression, but its enigma of loss" during decolonization, involving the realization that people "have allowed themselves to be duped, seduced, and deceived" (Mbembe 2010: 35). This (self-)critical scrutiny of complicity is not envisaged in current trauma theory. As Michael Rothberg states, traumatic memory in postcolonial terms may involve experiences of complicity under colonial oppression, and thus, "attentiveness to complicity marks one promising path for [such] a differentiated approach" (Rothberg 2008: 232).

All this is not to say that the C thought style is by definition that of a repressive and inimical authority. It is important at this point to bear in mind that the model itself is neutral: it does not express approval or opprobrium of any of the four major thought styles but poses that they are all intrinsic to any community, and thus mutually dependent. It is true that while the ideal situation is co-operation and mutual support, the reality almost inevitably involves conflict and competition between thought styles due to their distinctly opposite positions (Douglas 1996: 41).

What I wish to discuss briefly to complete my presentation of Douglas's model is an example of a fictional character that represents the A thought style and aspires to complete the A–C diagonal movement to reach a position of authority, and who, unlike the characters discussed above, is a morally outstanding protagonist, one who works towards the good of her community. Here, as before, colonial trauma is a factor in the character's personal and communal circumstances, and here, too, it is not negotiated or narrated so much as denied and ignored. This character is the young girl Kahu in Witi Ihimaera's mythopoetic novel *The Whale Rider*, set in Whangara, New Zealand. The book was well received by critics and readers after its publication in 1987, but it became a popular success only after its story had been made into the film *Whale Rider* in 2002. The success of the film led to a reissue of the novel and has made it a central work in the teaching and criticism of Ihimaera's important oeuvre. The narrative itself is easily summarized: a young Māori girl named Kahu (Paikea in the film) is next in line for the position of the leader of her tribe, but rejected harshly by her inflexible grandfather Koro, who represents patriarchial tradition. She strives to prove that she is worthy and eventually succeeds by rescuing and riding an ancient whale, as did her mythic ancestor Paikea. Kahu is then formally installed as the next leader of the tribe, thereby changing not only the grandfather's entrenched ideas of leadership, but also effecting an intrinsic change to patriarchal tradition.

The dramatic impact of Kahu's feminist revolt in the film (which earned young leading actress Keisha Castle-Hughes a nomination for the 2004 Academy Award for best actress) precisely derives its force from the relations between traumatic wounding and mechanisms of power and tribal authority. It is remarkable that protagonist Kahu and antagonist Koro are both firmly on the side of power, hierarchy, and authority. Indeed, Kahu's self-esteem, and her resilience in the face of adversity and rejection, are predicated on her loyalty to power, which is a loyalty to the tradition of the iwi (tribe) as embodied by the present leader, Koro Apirana. Her rejection is dictated by this tradition: while Kahu is the eldest grandchild, she is also a girl and in this patrilineal hierarchy, where only men are "sacred," she is "no good" to Koro (Ihimaera 1987: 35).

The cause of Kahu's childhood traumatization is therefore the intricate mixture of deliberate exclusion and the infliction of blame and guilt. From earliest childhood onwards, Kahu's attempts to bond with Koro are met with constant cruel rejection and outright accusations of causing the community's misfortune: "when she was born, that's when things started going wrong for us" (16). Forced to be an outsider and an individualist, but siding with power and hierarchy, Kahu, in terms of the grid-group diagram, starts out in the quadrant of the A thought style, but strives to approach the C quadrant, moving continuously on the A-C diagonal. Like Mda's characters Nefolovodhwe and Xoliswa Ximiya discussed previously, Kahu is also unwavering and steadfast in her loyalty to hierarchy; at no point in the story does she turn against Koro's authority and the power that he personifies, motivated by her (almost magical) conviction that her place is firmly in the upper echelons of that hierarchy.

It is useful to briefly consider this in theoretical terms, explaining the grid-group model's two dimensions of group (social cohesion) and grid (endorsement of belief system). In high-group, or strongly collective contexts (C), there are clear and strong boundaries. We see this reflected in Koro's strong imposition of rules to safeguard the traditional structures of hierarchy in the Māori community in Whangara. In low-group contexts (A), by contrast, persons interact as individuals in relatively unbounded social networks. This is shown in the situation of Kahu, who, as a girl, is excluded from traditional ritual training and forced to train on her own. High grid, which occurs when a thought style is strongly adhered to, certainly applies to Kahu, who displays an unwavering respect for the dignity of public roles and classifications, such as the genealogy of her tribe. Low grid occurs where such classifications play a minor role; it is obvious that Kahu never moves towards that position, even though her father is an exponent of that thought style (B). Forced by Koro's authority into a low-group position, Kahu nevertheless endorses high-group and high-grid positions; and when she eventually obtains her position of leadership (moving into the C quadrant), her triumph and that of the narrative itself is that the iwi's patriarchal authority structure has been expanded to allow female leadership.

As we have seen in the discussion of the similar characters in Mda's novel, there has been no working through of a trauma process; no resolution to the trauma of Kahu's long years of painful rejection. This confirms the notion that the A thought style derives from a sense of identity that remains focused on the move towards an alliance with power, rather than introspection, or the trauma process (the process of constructing trauma narrative as a way forward). Kahu's resilience, despite traumatic childhood experiences, is based on her conviction that she is the rightful heir to leadership as is confirmed by many instances such as her mystic communion with whales. The trauma of colonialism is felt throughout the novel in its references to Māori land claims, language loss, and racial discrimination as contextual elements in Kahu's story, serving to lend urgency to the need for a continuation of strong tribal leadership. Postcolonial trauma here thus underlies and intensifies the AC dynamic of the plot movement. It lends force to the narrative's climax which is more than merely the feminist triumph of a young girl over an older, overbearing relative: here the breaking of the cycle of patriarchal oppression is also the resolution and healing of trauma, both personally and collectively. This is the transformation that a working-through of trauma accomplishes, and what the narrative emphasizes is that such a recuperative process can be accomplished by ritual as well as by social, other-directed action.

What this analysis of trauma as an intergenerational conflict also demonstrates is that resilience is a major element in the positive adaptation to traumatic events or experiences. Resilience is at present not sufficiently incorporated in trauma theory, even though, as Luckhurst argues in *The Trauma Question*, it is acknowledged in psychiatry today as a common and healthy psychic response to trauma. Luckhurst points out that resilience is now being theorized, e.g. in studies of grief, and cases and images of resilience have been found empirically to be ordinary phenomena. This counters what Luckhurst terms "the default assumptions of the trauma model" that tend to argue a uni-dimensional and limited pattern of response to trauma in which resilience could even be seen as pathological (Luckhurst 2008: 210). This view contrasts sharply with my analysis of resilience as a major character trait in *The Whale Rider*, where it is a positive and recuperative factor. My analysis thus underscores Luckhurst's argument for a greater openness to the exploration of resilience in literary trauma studies, following the shift in psychiatry:

> The emphasis on resilience as a field of enquiry has led to a shift in psychiatric attitudes towards trauma victims; for instance, instead of active, immediate interventions after a traumatic event

aimed at "psychological debriefing" as many people as possible, there is now an awareness that victims' own "ordinary" resilience may make such interventions superfluous, and may in fact even induce or aggravate the syndromes they were meant to prevent, as studies confirm. (210)

Ihimaera's *The Whale Rider* places forgiveness in the centre of the trauma process as a potent force for good, as demonstrated by Kahu's unconditional and repeated forgiveness of Koro. The breaking of the cycle of violence, wounding, and suffering is effectuated by this forgiveness, which even annuls guilt. The problem with forgiveness is that it is not at present theorized in trauma studies and is not a recognized concept in trauma theory; this is partly due to what Julia Kristeva has diagnosed as the problem of Freudianism, which is that it has no place for forgiveness; "forgiveness is not a psychoanalytical concept" (Kristeva 1997: 14). Ihimaera's narrative, however, does allow a central place for forgiveness. Forgiveness is formally asked by Koro, expressed in his ritual words in Māori, translated as: "Wise leader, forgive me. I am just a fledgling new to flight." This ceremonial asking and receiving of forgiveness marks the end to Kahu's trauma of rejection and exclusion. Koro's enactment of the theme of forgiveness further reinforces the narrative's foregrounding of an alternative to the patriarchal cycle of exclusion and oppression. Forgiveness, in this ritual, is a very powerful psychological instrument, and, despite its complexity, and the potentially controversial nature of its theorization in view of Caruthian trauma notions, invites serious conceptualization in postcolonial trauma studies.

Ihimaera's story, furthermore, supports the conclusion that I have drawn on the basis of the novels by Mda and Ihimaera, which is that the thought style of the C sector is by definition traumatogenic: this culture typically inflicts trauma, prolongs it, condones it, or is complicit with agents of trauma. In Ihimaera's *The Whale Rider* where the C quadrant is that of the authority of indigenous tradition and culture, it is initially traumatogenic, when at the start Koro's attitude is repressively patriarchal, causing much hurt and wounding to Kahu. The eventual expansion of the C thought style at the end of the narrative, with the inclusion of the feminine, is the transformation that counters and removes the traumatogenic influence by subverting and overthrowing the traditional hierarchy. This further demonstrates the principle that none of the four segments of the diagram is by definition negative, oppressive or traumatogenic, and that the C thought style, too, can be beneficial to a society, if open to change and expansion.

One of the interesting conclusions to be drawn, is that in all three novels discussed in this essay the A–C diagonal movement towards the C thought style seems to preclude or remove the need for the individualized resolution of trauma. This may justify the conclusion that if identification of an individual is with the A quadrant, and if the goal is to move towards C, the construction of an individual trauma process has little significance or that in fact no such trauma process occurs, neither as personal "working through" nor in Alexander's broader definition as the sociocultural construction of trauma, but rather, that the desire to align with power and authority limits the trauma process. This relationship between power and trauma construction presents an interesting finding for further research in trauma theory in postcolonial literary studies.

A further conclusion that the above discussion justifies is that trauma has a far greater significance in quadrants B and D than in the A and C quadrants. The cultural type indicated by B is that of the isolated individual who withdraws from society, wishing to avoid "the oppressive controls of the other forms of social life" (Douglas 1996: 42). Here, typically, we find the traumatized victims of colonial repression: those denied their rightful place in society, and those that have chosen isolation from society in reaction to the "oppressive controls" of the post-colony. Erikson, in his pioneering work on collective trauma, speaks of "a gathering of the wounded" who have learned a "profoundly unsettling truth: that human institutions cannot be relied on" (Erikson 1994: 232, 239), which astutely describes the isolates of sector B. Those suffering from chronic or pervasive trauma will perceive the world as hostile and beyond their conscious control, influence, or knowledge. This is what Erikson terms the "traumatic world view" (239). However, in the fictional dynamic of plot movements, we see a tendency towards inclusion and connectivity, which is recuperative and leads to a coming of terms with trauma, often through social activism. A further expansion of trauma theory, as I have suggested, seems needed, not only to include resilience, but also the influence of forgiveness as a factor in the trauma process.

Douglas's theory of four thought styles enables insight into narratives of trauma and power in postcolonial literature, and her grid-group diagram offers an analytical instrument to explore how literature constructs, mediates, and comments on collective trauma. Postcolonial literary texts often engage with trauma in ways not envisioned in the currently dominant trauma theory, or in ways that reverse trauma theory's assumptions, for instance by depicting victims' resilience, resistance, and eventual triumph over trauma, or a community's increased cohesion and enhanced sense of identity after a traumatic event. Coping strategies of people in prolonged and severe circumstances vary according to a community's resilience and resourcefulness, but they are also influenced by the attributes of the thought style that a community identifies with. Douglas's model enables us to analyze the various ways in which narratives delineate resolution to individual and collective traumatic experiences and their resulting disorders in relation to power and authority. As Elleke Boehmer writes, the critical scrutiny of power relations remains a defining postcolonial concern. Drawing on key publications of recent years, she states that the postcolonial continues to signify "a theoretical and writerly force field preoccupied with resistance to empire and its post-imperial aftermath" and that it "correlates with struggle, subversion, the nation, the region, resistance to the global status quo—whether that be capitalist-driven colonialism or contemporary neo-imperial globalization" (Boehmer 2010: 143). Boehmer's emphasis on political contextualization thus further accentuates the need to theorize relations between trauma and power in postcolonial studies today.

Important aspects of Douglas's theory for postcolonial literary studies, therefore, are its inclusiveness, its wide applicability, its proven usefulness in a wide array of disciplines and interdisciplinary studies, and its flexibility and precision. Moreover, this flexibility and adaptability makes it potentially useful for the exploration of other themes in postcolonial trauma studies, such as guilt and complicity (Mbembe 2010) or "trauma envy" (Delrez 2011) which may further add to the ways in which postcolonial trauma can be theorized. The grid-group diagram presents a useful instrument for the analysis of narrative movements from trauma as isolation, numbness and stasis to trauma as itself an incentive to creativity, connectivity and moral and political action. It thus enables what Craps highlights as the commitment expressed by literary critics in postcolonial studies "to make visible the creative and political" rather than the "pathological and negative" in trauma literature (Craps 2012: 127). As a reliable framework to compare sociocultural constructions and representations of trauma in relation to power and authority, the grid-group theory invites comparative critical work in a diversity of areas, allowing us to explore, for instance, developments in early and recent postcolonial writing, in national literatures, or in a single author's oeuvre or major work. Douglas's "parsimonious" theory may thus be a useful instrument to open doors to richer analyses of postcolonial literary diversity.

Bibliography

Achebe, Chinua. *The Education of a British-Protected Child: Essays.* London: Penguin, 2009.

Alexander, Jeffrey C. "Toward a Theory of Cultural Trauma." In Jeffrey C. Alexander, Ron Eyerman, Berhard Giesen, Neil J. Smelser and Piotr Sztompka, eds. *Cultural Trauma and Collective Identity.* Berkeley: University of California Press, 2004, 1–30.

Baxter, Katherine. "Photography and Postcolonial Trauma in *The Bang-Bang Club.*" *Journal of Postcolonial Writing* 47.1 (2011): 18–29.

Bell, David. and J.U. Jacobs (eds.). *Ways of Writing: Critical Essays on Zakes Mda.* Scottsville: University of KwaZulu-Natal Press, 2009.

Bobis, Merlinda. "Passion to Pasyon: Playing Militarism." In Dolores Herrero and Sonia Baelo-Allue, eds. *The Splintered Glass: Facets of Trauma in the Post-Colony and Beyond.* Series Cross/Cultures—Readings in the Post/Colonial Literatures in English 136. Amsterdam: Rodopi, 2011, 57–80.

Boehmer, Elleke. "Postcolonial Writing and Terror." In Elleke Boehmer and Stephen Morton, eds. *Terror and the Postcolonial.* Malden: Wiley-Blackwell, 2010, 141–150.

Boehmer, Elleke. and Stephen Morton (eds.). *Terror and the Postcolonial.* Malden: Wiley-Blackwell, 2010.

Caruth, Cathy. "Introduction to Psychoanalysis, Trauma and Culture I." *American Imago* 48.1 (1991): 1–12.

Caruth, Cathy. *Unclaimed Experience: Trauma, Narrative, and History.* Baltimore: Johns Hopkins University Press, 1996.

Caulkins, D. Douglas. "Is Mary Douglas's Grid/Group Analysis Useful for Cross-Cultural Research?" *Cross-Cultural Research* 33:1 (February 1999): 108–128. 11 January 2013. http://ccr.sagepub.com/content/33/1/108.refs

Collins, Jo. "The Ethics and Aesthetics of Representing Trauma: The Textual Politics of Edwidge Danticat's *The Dew Breaker.*" *The Journal of Postcolonial Writing* 47.1 (2011): 5–17.

Courau, Rogier and Sally-Ann Murray. "Of Funeral Rites and Community Memory: Ways of Living in *Ways of Dying.*" In David Bell and J.U. Jacobs, eds. *Ways of Writing: Critical Essays on Zakes Mda.* Scottsville: University of KwaZulu-Natal Press, 2009, 91–114.

Craps, Stef. "Wor(l)ds of Grief: Traumatic Memory and Literary Witnessing in Cross-Cultural Perspective." *Textual Practice* 24.1 (2010): 51–68.

Craps, Stef. *Postcolonial Witnessing: Trauma Out of Bounds.* Basingstoke: Palgrave Macmillan, 2012.

Craps, Stef, and Gert Buelens. "Introduction: Postcolonial Trauma Novels." *Studies in the Novel* 40.1/2 (2008): 1–12.

Delrez, Marc. "'Twisted Ghosts': Settler Envy and Historical Resolution in Andrew McGahan's *The White Earth*." In Dolores Herrero and Sonia Baelo-Allue, eds. *The Splintered Glass: Facets of Trauma in the Post-Colony and Beyond*. Series Cross/Cultures—Readings in the Post/Colonial Literatures in English 136. Amsterdam: Rodopi, 2011, 191–204.

Douglas, Mary. *Thought Styles: Critical Essays on Good Taste*. London: Sage, 1996.

Douglas, Mary. "Four Cultures: The Evolution of a Parsimonious Model". *GeoJournal* 47 (1999): 411–415, available at http://www.springerlink.com/ content/dq79m65x7xapwqee/ [accessed 15 February 2013].

Douglas, Mary. *Implicit Meanings*. 1975. Repr. in Collected Works: Volume V. Selected Essays in Anthropology. London: Routledge, 2003.

Douglas, Mary. *Natural Symbols: Explorations in Cosmology*. 1970. Repr. London: Routledge, 2010.

Erikson, Kai. *A New Species of Trouble: Explorations in Disaster, Trauma, and Community*. New York: Norton, 1994.

Hartman, Geoffrey H. "On Traumatic Knowledge and Literary Studies." *New Literary History* 26.3 (1995): 537–563, available online at http://muse.jhu. edu/journals/new_literary_history/v026/26.3hartman.html [accessed 21 February 2013].

Herrero, Dolores and Sonia Baelo-Allue (eds.). *The Splintered Glass: Facets of Trauma in the Post-Colony and Beyond*. Series Cross/Cultures—Readings in the Post/Colonial Literatures in English 136. Amsterdam: Rodopi, 2011.

Ihimaera, Witi. *The Whale Rider*. 1987. Repr. London: Robson Books, 2003.

Kristeva, Julia. *Intimate Revolt: The Powers and Limits of Psychoanalysis*. Vol 2. Original French edition, *La Révolte Intime*, 1997. Trans. Jeanine Herman. European Perspectives: A Series in Social Thought and Cultural Criticism. New York: Columbia University Press, 2002.

Luckhurst, Roger. *The Trauma Question*. London: Routledge, 2008.

Mbembe, Achille. "The Colony: Its Guilty Secret and Its Accursed Share." In Elleke Boehmer and Stephen Morton, eds. *Terror and the Postcolonial*. Malden: Wiley-Blackwell, 2010. 27–54.

Mda, Zakes. *Ways of Dying*. Oxford: Oxford University Press, 1995

Mda, Zakes. *The Heart of Redness*. New York: Picador, 2000.

Mengel, Ewald and Michela Borzaga (eds.). *Trauma, Memory, and Narrative in the Contemporary South African Novel: Essays*. Amsterdam/New York: Rodopi, 2012.

Rothberg, Michael. "Decolonizing Trauma Studies: A Response." *Studies in the Novel* 40.1/2 (2008): 224–234.

Rothberg, Michael. "In the Nazi Cinema." *Wasafiri* 24: 1 (March 2009): 13–20.

Turner, Victor. *The Anthropology of Performance*. New York: PAJ Publications, 1987.

Visser, Irene. "Trauma Theory and Postcolonial Literary Studies." *Journal of Postcolonial Writing* 47. 3 (July 2011): 270–282.

Whitehead, Anne. "Journeying Through Hell: Wole Soyinka, Trauma, and Postcolonial Nigeria." *Studies in the Novel* 40.1/2 (2008): 13–30.

6
Voices of Survivors in Contemporary Fiction

Laurie Vickroy

Contemporary fiction by Jane Smiley and Margaret Atwood represents trauma within social contexts in order to emphasize the narrative and expressive aspects of severe circumstances. Although silence may accompany descriptions of the survivor's experience, fiction provides multiple perspectives that allow readers to meditate on the variety of human responses to shock. The various traumatic responses beyond the notion of the unspeakable cultivate the subtleties of experience, which are expressed through behaviors, bodies, provisional identities, and survival strategies. This chapter offers a multidisciplinary interpretive framework that appreciates the complex nature of these depictions by shifting beyond the traditionalist Freudian perspective that focuses primarily on childhood traumas, repression, and repetition. My analysis will focus instead on the social, situational, and narrative aspects of trauma to argue that fiction by Jane Smiley and Margaret Atwood depicts the many avenues for expressing the voices of trauma through the survivor's narrative.

Examining how cultural values influence traumatic experience is essential to understanding trauma's aftermath. Clinical psychologists, such as Maria Root and Laura S. Brown, argue that the socio-cultural contexts that shape individual identities may also shape how a survivor understands a traumatic experience. Understanding responses to trauma requires examining aspects of psychological functioning within the social or cultural environment that may suppress acknowledgement of trauma. Fiction that depicts trauma incorporates varied responses and survival behaviors within the characterizations of survivors. Writers such as Margaret Atwood and

Jane Smiley often depict characters as narrators of their own stories, after the fact, where they revisit their process of awakening.

The environment of social relations and cultural values can be a source of trauma or a force that silences victims out of denial or guilt. It can create veils of illusion, attempts to mask or reinterpret behaviors that induce trauma. Societies, communities, or families may want to preserve stability or be willing to sacrifice victims for other goals. Both writers covered in this chapter depict these sacrifices. However, individuals or circumstances within these same environments can be triggers for memory or encouragement because not everyone is silenced or traumatized by similar circumstances. Each writer provides their protagonists with insights by way of fellow characters similarly victimized who maintain their memories, and remain unpersuaded by the interests of those who create or refuse to acknowledge traumatic events. Atwood and Smiley create narrators, often the protagonists, who begin to piece together narratives of their lives in relation to their communities. Traumatized characters are offered clues and bits of memories to reassess survival and finally engage in new ways of thinking and being.

Trauma is an individual's response to events so intense that they impair emotional or cognitive functioning and may bring lasting psychological disruption. Survivors might live with a fragmented memory or a diminished sense of self, or might feel alienated (Herman 2009: 42–47). Traumatic responses may include shame, doubt, or guilt, or may destroy important beliefs in one's own safety or view of oneself as decent, strong, and autonomous (Janoff-Bulman 1992: 19–22). Trauma is located within a dynamic process of feeling, remembering, assimilating, or recovering from that experience. Trauma has a range of causes and effects, which moves away from a focus on internalized isolated psychic elements found in the traditional trauma mode and toward an alternative trauma model that considers the interaction of social and behavioral constructs associated with trauma. Learning theorists explain that trait-driven conceptions of personality are less accurate measures of behavioral causes than the individual's personal history of conditioning, personal constructs, and their psychological circumstances. Psychologist Walter Mischel notes that "conditions or 'situational variables' of the psychological environment provide the individual with information … thereby affecting cognitive and behavioral activities under those conditions" (376). Thus environmental contingencies are crucial to behavior.[1]

The social environment, the severity of the event, and the individual's characteristics and sense of control help determine how someone copes with trauma (Root 1992: 248; MacCurdy 2007: 17).[2] The social environment influences the causes and outcomes of traumatic experience in a variety of ways. It not only forms the circumstances out of which trauma is created, but can also provide or refuse the needed support for healing.[3] Cultural attitudes about trauma and family responses to it may either bring the victim together with healing connections, or may prevent them (Van der Kolk, McFarlane and Weisaeth 1996: 27). These attitudes and practices influence notions of expected behavior, responses, and even symptoms. Life roles and emotional management are "facilitated and ordered" within a culturally prescribed social and community structure where stress, illness, and grief are dealt with on personal and group levels (De Vries 1996: 401). Optimum circumstances for healing exist when a "society organizes the process of suffering, rendering it a meaningful mode of action and identity within a larger social framework" (401–402). When cultures do not function this way, individuals feel unprotected and are forced to cope in isolation.[4] Victims may respond to trauma in an unsympathetic environment by adapting as best they can with survival characteristics such as "egocentrism, quickness to anger, social and emotional withdrawal, rumination, or shutting down" (Root 1992: 248). These survival traits are demonstrated in Atwood and Smiley's novels that chart the emotions attached to victims' recovery.

Communities and societies can perpetuate the isolation felt by trauma survivors according to Root because communities want to protect themselves from vulnerability, avoid what survivors have suffered, and prevent survivors from sharing their experience with others. In an examination of the effects of trauma on personality, clinical psychologist Maria Root extends the range of traumatic experience to those suffering low status because of gender, class, or race (Root 1992: 230). Their experiences are "insidious" because they are endemic to particular class situations that are repeated in ways that maintain hierarchies of dominance. Root places more emphasis on victims' experience of events in trauma-producing environments rather than the events themselves in order to "depathologize" normal responses to "horrible experiences" (237). Further consequences of interpersonal traumas that involve betrayal or abuse of power include the impairment of an individuals' sense of trust, control, and self-worth (253). These dilemmas are found in fiction through the representation of traumatized characters, notably in their anxieties and problems with trust. These qualities are needed to survive, but impair the character's relations with others. Atwood and Smiley's texts indicate that traumatized characters confront and repair these psychological dimensions before reconciling with others.

Jane Smiley and Margaret Atwood establish well the social contexts of individual trauma by demonstrating how groups become invested in discouraging victims from speaking out. For example in Jane Smiley's *A Thousand Acres*, the plight of sexually abused and cancer-ridden women threaten a farm community's respect for the appearance of un-conflicted family life and the men who have built their farms from the raw earth, even if they had to use toxic chemicals to do it. To acknowledge those victims puts into question the value of their lives' work. Margaret Atwood likewise demonstrates how social and political structures are normalized by silencing victims in the fictional/speculative realm, the theocracy in *The Handmaid's Tale*. Atwood demonstrates that these structures are not absolute and do not traumatize everyone; they become vulnerable once their norms are questioned and lose power in the face of resistance. Her novels present cracks in the silencing armor, as other characters in the protagonists' sphere challenge the coercive lies of the powerful and provide a sense of reality and hope, allowing the protagonists to slowly recover a sense of self and voice. Often it is portrayed as an inner voice, working through trauma, and on the verge of being made public.

* * *

Margaret Atwood reproduces signs of trauma with narratives that highlight social aspects of her characters' minds as they endure and work through trauma in adverse social environments. In her characterizations Atwood also illustrates what Root calls the "survival schema[s]" individuals develop which determine their personalities and are predicated on the individual's "history of cumulative trauma, societal view of trauma, and preparedness for trauma" (Root 1992: 250). Atwood's work examines all these variables as they impact her characters' behaviors, associations, and imaginations. Atwood's novel *Cat's Eye* depicts an intricate social web of gender conformity in the Canada of her youth (the 1940s and 1950s), expressed in a range of forms from schoolgirls' rules of dress and conduct, to enforcement of adult cultural and religious ideologies, to media warnings of surveillance regarding proper female domestic practices ("the watchbird is watching you" states a popular women's magazine). Such social demands and punishments contextualize the protagonist Elaine Risley's traumas until she learns to recognize them and extricate herself from them; she will graduate from silence to defensive posturing to imagistic revelations of repressed emotion, to a real voice informed by recovered memory and mature perspective.

The product of a nomadic, irreligious, stable and supportive home life, Elaine proves inadequate to social conformities. The daily surveillance and abusive commands of her three girlfriends, particularly Cordelia, produce in Elaine extreme self-destructive symptoms (pulling her skin off) and constant fear and anxiety such that she loses any sense of the independent identity her parents have tried to instill. Peer pressure is merely an extension, Atwood suggests, of the larger societies' insistence on gendered, religious, and social conformity. That insistence becomes internalized, making women privilege men and blame themselves when they do not uphold the standards set for them. Elaine is bullied by her "friends" to the point of almost losing her life—they leave her in frozen water in a ravine—until she's saved by her own imagined vision of a mother figure (the Virgin) and her actual mother, who comes to save her and bears witness to the girls' appalling behavior. And though this close call makes her reject her friends, Elaine is forever marked by this early experience that continues to formulate her relationships to others for years to come.

After this period of her life she dissociates from the past and is unable to access painful childhood memories, not knowing what her mother means when she refers to "That bad time you had. ... I've forgotten things, I've forgotten that I've forgotten them. ... Time is missing." Amnesia makes her "happy as a clam: hardshelled, firmly closed" (Atwood 1998: 221). In adolescence she maintains emotional distance, protecting herself from others, mistrusting them and viewing relationships with girls and boys as pure power struggles, as she experienced with Cordelia. She avoids sympathy and empathy: "Knowing too much about other people puts you in their power, they have a claim on you, you are forced to understand their reasons for doing things and then you are weakened" (240). Though Elaine defends herself from the awareness and extent of her own earlier traumas, her defenses take over her mindset, such that she makes sure she is the one who judges, and not the vulnerable one. Upon escaping Cordelia she thinks, "I know she has expected something from me, some connection to her old life, or to herself. I know I have failed to provide it. I am dismayed by myself, by my cruelty and indifference, my lack of kindness. But also I feel relief" (284).

Elaine is particularly judgmental of other women, both needing their camaraderie and bravery during the early days of feminism, but also holding them to society's standards, hating their and her own helplessness to prevent pregnancy, for instance. Her mistrust, really fear, of women also makes her overlook the sexism and condescension from the men in her life, her first lover Joseph (her art professor) and Jon, her husband and fellow art student. After putting up with two bad relationships (with blame on both sides), she will take enormous pleasure from walking out on these men when they show signs of weakness: "I'm good at leaving. The trick is to close yourself off. Don't hear, don't see. Don't look back" (411). Not until middle age will she understand the fearful place from which her behavior originates.

Her relationship to Cordelia will continue to haunt her; it is both her closest relationship to anyone and the most painful. At a vulnerable point in Elaine's life Cordelia asks again for help; that is, for Elaine to help her escape a mental institution. Elaine is furious at this imposition, fearing for her daughter if Cordelia should attempt suicide again. Though Elaine's hesitation seems reasonable, her emotions are over-determined and her reference to want to "rub [Cordelia's] face in the snow" recalls her own life-threatening experience on that snowy day in the ravine in their youth. Elaine must eventually return to that place to be reunited with the context and her own emotions. After recovering some of her memory with her mother as they go through her old things, Elaine finds herself "Looking for something that's been thrown away as useless, but could still be dredged up and reclaimed" (422). When she revisits the ravine at the end of the novel, she contemplates Cordelia's emotions:

> I know she's looking at me, the lopsided mouth smiling a little, the face closed and defiant. There is the same shame, the sick feeling in my body, the same knowledge of my own wrongness, awkwardness, weakness; the same wish to be loved; the same

loneliness; the same fear. But these are not my own emotions any more. They are Cordelia's; as they always were. (459)

To reclaim her past and not be unconsciously ruled by it, Elaine has to overcome her fears. Because of this past, Elaine dreads being back in Toronto, a place she left decades before, where she feels "overwhelmed" by "old time." It's the restrictive scene of her childhood traumas, a reminder of when she lost herself, and of broken relationships and lost connections. She must return to be honored for a retrospective of her paintings: conservative, provincial Toronto can now appreciate the unconventional woman artist. She must now face the past with a new perspective, revisit the ravine and what happened there, and reconcile with (but not return to) her first husband, Jon. Once she understands more of her past, what motivated her and her art, Toronto becomes drained of much of its traumatic force. She still does not wish to linger, but she cannot reach the necessary insights without being there.

The impact of early traumas on the protagonist's imagination is crucial to her development as an artist, with some drawbacks and benefits: the defensive narrowing and focus of her vision has protected her from harm (but also feeling at times). The ability to see and to focus in such detail has made her into a gifted painter of physical details, and creates what seems to her an emotional distance. However, these paintings in fact carry the feelings from which she's become estranged. The process of creating these paintings stems from anxiety that is a sign of emerging memory.

Before she marries Jon and is worried about being pregnant, she suddenly begins to paint domestic items from her own and her friends' homes during the early traumatic period; their appearance represents the kind of visual, involuntary memories characteristic of trauma, and they remain dissociated from her own emotional context at that time. "I have no image of myself in relation to them. They are suffused with anxiety, but it's not my own anxiety. The anxiety is in the things themselves" (367). It is really in her, but her artistic forms enable her dissociation and yet express her deepest emotions, such as her grotesque portraits of the hateful Mrs. Smeath, who condoned the girls' humiliations of the "heathen" Elaine. Her vision allows her a kind of revenge that in the end Elaine must recognize, as well as her own cruelty, as she tries to understand what might have motivated

Mrs. Smeath and later, Cordelia. Looking again at her paintings in the retrospective, she examines Mrs. Smeath's eyes: "I used to think these were self-righteous eyes, piggy and smug inside their wire frames; and they are. But they are also defeated eyes, uncertain and melancholy, heavy with unloved duty. The eyes of someone for whom God was a sadistic old man" (443). In acknowledging the limits and vulnerabilities of these women, Elaine is able to begin freeing herself of some of this past baggage. What has made her a strong artist in some ways has also affected her ability to be compassionate, which she reclaims at the end of the novel: the ability to see in a new light.

* * *

Fiction provides readers a wealth of thick description of the conditions and characteristics of traumatic experience. With its unique capacity to represent the interweaving of the environment and human responses, fiction illustrates the creation of emotional and cognitive patterns arising out of trauma that in turn shape social attitudes and structures of living. The mechanisms of trauma, how it is caused and perpetuated, and the possibilities for healing often depend upon social interconnections, through acts of witnessing or sympathy. Unfortunately, social opinions can re-traumatize or undermine victims. Trauma in texts by Atwood and Smiley feature adverse social environments where trauma is denied and healing is thwarted. Denials, revulsion, and scapegoating characterize the responses of witnesses, and implicate them in victims' further suffering. Though depicted as normative responses, texts also offer a critique of them in light of the devastating isolation and abandonment others inflict on the wounded. Trauma in fiction can demonstrate the silencing power of the environment, but also the possibility of critiquing its delusional premises; often only a few characters who are able to break out of the established patterns.

Potentially literature can imaginatively place readers into difficult and alienating situations. The degree to which this is possible must be qualified. For instance, Dominick LaCapra believes fiction can reveal the emotional experience of historical phenomena such as slavery (LaCapra 2001: 13–14), but he favors texts that put readers into a position of "empathic unsettlement," that is, that take readers through a process of working through trauma that put readers into a critical as well as an empathic mode of thought that does not entitle readers to be in the "victim's ... position" (78). Much of the trauma in literature analyzed here undercuts any uncritical sentimentality readers might feel, by creating characters that are sympathetic but problematically complicated, behave unethically, and are often unable to bond with others.

Effective trauma texts engage readers in a critical process by immersing them in, and yet providing perspective on, the flawed thinking, feeling, and behavior of the traumatized individual. E. Ann Kaplan measures this success in the ways readers/viewers are interpolated in the story, or even become implicated in some way. She concurs with Jeffrey Alexander that our views of trauma are culturally constructed and cultural representations inform public consciousness: "Genres shape how we think about our lived worlds through establishing certain kinds of story, certain repeated narratives and situations, leading to well-defined expectations" (Kaplan 2013: 55).[5]

Authors who want to adapt readers' cognitive frameworks towards victims must signal for readers the effects of trauma on characters by engaging readers' cognitive and emotional responses in their depictions. Thus writers can affect the ways readers usually attribute mental states to characters. Narrative theory methods provide tools for analysis that help identify how writers produce textual material that stimulates readers to envision these mental states. Their methods for detecting these will help readers look at the storytelling features and interpretive possibilities for trauma literature, including analysis of: how characters' cognitions, emotions and behavior are shaped by wounding; how unrecognized memory and its affects emerge in the narrative; and evidence of defenses that suggests characters' mental states. Through familiar literary elements trauma fiction creates constructs of that experience with prototypically imagined situations and symptoms, metaphoric dreams, death imagery, and narrative styles that mimic such experience, for example, fragmented thoughts, dissociative outlook, de-contextualized visualization, etc.

Cognitive scientists emphasize the role of the environment in cognition, finding that the mind is more "social, embodied, concrete, located, engaged and specific" than individual, rational, or abstract, as the classical view has it (Smith 1999: 769). Alan Palmer's *Fictional Minds* examines narrative techniques writers use to show connections of the "internal consciousnesses of characters to their external social and physical context" (Palmer 2004: 49). The narrative vehicle for expressing these connections are the "thought reports" of characters, which he describes as having:

> a linking function whereby the narrator, in presenting a character's consciousness, connects it to its surroundings. The use of this device emphasizes the nature of consciousness as mental action and thereby brings together consciousness and physical action. The mode of thought report is ideally suited to informative presentations of the purposive and directive nature of thought as well as its social nature. (76)

Authors also provide reasons and motives for characters' actions by demonstrating their mental functioning and dispositions in first person narratives (Palmer 2004: 81–84). Tracking these thoughts is useful to interpreting trauma, because though it is isolating, trauma makes us confront how the individual mind is situated in larger contexts because its causes and consequences are rooted in the social world. For example, in many of Atwood's texts such as *The Handmaid's Tale* and *The Blind Assassin* the principle narrator's mentality has been afflicted by a gender and class-driven world order; her mind is social in its inhibitions and sense of duty or fear, and operates within places of confinement (such as imprisonment, domestic space, an asylum, etc.), to which the society has relegated her. By analyzing the social influences on these characters' thinking, readers can link some of these to the causes of traumas, and consequent coping mechanisms. And yet social connections can also provide pathways toward awareness.

Other textual details also prompt readers to create in their minds a sense of a thinking being and their mental processes. These details that resemble lived experience are called qualia, a term coined by philosophers of mind and used by narrative theorists focusing on consciousness.[6] Philosopher Janet Levin describes qualia as "the qualitative, experiential, or felt properties of mental states." When reproduced in narrative, these help readers envision a character's experience, and by extension, his or her consciousness (D. Herman 2009: 143). Monica Fludernik explains that "the protagonist's emotional and physical reaction to [events as they impinge on her situations and activities]" is integral to creating this sense of a living mind: "since humans are conscious thinking beings, (narrative) experientiality always implies—and sometimes emphatically foregrounds—the protagonist's consciousness" (Fludernik 1996: 30). One way qualia is illustrated is in the depiction of visceral reactions to traumatic memory that acknowledge its sensory nature and how reactions are often physical and unconscious because of the ways trauma is encoded in the brain (MacCurdy 2007: 21).

Many fiction writers portray their traumatized characters in the midst of this dilemma as they perform their symptoms. However, the writers make connections for readers that victims cannot, or portray victims trying to fit the pieces together, with some partial success. They do not always offer readers answers, but allow the reader into that uncertain experience and try to reconnect characters' memories and emotions.

* * *

Contemporary fiction depicts the struggle with memory and avoidance that characters undergo, but these representations move beyond the repetitive-performative image found in the classic model of trauma to accommodate the ambiguous aspects of traumatic experience that include limited remembering in contrast to a fixed state of forgetting. Texts by Atwood and Smiley indicate that one sympathetic ear or one different variable in the environment that invites memory and telling one's story can alter a character's defensive patterns, which brings them through a process of resituating themselves in relation to their traumatic experience and society. Both writers feature helpers or witnesses to traumatic events who importantly make the protagonists more aware so they can work their way out of denial, and discover ways of rejecting and resisting people and situations that silence and devalue them, as well as redefining and reclaiming in words their own value and agency in the process. By seeing trauma as collectively and situationally-driven, the possibilities for telling increase. These writers question or counter narrowly dominating viewpoints; they articulate some of the implications of traumatic history via multiple viewpoints; and give readers a sense of the many contingencies upon which individual traumas and history are predicated upon.[7]

In Jane Smiley's *A Thousand Acres* the narrator/protagonist, Ginny, goes through a process of remembering her trauma and reevaluating her life with fellow trauma victims—Jess and her sister Rose—who propel her out of amnesia, dissociation and stasis. Smiley makes farm women's predicaments part of a larger American story of Westward expansion, capitalism and human spoilage of the environment within the specific context of an Iowa farming community. Women's bodies endure traumatic assaults, as women on the farm regularly die of cancer or miscarry because of the poisonous chemicals used for farming.

Women become passive, worn down by men's wills: generations of women, including the protagonist's own mother, cannot defend themselves or their daughters from a father's need to dominate them and his land. Women's traumatic responses are due to this wearing away of their individuality, and, after their mother dies, due to the father Larry's incest of the eldest daughters, Ginny and Rose. As the novel begins, Ginny, the narrator/protagonist, has dissociated from her past (good and bad experiences) forgotten the abuse, and fallen into the passive farm wife pattern of her mother. She gains some agency as Larry, in Lear-like manner, gives over his property to his daughters early in the novel (the youngest, Caroline is left out after she expresses doubts). After that, the two elder sisters begin to assert themselves more, and break the taboo of crossing the father, who becomes self-destructive and eventually mentally incompetent after giving away the farm. Their assertions begin a chain reaction of rebellion, memories, and betrayals that bring Ginny to awareness of her traumas and some healing, but not without enormous personal losses.

Smiley contextualizes trauma in a particular geographical and cultural setting. Place becomes the locus to organize memories and feelings as Ginny nostalgically remembers enjoying with Rose the hidden places on their land, like the pond, before her father drains it for more farm land and riches. Such instances provide analogies to a hidden and destructive past, foreshadowing some of the sacrifices she and other women have made to the building of the farm, including the devastating effects of farm chemicals on their bodies. These place memories also help Ginny piece together a history of abuse, observes Marinella Rodi-Risberg (2010: 206): "Ginny imaginatively transforms uncultivated areas from her childhood days—uninscribed with patriarchal values and abuse—into sites of memory. ... [and] even the tamed areas [of land] ... powerfully demonstrate the connection between place and Ginny's trauma" (203).

The father's stranglehold is threatened by the generational divide that opens up in the 1970s when members of the younger generation begin to think for themselves and reject old patriarchal values like going to war in Vietnam and denying their feelings. Jess embodies these feelings, telling Ginny of his own traumas of avoiding the draft alone in another country and being rejected by his mother who would not defy her husband's views to reach out to her son. "What ideal did she sacrifice me to? Patriotism? Keeping up appearances in the neighborhood? Peace with Harold?" (Smiley 2003: 55). The price their generation paid for their parents' rigid behavioral demands that made the farm successful came at great emotional and physical cost.

Smiley brings readers into the workings of Ginny's mind by making her the novel's narrator demonstrating the cognitions and emotions of someone who is undergoing a gradual transformation of remembering and only beginning to face her life traumas as a woman in her 30s. Through her impressions, gradual remembering, and the increasingly recognizable patterns of behavior Smiley recreates a state of mind shaped by wounding. We are first struck by her defensive mentality: like her mother, Ginny consistently avoids conflict with her husband, Rose and her father. "I was, after all, my father's daughter, and I automatically did believe in the unbroken surface of the unsaid" (94). She is emotionally distant from her husband, demanding nothing except to attempt pregnancy after five miscarriages, against his wishes. She is desperately trying to recreate the life of family and farm her parents had. Referring to her secret attempts at pregnancy as a life of "untapped possibilities" (26), she tries to maintain a defended life: "my worst habit ... was entertaining thoughts of disaster" (65), and slowly admits her isolation: "I really didn't believe in myself ... my life [was] an unending battle to make friends" (86). She does not merely repeat or reenact her mother's life (she protects her sister Caroline from Larry while her mother did not protect Ginny and Rose), but Ginny does engage in avoidant behavior, and experiences dissociation and failed relationships because of her self-protective survival mode.

Revelations of the past begin as Smiley presents readers with the emotional undercurrents of Ginny, Rose, and Larry. The over-determined feelings of the characters indicate that there is more than meets the eye before Ginny's memory returns. When her mother's friend Mary expresses to Ginny that her mother was worried about the girls after her death, this makes Ginny feel vulnerable: "That that young woman foresaw my life so clearly unnerved me, as if something intensely private had suddenly been exposed and discussed by people I barely knew" (93). Ginny also vividly talks about totally disproportionate feelings of shame about her body's awkwardness as she imagines Larry's critical eye as she gets eggs for his breakfast: "The whole way I was conscious of my body—graceless and hurrying, unfit, panting, ridiculous in its very femininity. It seemed like my father could just look out of his big front window and see me naked, chest heaving, breasts, thighs, and buttocks jiggling, dignity irretrievable" (Smiley 2003: 114–115). This is a key instance of how qualia, the experiential qualities of mind (and body), can be depicted narratively and will be followed later by a similarly sharply rendered but more horrific involuntary sense memory of Larry sucking her breasts 20 years before. Readers also encounter over-determined emotions with Rose's constant anger, and their father's fury, expressed in inappropriately sexualized terms, over daughters who no longer obey him, which overturns his idea of universal order. These conflicts will pave the way for more revelations.

Once Jess begins to open Ginny up emotionally, and her sister Rose admits she remembers their father sexually abusing them, only then can Ginny's memories slowly return, confirming the social aspects of memory and healing. Throughout the book Ginny undergoes glimpses of memory or feeling that make her deeply uncomfortable or upset, but only after Rose tells her and she returns physically to the house and room where her father's abuses of her occurred, does she have the vivid, intrusive memory of one of these encounters: "That was the only memory I could endure before I jumped out of the bed with a cry" (228). She continues to fight off these memories, but refers to how "another new life" had begun that day. She will remember enough that she can piece together her realizations about the nature of Larry's demands, and how everyone is sacrificed to his status as the prominent farmer of the county (and eventually she will pass beyond this to also see his isolation and loneliness). She eventually recognizes the broader inherited pattern of all their lives, and becomes determined to break away from it.

Rose instigates Ginny's confrontations with the truth about her father and their lives. Rose is often angry over the injustice of being beaten by her husband (which she stops), and is then able to express her feeling about their father beating them in the past. Rose seems more in control and less damaged initially, as she can remember and admit that Larry incested them. However, as the novel goes on, we recognize Rose is perhaps more damaged than Ginny, because, despite her awareness, she cannot bring herself to leave the situation and the patterns of their lives. "That's the thing that kills me. This person who beats and [rapes] his own daughters can go out into the community and get respect and power, and take it for granted that he deserves it" (302). Rose is characterized primarily in her justified, self-righteous anger, which brings her some temporary relief and some satisfaction in speaking the truth, but unfortunately it also alienates her family and community from her and Ginny. She is a voice of social injustice that Ginny will later take up as well.

However, Rose also illustrates how traumatic patterns endure and become deeply embedded in personality such that she also takes after Larry in going after whatever she wants; Rose reenacts their father's betrayal of her and Ginny by betraying Ginny with Jess, knowing Ginny loves him. She loses her husband, Pete, who, under the pressure of knowing what Larry did, and how it affected Rose's personality (her anger and adultery with Jess), blinds Harold (intending to blind Larry) and probably kills himself in a car accident. Tragic events set off others, and though the novel is structured on Shakespeare's tragedy *King Lear*, and follows many of its plot lines, Smiley is also acknowledging trauma's repercussions, the effects on personality and relationships that cause others not so much to inherit traumas as to suffer blowback from them. Rose particularly exemplifies the complicated identities of the three sisters in relation to Larry. They all identify with his point of view, often see their lives according to his, but they all seek refuge from him as well, from his needs and demands, which they have tried to fulfill. He remains for them, psychically, the largest force in their lives, even as they achieve more independence.

Ginny must confront the past once she learns it from Rose. Part of this will be confronting her bond with Rose, forged in abuse, and apparently has maintained them in the prison house of their pain. Except for Rose, Ginny has always had trouble bonding with others. She must begin to face life with full knowledge of her situation. Her progress in the novel takes the form of a growing awareness of her past, the family's past, the illnesses and disadvantages of the women in the family, as well as harsh assessments of each family member:

> Maybe if we had conducted our lives differently in the past, had not been so accommodating, nor so malleable—how was it that

everyone had left the land and we had stayed behind? How was it that I had not even thought of college, of trying something else ... Then there was the image that things always looped back to those five miscarried children ... No! It was time to set up, to reach out, to choose this and not that! Ty's steadiness was getting us, getting me, nowhere. (147)

As she becomes more aware, the farm, the family and her relationships all become tainted for her. She falls for Jess, risking her heart and she is unfaithful to Ty with him, but Jess does not share her deeper feelings. When she learns Rose has betrayed her with Jess she recognizes in herself a whole different way of thinking:

It was a state of mind in which I "knew" many things, in which "conviction" was not an abstract, rather dry term referring to moral values or conscious beliefs, but a feeling of being drenched with insight, swollen with it like a wet sponge. Rather than feeling "not myself," I felt intensely, newly, more myself than ever before. The strongest feeling was that now I knew them all. (305)

Ginny's willingness to take on conflict more as the story unfolds indicates an unveiling of the anger she was never able to express. Her niceness was part of her defense, but now the realities overwhelm her for a while as she is now able to see the self-interests driving Ty, Rose, and her father. She goes through a stage of the kind of anger Rose exhibits and attempts unsuccessfully to poison Rose, to feel some sense of agency. After she loses Jess, Ginny feels like a failure, like she's never succeeded in having a loving relationship:

My love, which I had always believed could transcend the physical, had failed, too—failed with Ty, failed with my [unborn] children and Rose's, failed, in a bizarre way, with Daddy, who in his fashion loved Caroline and Rose but not me, failed with Jess Clark, and now had failed with Rose herself, who clearly understood how to reach past me, to put me aside, to take what she wanted and be glad of it. (307)

Her survivor's defenses have been a part of her trauma, separating her from others. At this point she's still confronting her wounds and misconceptions, and preparing herself for a new life without them.

The protagonist must reassess the meaning of her life on that farm and the relationships connected with it.

> What was transformed now was the past, not the future. The future seemed to clamp down upon me like an iron lid, but the past dissolved beneath my feet into something writhing and fluid, and at the center of it, the most changed thing of all, was Rose herself. It was clear that she had answered my foolish love with jealousy and grasping selfishness. (308)

Ginny takes care of Rose's girls after her cancer returns and Rose dies, but they don't fully trust her after she's abandoned the family for the past few years. The narrative makes it clear that Ginny is justified to remove herself from this family—a patriarchal nightmare that evolves into dissention once the father ceases to dominate them—that has been very destructive to her and now has imploded. By the end of the novel they all have betrayed each other out of self-interest or emotional need.

The whole notion of family has become tainted for the protagonist because the family only valued her insofar as she did its bidding. There was no recognition of her self except in relation to the family entity. Ginny finally resists her own commodification. Larry used Ginny and Rose like objects: part of his property, like the farm, the equipment, and so on, Rose observes (though she tries to cling to this property). Acquisition is synonymous with the success of the family, often at the expense of other, less relentless farmers and land grabbers. After the father's misguided lawsuit to get the farm back (abetted by Caroline) Ginny no longer wants to own it. The courtroom scene provides her more evidence of family division as her demented father only remembers Caroline, not her and Rose: "I felt icy shakes descend in waves through my body" (321). The farm was created in a family context that the family's breakup nullifies; she can now escape what was an emotional and acquisitive trap. She rejects the farming empire for a basic life as a waitress while she regroups. Ginny realizes that as members of his family they cannot help but recreate versions of his dominance. Ginny can only free herself by breaking the pattern even if it means she loses her family.

Smiley illustrates how communities and individuals protect themselves from a sense of vulnerability by suppressing or ignoring trauma victims' experience. The male dominated farming community is quick to blame the sisters for their father's downfall; it cannot even imagine the women might have grievances against their father. The sisters receive little support or few friendly ears beyond each other: only Jess, and a friend of their mother's, Mary, who knew how tyrannical and abusive the father was. The community does not want to hear about personal matters, especially incest. Even Ginny's husband Ty thinks people should "keep private things private" (340) and resents Rose for telling everyone she could about it. This demonstrates that silencing and the unspeakability of trauma can be the outcome of cultural values and ideologies. In her final encounter with Ty, years later, Ginny echoes Rose in articulating her sense of injustice to the unwilling Ty:

> You see this grand history, but I see it blows. I see taking what you want because you want it, then making something up that justifies what you did. I see getting others to pay the price, then covering up and forgetting what the price was. Do I think Daddy came up with beating and fucking on his own? ... No. I think he had lessons, and those lessons were part of the package, along with the land and the lust to run things exactly the way he wanted to no matter what, poisoning the water and destroying the topsoil and buying bigger and bigger machinery, and then feeling certain that all of it was "right," as you said, (342–343)

Ginny finds some healing in the end, but when she realizes she would have to force her unsympathetic sister Caroline (in denial about father) to listen, Ginny cuts her losses, realizing the truth would only ruin Caroline's memories (her relationship to their father seems different), emblematic of how Caroline does not want to face how Ginny and Rose protected her from the father. Smiley acknowledges this need for denial that prevents trauma victims from recovering. In the late scene with Caroline, after Rose's death, neither Ginny nor Caroline can clearly identify family heirlooms or family members in old photographs: "These are our ancestors, but they don't look familiar" (361). Ginny asks Caroline why she wants things she cannot remember. Caroline clearly wants a fantasy version of the family; she remembers reconciling with the demented Larry and cannot fathom the different past with him that Ginny and Rose had. There is not an absolute truth in these matters: Ginny realizes she cannot impose her truth onto Caroline who is not sympathetic enough to hear Ginny's version.

The reconstruction of trauma's significance changes with different recollections, as depicted by Ginny slowly coming out of repression and denial, through anger and a taste for vengeance, avoidance of the painful environment, and then to her own ways of acceptance. She moves from unconscious patterns and reactions to shocking memories to an ability to analyze her family's lives and figure out what she needs to avoid. She ends her narration with the image of a black "shard" of her painful memory of her father's actions, always sharply there, but somewhat mitigated by knowledge of his isolation and desolation as a widower. The protagonist recovers from trauma through escape, breaking patterns, and shifting her life into a new set of variables as she develops an interest in the exploration of human motivation. Importantly, the text explores the consequences when those around the victim are unsympathetic or refuse to listen. As most of the characters in the story deny, reject or are overwhelmed by the protagonists' incest experience, the text counters these disconnections by directing readers to be invested in Ginny and Rose's perspectives. Smiley's fiction tries to produce in the reader a locus of understanding the sisters' anguish in the face of others' discomfort. The text critiques family members and the community for willingly accepting women's illness and exploitation in exchange for prosperity.

Contemporary novels by Margaret Atwood and Jane Smiley demonstrate the capacity of trauma in literature to engage the reader's empathy by closely examining the personal and community contexts of trauma and its psychological ramifications. These texts provide narrative means to articulate trauma's effects even when dissociation may occur or when victims face denial and hostility in the social environment. Fiction thus explores trauma as the crucible of human survival and growth. Novels by Atwood and Smiley represent trauma beyond the unspeakable and repetitive by depicting survivors as deeply interconnected to social networks. These social networks can cause trauma, limit expression, or offer resources that provide avenues toward healing. The social environment is not uniform in the novels; it provides many types of experiences that motivate individuals to maintain or discard protective survival patterns. In fiction by Atwood and Smiley, suffering is shown to be the basis for social critique by demonstrating the ties between individual trauma and larger social injustices.

Notes

1. Sociologist Kai Erikson emphasizes that the causes of trauma can be entrenched in daily life as well as from horrific events like the Shoah, war, or rape. Trauma can result "from a continuing pattern of abuse as well as from a single assault, from a period of attenuation and wearing away as well as from a moment of shock" (Erikson 1991: 457).
2. Some victims may dissociate themselves from physical and emotional self-awareness to avoid pain in order to endure the situation (Herman 43, 2009: 101–102).
3. Psychologist Laura S. Brown asserts that the currently limited therapeutic parameters in use minimize the effects of constant stress and humiliation associated with poverty and low socioeconomic status. (Brown 1995: 102–103).
4. In U.S. culture, ideologies of individual responsibility once impeded recovery of veterans and rape victims. However, in recent decades the openness to hearing personal stories as well as literature, autobiography, and writing courses that invite trauma writing offer new possibilities of supportive communities. Along with assorted variables of memory retrieval, these contexts indicate possibilities for remembering, witnessing, and telling trauma.
5. Kaplan also indicates how critical scholarship (and I would add teachers) can help this learning process: "In the case of Trauma Studies, arguably, humanist scholars produce new knowledge about trauma and its cultural ramifications through studying the contribution of art about atrocity in processes of memory, witnessing, healing, and the working through of national and international catastrophes" (Kaplan 2013: 55).
6. See discussions of qualia as part of consciousness in Palmer's *Fictional Minds*, Damasio's *The Feeling of What Happens*, and D. Herman's *Story Logic*.
7. Many contemporary writers address the process of coming out of trauma, whereas in the literature Caruth addresses the characters remain in thrall to it.

Bibliography

Alexander, Jeffrey C., Ron Eyerman, Bernhard Giesen, Neil J. Smelser, and Piotr Szompka. *Cultural Trauma and Collective Identity*. Berkeley: University of California Press, 2004.

Atwood, Margaret. *Alias Grace*. New York: Random House, 1996.

Atwood, Margaret. *Cat's Eye*. New York: Anchor Books, 1998.

Brown, Laura S. "Not Outside the Range." Cathy Caruth, ed. *Trauma*. Baltimore: Johns Hopkins University Press, 1995, 100–112.

Bucci, Wilma. "The Power of the Narrative: A Multiple Code Account." In James W. Pennebaker, ed. *Emotion, Disclosure, and Health*. Washington, DC: American Psychological Association, 1995, 93–122.

Caruth, Cathy. *Trauma: Explorations in Memory*. Baltimore: Johns Hopkins University Press, 1995.

Caruth, Cathy. *Unclaimed Experience: Trauma, Narrative, and History*. Baltimore: Johns Hopkins University Press, 1996.

Damasio, Antonio. *The Feeling of What Happens: Body and Emotion in the Making of Consciousness*. San Diego: A Harvest Book, Harcourt, 1999.

De Vries, Marten W. "Trauma in Cultural Perspective." In Bessel Van der Kolk, Alexander C. McFarlane, and Lars Weisaeth, eds. *Traumatic Stress: The Effects of Overwhelming Experience on Mind, Body, and Society*. New York: Guilford, 1996, 398–413.

Erikson, Kai. "Notes on Trauma and Community." *American Imago*. 48.4 (1991): 455–471.

Fludernik, Monica. *Towards a 'Natural' Narratology*. London: Routledge, 1996.

Heinemann, Larry. *Paco's Story*. New York: Penguin, 1986.

Heinemann, Larry. *Story Logic: Problems and Possibilities of Narrative*. Lincoln: University of Nebraska Press, 2002.

Heinemann, Larry. "Stories as a Tool for Thinking." In David Herman, ed. *Narrative Theory and the Cognitive Sciences*. Stanford, CA: Center for the Study of Language and Information Publications, 2003, 163–192.

Herman, David. "The Nexus of Narrative and Mind." In David Herman, ed. *Basic Elements of Narrative*. West Sussex, UK: Wiley-Blackwell, 2009, 137–160.

Herman, Judith. *Trauma and Recovery*. New York: Basic, 1992.

Herrero, Dolores. and Sonia Baelo-Alluè (eds.). *Between the Urge to Know and the Need to Deny: Trauma and Ethics in Contemporary British and American Literature*. Heidelberg: Universitatsverlag Winter, 2011.

Janoff-Bulman, Ronnie. *Shattered Assumptions: Toward New Psychology of Trauma*. New York: Free Press, 1992.

Kaplan, E. Ann. "Trauma Studies Moving Forward: Interdisciplinary Perspectives." *Journal of Dramatic Theory and Criticism* 27.2 (Spring 2013): 53–65.

Keen, Suzanne. *Empathy and the Novel*. Oxford: Oxford University Press, 2007

Kincaid, Jamaica. *The Autobiography of My Mother*. New York: Farrar, 1983.

LaCapra, Dominick. *Writing History, Writing Trauma*. Baltimore: Johns Hopkins University Press, 2001.

MacCurdy, Marian M. *The Mind's Eye: Image and Memory in Writing About Trauma*. Amherst: University of Massachusetts Press, 2007.

McNally, Richard J. *Remembering Trauma*. Cambridge: Belknap Press of Harvard University Press, 2005.

Morrison, Toni. *Paradise*. New York: Knopf, 1998.

Palmer, Alan. *Fictional Minds*. Lincoln, NB: University of Nebraska Press, 2004.

Rodi-Risberg. *Writing Trauma, Writing Time and Space: Jane Smiley's A Thousand Acres and the Lear Group of Father-Daughter Incest Narratives*. ACTA Wasaensia no. 229. Literary and Cultural Studies 5 English. Vaasa, Finland: Universitas Wasaensis, 2010.

Root, Maria P.P. "Reconstructing the Impact of Trauma on Personality." In Laura S. Brown. and Mary Ballou, eds. *Personality and Psychopathology: Feminist Reappraisals.* New York: Guilford P, 1992, 229–265.

Smiley, Jane. *A Thousand Acres.* New York: Anchor Books, 2003.

Smith, B.C. "Situatedness." In Robert A. Wilson. and Frank C. Keil, eds. *MITECS The MIT Encyclopedia of the Cognitive Sciences.* Cambridge: MIT Press, 1999, 769.

Taylor, Marjorie, Sara D. Hodges. and Adele Kohanyi. "The Illusion of Independent Agency: Do Adult Fiction Writers Experience Their Characters As Having Minds of Their Own?" *Imagination, Cognition and Personality* 22.4 (2002–2003): 361–380.

Van der Kolk, Bessel. and C.R. Ducey. "The Psychological Processing of Traumatic Experience: Rorschach Patterns in PTSD." *Journal of Traumatic Stress* 2 (1989): 259–274.

Van der Kolk, Bessel A. and Onno Van der Hart. "The Intrusive Past: The Flexibility of Memory and the Engraving of Trauma." *American Imago* 48.4 (1991): 425–454.

Van der Kolk, Bessel, Alexander C. McFarlane, and Lars Weisaeth. *Traumatic Stress: The Effects of Overwhelming Experience on Mind, Body, and Society.* New York: Guilford, 1996.

Vickroy, Laurie. "Sexual Trauma, Ethics, and the Reader in the Works of Margaret Atwood." In J. Brooks Bouson, ed. *Critical Insights: Margaret Atwood.* Ipswich, MA: Salem Press, 2013.

Vickroy, Laurie. "Seeking Symbolic Immortality: Visualizing Trauma in *Cat's Eye*." *Mosaic* 38.2 (June 2005): 129–143.

Vickroy, Laurie. *Trauma and Survival in Contemporary Fiction.* Charlottesville, VA: University Press of Virginia, 2002.

Vickroy, Laurie. "That Was Their Deal" In Dolores Herrero and Sonia Baelo-Alluè, eds. *Between the Urge to Know and the Need to Deny: Trauma and Ethics in Contemporary British and American Literature.* Heidelberg: Universitatsverlag Winter, 2011, 37–52.

7
Memory and Commemoration in the Digital Present

Paul Arthur

The deceased can always be provided with a here and a now [via the Internet], something which is increasingly evident in the appropriation of public space for private grief, at times of ... traumatic loss.

—Elizabeth Hallam and Jenny Hockey

The first "Digital Death Day," held on 20 May 2010, brought together world experts in the fields of death studies, social networking, and data management. Promoting the event, coordinator Jennifer Holmes commented, "The online memorial has already become the new grave" (Andrews 2010). How seriously should we take such a statement? Was this turn of phrase simply intended to indicate the increasing dependence on digital media for performing social rituals? Or has online memorialization in fact created a new kind of "resting place" for the deceased, and if so what is the nature of that place and how do the living relate to it? Whether through intentional online memorialization or through the unplanned bestowing of an afterlife on anyone who has had an active online presence in life, it is now indisputable that the digital world is being populated, at an exponentially growing rate, by the stories, images, traces, and voices of the dead—so much so that this digital afterlife can be seen as a new kind of immortality. Drawing upon several kinds of digital memorialization, this chapter considers the influence of these new forms—that create a perpetual "here and now" for the dead—on the way people experience and communicate grief and the implications, more broadly, for trauma theory.

In the twenty-first century, trauma associated with death is increasingly being worked through in communal spaces and collective formats through online memorialization. Ongoing connections with the deceased are being enabled through memorial websites and social media, and this is re-contextualizing and even normalizing trauma by bringing it into everyday social settings—reducing the privacy and distance once thought to be requirements of the grieving process. Today's media technologies do more than mediate: they are the mechanism both for recording or conveying news about death, and for remembering and memorializing. The incorporation of the deeply personal into the everyday is central to the therapeutic aspect of online memorialization. Through online memorialization memorial practices are increasingly integrated into everyday social interactions via social media.

Online memorials are "sites" of trauma in more than the sense of "website." What are these "sites"? What forms do they take? How are they functionally different from physical sites of remembrance? These questions are addressed in an opening discussion of the features of physical memorials and an overview of online memorialization since the early 1990s. The focus then turns to social media and networking. What is striking today is that the same social media services that are being used in life are also used after death, fulfilling different functions. In this way it becomes clear that memorialization online does not have an easy equivalent in the gravestone; rather, it relates more closely to grief therapy. In other words, online memorialization is not a matter of supplanting the real with the virtual; it is more complex than that, and this chapter explores that complexity.

In a recent paper on "Internet Memory and Life after Death," Bryson asks, "Can the digital revolution lead to permanent memorials, or even a sort of internet-based immortality?" (2012: 70), and more broadly, "How does widespread access to computation and the Internet affect what it means to be dead?" Online memorials may appear fleeting and impermanent. However, their value grows over time and the responsibility to preserve, maintain and add to these digital life archives increases rather than decreases. Online memorials continue to write the life after death, in relation to the living, in the context of an extended present. Moreover, the possibility of "continuing bonds" represents a new form of grieving and working through trauma that would have once been considered ineffective and aligned with denial or psychological damage (Kasket 2012: 63).

This chapter argues that there are at least two kinds of working through trauma that online memorialization allows. In the first, there is a normalization of death through "continuing bonds." This entails taking over the voice of the deceased and bringing it into the ongoing chatter of real life; while this process takes place, time can perform its healing function. The "continuing bonds" approach engages more than immediate family, and while this has the positive effect of drawing family and friends together, it also opens the process to risks such as that of online memorials being diluted or "defaced." In the second, a dynamic is created that enables extreme expressions of intimate testimony or reflection to be shared in a largely public space. This is coming to be seen as constituting a lasting, even permanent, memorial and is for some as important as a physical memorial. Moreover, the integration of personal and public enables the formation of communities in a complex, new sense of the idea of "community." Public exhibition of deeply private trauma brings together two categories that would not be compatible without Web 2.0 technologies and so this duality characterizes a form of communication that is without precedent; it is leading to new notions of identity, and hence of memorialization. The public "place" paradoxically becomes a "safe" haven where trauma can be expressed, *as though privately*, and yet, within the supportive framework of a community of other victims of trauma, to the wider world.[1]

Online memorialization remains a very new field of critical inquiry in relation to trauma and bereavement care. These practices have been the focus of sociological and psychological studies, and they have also been considered in terms of interaction design and human-computer interaction, but they have not received the same attention from the wider interdisciplinary perspectives of trauma studies and life writing. The implications of this research are wide. The topic has relevance for fields ranging from journalism and media studies to clinical practice. For biographers and scholars of life narrative, online memorialization opens up new opportunities for understanding changing concepts of identity and community in the digital era.

Memorial sites

Culturally specific practices to mediate memories of the dead have developed over thousands of years, and memorialization is linked with rituals that have been dated as far back as 35,000 BC. Estimates of the total number of deaths of our ancestors worldwide over human history run to over 100 billion (Davies 1994). Commonplace ritual practices and memorial markers in western cultural contexts include funeral ceremonies, wakes, eulogies, tombs, head stones, monuments, plaques, epitaphs and inscriptions, funerary wreaths and objects placed on graves, roadside crosses at sites of fatal accidents,[2] and participation in grieving practices such as writing condolence cards and letters to the families of the deceased, as well as published death notices, obituaries, and biographies. The forms these various expressions of memorialization take are governed by systems of cultural and social conventions and traditions. It is rare to find extended commentary on a headstone, for example, or on a cathedral tomb; lengthy text is usually saved for monuments marking events rather than individual people or for written genres such as obituaries or biographies. However, for all their variety, built memorials have generally had in common the fact that each exists in a meaningful location, a specific site that has an intrinsic connection, or creates a connection, with the dead whom it honors: "Memorials provide a permanent place for those left behind to connect emotionally and spiritually with their loss" (Veale 2004: 1–2). While nothing is truly permanent, memorials are usually intended to be as enduring as possible and the sense of stability is reassuring. Monuments gather in, accumulate, and concentrate memory and history into the spaces they occupy. Although the sites of monuments are especially resonant, space is never simply space; space is heavy with history; or, to use Bachelard's words, "space contains compressed time" (Bachelard 1994: 8).

Once reserved for the wealthy and elite, by the fourteenth century memorials in England included "ordinary" people. Commonly displaying "name, date of death, words of praise, profession (and indirectly rank and status), and prayers to God for the soul," many also offered humorous rhymes, as though in an attempt to engage with future audiences in a jocular way.[3] The wealthy commissioned the countless fine tombs, with their beautifully crafted effigies of the dead, which still grace the cathedrals and churches of England and Europe.[4] During the seventeenth century, many memorials included text connecting family members to the deceased and biographical accounts also featured (Veale 2004: 1). Whatever form they take, the messages and artifacts left by or on behalf of the dead reach out to the future, to imagined communities of the living, in a gesture that seeks a connection beyond the grave. By 1850, according to *The Times* newspaper, "Britain was in the grip of 'Monument Mania' ... with a proliferation of 'sacro-secular' sites in the public sphere" (Pickering and Westcott 2003: 1).

In the early nineteenth century in Britain the most famous of the dead re-entered "life" as life-like replicas of themselves at Madame Tussaud's wax museum, which continues to operate to this day, billed as "the place where time stands still" (*Metro* 2012) (Madame Tussaud's has also always exhibited wax replicas of the living). The philosopher Jeremy Bentham, in the 1830s, notoriously, went even further, by requesting in his will that his own body be mummified and displayed as its own monument, "*his own statue*" (quoted in Pickering and Westcott 2003: 3).[5] Kept on public display in the famous "auto-icon" cabinet at the University College London, the body was reportedly brought in to "attend" the College Council meetings held on the institution's 100th and 150th anniversaries, where it was registered as "present but not voting."[6]

Although Bentham did not believe in an afterlife, he went to extraordinary lengths to achieve a physical posthumous presence in the world. His extreme example supports the idea that all forms of self-memorialization, regardless of their framing systems of belief, are driven by a desire for some kind of continuing presence in the world beyond death. Indeed, Bentham's act has been described as a "consciously positioning of [himself] as an archive" (4).

Monuments are most commonly the material expression of the desire to leave an enduring symbol, honoring a life or the lives of many.[7] Built to last, they can play an important public role in that they are often designed to be "permanent statements of a particular nexus in the narrative of a nation" (4). In their static solidity and "permanence," built monuments, both public and private, can be viewed as the antithesis of online memorials, which partake of the Internet's qualities of instability, fragmentariness, diffuseness, and interactivity. In Christian settings the solidity and lastingness of monuments were a metaphor for life after death. Looked at from this perspective, online memorials, by their very nature, appear to be dismantling those qualities and so abandoning the traditional principles by which the quest for eternity was outwardly expressed; looked at through another lens, online memorials, in their multiple forms, can be seen to be creating a parallel memorial universe that is very different but may, in fact, be more enduring.

Ultimately, while their focus is on the deceased, memorials are primarily for the living. Traditionally, what they have offered is closure in that they look back from an immoveable vantage point—the moment of death.[8] They draw a clear line between life and death. In each individual case, they make it possible for the living to retrospectively shape and round off the story of the life that has ended and allow it to take up its new fixed position and its finalized identity—in their own historical past. In the process they can begin to "deal with" and reshape their own identity in relation to the finished life or lives and the related events.[9] The same can be said of public memorials to war and other traumatic events in the context of a nation. A monument of this kind typically makes a powerful statement that is imbued with the authority of the State. It summarizes; it tells a story and raises it to prominence. It creates a framework for accepting, letting go, and coping with personal or communal loss and trauma. It also closes off other possibilities.[10]

Memorials, whether private or public, are always partial. Their story is one of many that could be chosen to be told and the selection is driven by a range of factors that include political, social, historical, and more specifically contextual local issues.[11] The Lincoln Memorial in Washington, for example, does not refer to slavery, and the Vietnam Veterans' Memorial in the same city "expressly prohibits individual citation of those who died later of the effects of Agent Orange or suicide" (Pickering and Westcott 2003).[12] Erasures and elisions such as these, relating to trauma suffered on a vast scale, are a common feature of public memorials.[13] The solidity of their physical presence has the effect of shutting down or, at least, tidying up the moral, emotional and social turmoil from which they arose. The story they tell is strong and clear.

The most notable feature of online memorialization, on the other hand, is open-endedness—the opposite of closure and, indeed, the impossibility of closure in many cases. The worlds of the living and the dead, the past and the present, interpenetrate, interact, and blend. Permanence takes on a different meaning. Far from being cast in stone, the online memorial is *not* an object in space, but a "live," endlessly changeable and fluid set of connections. In the online arena a monument is not a thing to be *looked at* by those who wish to remember the dead; it is a *process* to participate in. It does not impose a single story; it encapsulates a multiplicity of stories, potentially without end. It does not depend on a physical site, although it may relate to one; its site exists in infinite space.

The integration of the intensely personal and painful into the everyday is key to the therapeutic dimension of online memorialization. Online engagement provides a neutral space where the experience of trauma can be spoken about and shared without the participants being constrained by long-held social conventions and taboos surrounding grief and its expression. In other words, online memorial practices are allowing grief to be increasingly integrated into everyday social interactions, via social media, and in the process, they are changing social attitudes to death. While the prevailing view has been that post-death rituals "are most effective when the bereaved are allowed to remove themselves from everyday life ..." (Roberts 2004: 58, citing Kollar 1989),[14] the rise of online responses to death is challenging that view. There is a complex relationship between public and private expressions of grief and mourning when a life is lost. New forms of communication technology are eroding and collapsing boundaries that were very clear in the past.

All death is, to a greater or lesser extent, traumatic for the living, and yet some deaths are more shocking and catastrophic than others and they require different kinds of memorialization. Physical memorials provide tangible sites for family, friends, and colleagues to visit and to express deeply felt emotion as part of the process of coping with grief and loss.[15] The place and positioning of a memorial is a significant part of the messages it is intended to convey and for its reception. A cemetery, for example, demarcates multiple sites of individual memorialization, each of a certain size, clearly bounded, and signed by an inscribed gravestone or memorial marker. In the peace of removal from everyday activities, cemeteries are intended to be reflective places. Although open to the public, they are primarily designed for individual rather than collective memorialization. By contrast, large memorials to collective traumatic experience, such as monuments to war or other catastrophes of great magnitude, are designed to have high visibility, with many of them, controversially, becoming major international tourist attractions. In these cases, the penetration of digital technologies into the realm of remembering and grieving has facilitated new levels of realism and interactivity, whose value and motivation is the subject of critical debate. Writing about the ethical contradictions and dilemmas inherent in the public display of "heart-rending subject matter" in museums that memorialize disasters, Susan Sontag makes the comment, "the museum has become a vast educational institution-cum-emporium. ... The primary function is entertainment in various mixes, and the marketing of experiences, tastes and simulacra" (Sontag 2003: 109). In a similar vein, Baudrillard deplores the "assumption of human suffering into the heaven of the media and the mental space of advertising" (Baudrillard 1996: 138).

Memorialization online

The first online memorials date from 1993, that is, from the beginning of the World Wide Web. The earliest known example was a bulletin board devoted to the memory of an online community member (Roberts 2006: 55). In the first decade of the Web, memorials tended to be created as spontaneous tributes to the deceased rather serving as long-term memorials, although as the practice grew, tributes became more formally organized as discreet memorial sites, and were known collectively as "web memorials" or "web cemeteries." Many early examples of web cemeteries were also for pets. Cyberspace quickly became "a repository for immense spiritual yearning" (Wertheim 1999: 61).

There is no limit to the range of applications of online memorialization; free from the constraints, taboos, and conventions of physical memorials, they can specify and expound on causes of death and include every kind of cause from still birth to terminal illness, natural disaster to torture. Online memorials can take many different forms including: webrings; dedicated web memorials and cemeteries; social networking sites, including photo and video sharing archives (Roberts 2006: 55); and larger institutionally supported collective memory projects. Most research to date has been on dedicated web memorials and cemeteries, but the focus has turned to social networking sites. Webrings, which allow individually created web pages to be joined together in a circuit or sequence, were popular in the 1990s and early 2000s but are now rare. Web memorials and cemeteries refer to websites designed specifically for memorialization, rather than to other kinds of sites that are colonized for this purpose. The examples below provide insights into way some of these new forms function and the purposes they serve. Increasingly integrated into everyday social interactions via social media since around 2004, online memorial practices are gaining widespread acceptance and popularity and new opportunities are appearing "at a dizzying pace" (Roberts 2006: 55–66).

The Virtual Memorial Garden (http://catless.ncl.ac.uk/vmg) has operated continuously since it was formed in 1995. Even a cursory look at the content in this long established archive shows the importance of the *site* of memorialization and a sense of *place* even in online form, especially, it appears, for the more recent visitors. The visitors' book, which has comments fully open to public view, includes messages from appreciative return visitors, such as the one below, who relate to the site as place where loved ones are "placed":

> 1 Feb 2011, 16:15, Georgia K-N. < ***@gmail.com >, from 99.169.42.134:
> Thank you so very much for operating this site, I have my Mother and two brothers here and two beloved pets a cat and a dog.

In other comments the language of marking, inscribing, suggests permanency comparable to inscriptions on gravestones:

> 11 Jul 2011, 23:15, ****@cyberon.com, from 98.118.53.19:
> I visit this site each year on the death anniversaries of my relatives. It gives me great comfort to see the words etched [sic] on the page and the love i felt for them at their passing. Thank you for keeping this up.

In the following example the site provides a memorial that could not be offered in physical form at an earlier time and in another place:

> Napoleon L.
> 29 Mar 1857–23 Apr 1936
> Buried in St Mary's Cemetery, North Bay, Ont. Here's the gravestone you never had. Thank you for helping me to find my roots.

I couldn't have done it without you. Your great-granddaughter Michelle.

The Virtual Memorial Garden was recognized as the largest web cemetery in 2005 when a study was conducted of 244 of its memorials. Findings included that children (who, it was speculated, had better computer skills), were responsible for the greatest number (33%), followed by friends (15%), grandchildren (11%), parents (10%), siblings (8%), and spouses (4%). This study also investigated the content of memorials, reporting that cause of death was rarely referred to, and there was little mention of God or religion. Most importantly, in the context of this chapter, the study also found a marked difference in mode of address: "Memorials were more likely to be written to the deceased (e.g., in the form of a letter) rather than about or for the deceased (e.g., eulogy/obituary or tribute)" (deVries and Rutherford 2004: 5–26).

Writing letters to the dead has a recognized cathartic effect, which has been well studied in pre-digital contexts. However, Internet communication has allowed this letter writing to be made far more public than was previously possible. In the example below a son is willing to provide his email address but he also, perhaps unwittingly, has his computer's IP address recorded. In our era of concerns over breaches of digital privacy and misuse of data, the full disclosure of personal information online is both risky and naïve, as well as perhaps indicating emotional vulnerability. There is also something poignantly hopeful about sharing one's computer IP with the dead:

10 Apr 2012, 13:45, Charles E. P. **@yahoo.com, from 173.67.22.118:
Mom, you left us so unexpectedly. I remember your last words to me, "I LOVE YOU VERY MUCH." I still hear the sweet sound of your voice uttering those words to me. I love you too Mom and I miss you so much. When you left us, you took a part of me with you, a part I will never get back. Your memory lives on in my heart and I call on you often. Thank you for being MY Mom and thank you for all the things you have done for me throughout the years. I only wish you were here to talk to me. I know we will all

be together again someday, until that day, I will continue to pray for you and keep you in my thoughts daily. I love you Mom and I miss you. Love Bookie.

Some letters more clearly than others take the form of communication with the afterlife, as in the following example:

Vernon L.

28 Jul 1923–22 Apr 1984

Dear Dad, It has been so long since you passed away on that Easter Sunday. We had no clue that the end was near the morning of Easter when me and my family talked with you on the phone. My heart about broke when I heard you had died. But, you went so fast, I know you must not have had any pain or fear. It was a little over 17 years before Mom joined you … and you know losing her really did break my heart. I am happy to know you are both finally back together and enjoying heaven together. My son, Jason is a great bowler (he has bowled 27 300 games!!) and he always tells people he gets it from his grandpas. My kids are adults now and I have 3 grandkids and a step-grandchild … boy, alot has changed hasn't it?? Remember always that I am your "little girl" and I miss you as much now as I did in 1984. Take care of Mom for me. … I love you. … Cindy & family

Pamela Roberts' pioneering study of web cemeteries (2004) revealed changing patterns of language use in online memorialization. She traced differences in language use to generational preferences and familiarity, with older users preferring the "condolence letter" form, and younger users tending to write more directly to the deceased as though they were speaking to them, in the common vernacular of social media communication.

Social networking in the afterlife

SNS [social networking sites] memorials … stand in the middle of the town square, surrounded by the busy profiles of the living; short of searching for likely terms (eg. RIP, In Loving Memory), there is no easy way to find other SNS memorials to the dead and, even if one does, it is quite likely that they will be denied access. As a result, the slow leave-taking afforded by cemeteries is less possible there; instead, one is immediately thrown back into the here and now, a different neighborhood altogether. (Roberts 2004: 59–60)

Facebook was launched in 2004, but it was not accessible to everyone with an email address until late 2006. Since 2009 Facebook users have been given the opportunity to "memorialize" a user profile, an action that triggers some immediate practical effects: the memorialized user no longer appears as a "suggested friend" on other users' news/status feeds/updates (or equivalent); their profile is locked in an "as is" state but minus sensitive information such as contact information and status updates; the profile can only be viewed by confirmed friends, and is not findable in general searches; and no-one is able to log into the account in the future. The one feature that is left open is the ability for family and friends (that is, Facebook friends confirmed prior to the user's death) to leave posts on the profile Wall in remembrance. The page can remain as a memorial for as long as the family gives permission, and they can also request that it be removed at any point. Although this online facility is in its infancy, samples of usage already show that the sites are serving a beneficial therapeutic purpose, in terms of the process of working through trauma, particularly at the time immediately after a death. They are also showing that people feel freer to express their pain, and to communicate messages to the dead, in these ambiguous virtual spaces where traditional lines between public and private dissolve away.

The memorialization of Facebook pages has been described, by Richard Allan, European Director of Public Policy at Facebook, as "a new form of mourning" (*i-Shrine* 2010). An estimated three Facebook users die per minute. In 2011, 1.78 million Facebook user accounts become deceased persons' accounts. There is a demographic shift in new Facebook users toward older people, and existing users are aging. The overall shift means that in time the number of deceased Facebook users may outnumber the living. MySpace, home to many memorials and the subject of earlier research, has relinquished its position as the most popular social networking service. However, despite differences in functionality and interaction, MySpace and Facebook are generically similar. Both allow for profiles to become memorials after their creator has died.

Social networking sites have a wide range of user privacy preferences that control who can view content, including that of memorialized sites. This makes them less accessible, in one sense, than dedicated web memorials and cemeteries, which are, by and large, open to all. And yet, because user profiles of the deceased can be "memorialized," there is continuity between the living person's profile and the memorialization and so there is unlimited access to "friends." There is also, unavoidably, an unplanned residue of online information and activity that is simply left "lying about" as a scattered inadvertent posthumous archive. The result is that there are "...billions of pages held by Facebook and other social networking sites ... basically anything into which we put data ... data which, in most cases, remains after we die" (Andrews 2010). Can this bequeathing of bits of one's past to the future offer a sense of connection and continuity with the living world, or is it closer to what Baudrillard describes as "traces and dregs" which represent "the derisory mirror of your lost identity, your dejecta" (Baudrillard 1997: 42).

More recently established web memorial sites have templates and tools as well as the option of social networking features such as secure feeds to or full integration with Facebook and Twitter. In other words, there is now less to distinguish web memorials and cemeteries from social networking sites such as Facebook. The most recent examples are using common technological platforms for communication. This digital convergence in the posthumous world further erodes traditional partitions between notions of public and private and also, strangely, and to some disturbingly, between the living and the dead.

In purely practical terms, there are obvious benefits in online memorialization in its many forms. The Internet allows access to the memorial regardless of physical location, and it allows users to visit at any time, and more regularly. "In a society that is increasingly fragmented—where families and friends, often separated by significant distances, cannot actively participate in memorializing their deceased—an alternate space to the physical needs to be provided" (Veale 2004: 1).

Futhermore, as we live increasingly in and develop greater reliance on and trust in digital environments, the relationship between notions of permanency as relating to the physical, and impermanence as relating to the virtual and intangible online, is being disturbed and even inverted. Online memorial sites are now commonly assumed to last "forever," as in the following example:

Keith F. L.
13 Jun 1950–27 Feb 1988
   It gives me great comfort to put you here on the internet so you will never ever be forgotten. You were very special to me. The best brother anyone could ever have.

Roberts' most recent published study found that users "tend to see [onlinememorials]aspermanenttributestothedead"(Roberts2006:55); they were attracted to the notion of leaving "'permanent' evidence of the visit (that will not wilt or blow away)"; and they liked being able to visit without others seeing or knowing if, when or how often a visit is made (58). Her latest analysis of early forms of web cemeteries/memorials (such as Virtual Garden and World Wide Cemetery) showed that few follow the obituary format; messages are more personal, with a third to a half writing letters to the dead. Because the newer iterations of web cemeteries (dedicated memorial sites) include more templates, they influence the structure of what is written and arguably the content. Roberts suggests that, while it has not been studied, it is likely that the "tab" approach (requiring filling out of multiple fields) may produce "something closer to an obituary." It is also likely to lead to increasing homogenization of forms of communication with the dead or, in other words, the formation of genres. However, even when tabs suggest that particular content should feature, much freedom remains (57). We are yet to see the full extent of how these developments will reconfigure modes of mourning and so potentially provide new frameworks for understanding processes of healing, but if popularity is any guide, they are already answering to a significant need.

Continuing bonds with the persisting digital self

In a recent study of online memorialization on Facebook, Kasket presents an analysis of 943 posts on "in-memory-of" Facebook groups and uses the frame of the "continuing bonds theory of bereavement" (referring to Klass et al. 1996; Klass and Walter 2001; and Klass 2006). She explains:

> [t]he notion that "healthy" resolution of grief involves breaking bonds and letting go of the relationship with the deceased person is a 20th century phenomenon and is largely due to the influence of Freud, who felt that to hold on to such connections was pathological, and that it was important to invest one's energies fully into other things, other relationships. Continuing bonds theory is an increasingly influential alternative to this view and holds that, while relationships necessarily do change, they do not end as such, and that this can be normal, adaptive and comforting. (Kasket 2012: 63)

Kasket explores four themes in Facebook memorialization, relating to (1) Modes of address, (2) Beliefs about communications, (3) Experience of continuing bond, and (4) Nature and function of Facebook community. Most relevant in the context of this chapter are the observations on the theme of "Experience of continuing bond," which relate to: "comfort of communication," "vividness of deceased person's telepresence," "investment in maintenance of bond," "sense of 'everydayness'," and "fear of bond breaking" (64). Also relevant (under theme 4) is the observation that one of the main roles of participants in the Facebook community was found to be "as co-constructors of deceased person's biography" (64), highlighting the communal construction of life stories as part of the grieving process. A memorialized Facebook site is not newly set up to eulogize; the identity construction of the deceased has a direct continuity with the living identity:

> (a) the mourning takes place in the same "place" or "space" as formerly, rather than in a new "place" such as a virtual memorial site, and (b) interaction continues with the same co-constructed representation of self created during that person's life, rather than with a new, eulogised representation of the person created by someone else in a virtual cemetery. (63)

Mixing the metaphors of burial and cremation, Kasket refers to these as "gravemarkers of the dead, scattered among the profiles of the living" (62).

Kasket found that statements from users suggest there is comfort in imagining or believing that the dead person can actually receive the messages being written. For many there is such a strong commitment to continuing the online bond that "The persisting digital self and the mourner's bond with it is experienced as somehow 'real', and there is as terrible fear of that bond being broken" (66). Examples given include:

"I know u can read this, it just sux that u can't
talk back … thanx for lettin me talk to u again [on
Facebook]."
"I know you are reading this."
"Sorry I haven't been around in a while to say hi." (65)

The "in-memory-of" group may more properly resemble the space of a wake, a "communal space, allowing a more 'complete' picture of the person to emerge" (63). On Digital Death Day 2010 Kasket was quoted by the BBC as saying, in relation to online memorialization, "It's perhaps the best example so far of continuing bonds after death." Messages are written to the deceased as though they are still present in some way, "logging on from some internet cafe in heaven" (Andrews 2010). In some cases people write on the memorial "wall" of someone they never knew. This is discussed by Kasket, who found that although 7% in her study fell into this category, many felt uncomfortable about it and said this directly in statements such as, "I don't feel like I should be writing here as I didn't know you as a friend" (Kasket 2012: 65).

A key phase of Kasket's research involving participant interviews provided insights into the perceived differences between traditional practices such as visits to gravesites and writing of letters, for example, and online activities such as posting messages on Facebook. Responses included feeling that the deceased are more likely to "see it" if it is on their wall and that the act of writing, rather than thinking thoughts or speaking aloud, is a "more tangible" way to communicate. This contrasts with one respondent's reverse perception that "… when I see his name on his headstone in a silent cemetery or I see his room frozen in time, it's more in-your-face." Within these reflections there are many complex and contradictory strands. On the one hand there appears to be comfort to be gained from having the deceased "see" the words written on the Facebook wall; on the other the living person doesn't want to have the fact of death, as marked by the gravestone, "in-your-face," or in other words does not want to see it or at least not to see the marker of the death of the other, preferring the reassurance of continuing communication via the wall, even it is only one-way (on the wall, at least). Many respondents do in fact report that messages come back in other ways, through dreams, for example, but this is a common feature of the experience of bereavement with or without online "contact."

Posthumous connectivity is not new to social media and Web 2.0. It was identified as a key feature of memorials from the earlier era of the Web. Veale refers to the example of an online memorial for a young woman who died in 1997 ("Amanda Joy Alstatt, March 15, 1981–June 05, 1997", n.d.), where her father and brother regularly left messages on her memorial message board. These are conversational, talking about family news and everyday happenings:

> Amanda. Yea, it is me Daddy ... I know you know about the new and wonderful
> news. Pretty awesome Huh! That is it for now!...
> Hi Amanda its me Matthew, I started highschool (sic) on August 11th. Im (sic)
> now in 9th grade and im 14...
> It is me!. So much to say, but not enough room or time, right here, right now.
> (cited in Veale 2004: 4)

User motivations for creating or posting on memorial websites are wide-ranging. Veale formulated a "Memorial Attribute Model" based on "analysis of the work of several authors, using their definitions of memorialization and their discussions of the motivations and characteristics of traditional memorial practices" (1). First, memorials manifest online as a result of one or more of four motivations: grief, bereavement, and loss; unfinished business; living social presence; and/or historical significance. Secondly, online Memorials adhere to one or more memorial characteristics: invoking remembrance, a demonstrable array of kinships, and/or as a surrogate for the deceased (2).

When Kasket refers to traumatic experience, it is not only in relation to the immediate family. She also identifies the distress that can be inflicted on the wider social network of friends when a profile is removed at the request of the family: "Friends have traditionally been a disenfranchised group of mourners" (Kasket 2012: 66). Facebook's policies recognize this issue. It is central to debates over the right to grieve. The severing of online existence, the annihilation of the site where friends can retain a connection with the dead, leaves a disturbing sudden absence which is experienced like another kind of death, in some cases as a traumatic loss, for the Facebook friends: "A piece of who he was is still going to live on, his heartbeat will always be with his family ... but for the rest of us, as a friend, or the people who sat next to him in class, it's a way for them to remember him too ... to feel connected. ('Ruby')" (66). And:

> I would be close to inconsolable. Having something that may seem so small to some people is everything to me. [His profile] is the one last thread of him that I have. If we lost it, it would be like losing him all over again. There are just certain things that rip the wounds open. ("Ava") (66).

In another recent quantitative study that can inform further qualitative research, Carroll and Landry combined ethnographic study (of 200 Myspace memorial posts) with quantitative analysis (of 100 undergraduate university student Facebook users). They reported that 60% had visited a profile of a person after their death, but only 10% had posted messages and that there was a higher likelihood of young users visiting memorialized Facebook pages than reading obituaries. Most importantly, Carroll and Landry's study acknowledged "the ability of the [online] medium to facilitate connection with the deceased person, with memories, and with the community of mourners" (343). This process is identified by Kasket as "the phenomenon of the persisting digital self" (63).

The nature of that self and what impact its persisting digital "life" has upon the living remain open questions—and they relate as much to the fundamental social questions, conundrums and dilemmas that the digital revolution has thrown up as to the domain of death and commemoration. If we ask the question: Is the persisting digital self a blessing or a curse?, we can only answer obliquely and provisionally, by following two divergent trajectories and two opposing sets of values in relation to digital communication.

On the one hand, there is plenty of evidence that, for many, there is comfort and healing power in the continuing contact with the dead that the perpetual digital self seems to promise. Trauma is lessened by the very fact of continuity, even if it is an illusion created accidentally as a by-product of technologies designed to serve very different purposes. More than half a century ago in his essay "The Storyteller," Walter Benjamin lamented the fact that "dying has been pushed further and further out of the perceptual world of the living." In the past, as he explains:

> There used to be no house, hardly a room, in which someone had not once died. ... Today people live in rooms that have never been touched by death, dry dwellers of eternity, and when their end approaches they are stowed away in sanatoria or hospitals by their heirs. It is, however, characteristic that not only a man's knowledge of wisdom, but above all his real life—and this is the stuff that stories are made of—first assumes transmissible form at the moment of his death. (Benjamin 1973: 93, 94)

Has Facebook, or its equivalent, become the new "room" that provides a reassuring and safe place for dying amongst family and a community of friends? Or has the realm of social media already become, in the short time since it was born, so debased, so overwhelmed by banality and trivia, and so much a shrine to hyper-consumerism, that it is not a fit place for honoring the dead and exposing the pain of the living?

Jean Baudrillard's vision of the mid-90s was prophetic:[16] We are, in effect, persisting in the increasingly sophisticated deconstruction of a world which can no longer secrete its end. So everything is able to go on to infinity. We no longer have the means to stop the processes which now run on without us (Baudrillard 1997: 47). Baudrillard's words take us back to the epigraph at the beginning of this essay, "The deceased can always be provided with a here and a now [via the Internet]." If, as it seems, the Internet has given us the hope (or threat) of a new kind of immortality, it has done so through flattening out time and space and changing our experience of memory and history, and if we listen to Baudrillard, built into the new digital eternity there may be another kind of death. In the early years of the Internet he wrote:

> What is impossible at the cosmic level (that the night should disappear by the simultaneous perception of the light of all the

stars) or in the sphere of memory and time (that all the past should be perpetually present, and that events should no longer fade into the mists of time) is possible today in the technical universe of information. The info-technical threat is of an eradication of the night, of that precious difference between night and day, by a total illumination of all moments. In the past, messages faded on a planetary scale, faded with distance. Today we are threatened with lethal sunstroke, with blinding profusion, by the ceaseless feedback of all information to all points of the globe. (53)

Notes

1. Baudrillard is especially negative about this kind of display of victimhood. See "The New Victim Order" (in Baudrillard 1997: 131–141). In a similar vein, Susan Sontag points to the fine line between voyeurism and empathy in relation to photographically exhibited suffering.
2. The play *Shrine*, written by the Australian writer Tim Winton and performed in Perth, Western Australia in September 2012, focuses on the way people commemorate their dead and memorialise road trauma with roadside crosses, flowers and mementos. "I guess it is about the way in which we try to own our dead and the way they come to own us," Winton said ahead of the launch (*West Australian* 2012: 55).
3. For example see Shushan 1990.
4. One such tomb inspired Philip Larkin's poem, "An Arundel Tomb" whose first two stanzas read:

> Side by side, their faces blurred,
> The earl and countess lie in stone,
> Their proper habits vaguely shown
> As jointed armour, stiffened pleat,
> And that faint hint of the absurd –
> The little dogs under their feet.

They are followed towards the end by:

> And up the paths
> The endless altered people came,
> Washing at their identity.
> Now helpless in the hollow of
> An unarmorial age, a trough of smoke in slow suspended skeins
> Above their scrap of history,
> Only an attitude remains.

5. In a similar vein, Balaev refers to "personal and cultural histories imbedded in landscapes" (149).

6. In spite of Jeremy Bentham's intense promotion of self-museumization the practice did not win popularity.

7. It is useful to note that closely related to memorialization is the concept of "legacy". Memorials protect and recognize the legacy a person leaves behind. The qualities and character of the deceased—the "mark" they left—is captured and contained and in the traditional processes of memorialization, that is, set in a mould, preserved, objectified, distanced from the everyday.

8. Walter Benjamin wrote, "Death is the sanction of everything that the story teller can tell" (Benjamin 1973: 94).

9. Discussing the fiction of trauma, Balaev refers to "the reformation of self and world" and "the reformation of identity" that can occur in the process of remembrance (Balaev 2008: 161).

10. Relevant to monuments commemorating traumatic events is Kali Tal's comment on written representations: "Representation of traumatic experience is ultimately a tool in the hands of those who shape public perceptions and national myth" (Tal 1996: 19).

11. As Michelle Balaev states: "the story's meaning changes depending on the historical time and place" and "memories of the traumatic experience are revised and actively rearranged according to the needs of the individual at a particular moment" (Balaev 2008: 160).

12. However, there are also innumerable cases of denial or belatedness, where there are no monuments, and sometimes long-term official suppression, of trauma and suffering on a massive scale. See, for example, Melnyczuk (2012), which documents, through interviews with survivors, the enforced hunger, now acknowledged as genocide, that was inflicted on the people of rural Ukraine in 1932–1933 by Stalin's regime. The history of this event was suppressed for more than half a century. My grandfather's family, who lived in Rublivka, near Kharkiv, experienced the famine. A monument was finally erected in Kyiv in 2009, 77 years after the event, Memorials to the Victims of Holodomor in Ukraine National Museum. See http://primetour.ua/en/excursions/museum/Natsionalnyiy-muzey--Memorial-pamyati-zhertv-golodomorov-v-Ukraine-.html (accessed 2 February 2013).

13. The need for privacy by mourners has traditionally been expressed in some cultures in symbolic ways such as the wearing of mourning clothes that set them apart and through social codes requiring withdrawal from normal community interaction for a specified period of grieving.

14. The etymology of the word "site" can be traced to the Latin *situs*, referring to "place" or "position." It is ironic that the word "site" has been adopted, along with related words such as "build" and "landscape," as a key term in the virtual world, operating as a metaphor that bestows the appearance of substantiality to something that is ephemeral and placeless.

15. Elsewhere Jean Baudrillard makes this observation: "Whether an organism dies a natural death, or perishes because it carries within it from the outset genes and cells whose function is to put an end to it, are very different things. The latter is an automatic programming, without which life itself, the living organism, would be immortal. *Without this specific, inhibitory*

action, life would be incapable of stopping on its own; it would proliferate to infinity ... Our present pathology is one of the failure of these inhibiting agents, opening onto a prospect of exponential development of all functions" (emphasis added, Baudrillard 1996: 43, 44).

Bibliography

Andrews, P. *Virtual Life after Death. Radio 4's i-Shrine.* BBC News. 22 May 2010, available at http://news.bbc.co.uk/2/hi/technology/8691238.stm (accessed 2 February 2013).

Bachelard, G. *The Poetics of Space.* Trans. Maria Jolas, Boston, Massachusetts: Beacon Press, 1994.

Balaev, M. "Trends in Literary Trauma Theory." *Mosaic* 41.2 (2008): 149–166.

Baudrillard, J. *The Perfect Crime.* Trans. Chris Turner, New York and London: Verso, 1996.

Baudrillard, J. *Fragments—Cool Memories 111, 1991–1995.* Trans. Emily Agar, London and New York: Verso, 1997.

Benjamin, W. *Illuminations.* Ed. Hannan Arndt, trans. Harry Zohn, London: Collins/Fontana Books, 1973.

Boyd, D. "Social Network Sites as Networked Publics: Affordances, Dynamics and F>Implications." *A Networked Self: Identity, Community and Culture on Social Network Sites.* ed. Zizi Papacharissi. 39–58. New York: Routledge, 2011.

Brubaker, J.R. and G.R. Hayes. "We Will Never Forget You [Online]: An Empirical Investigation of Post-Mortem *Myspace* Comments." Proceedings of the ACM 2011 Conference on Computer Supported Co-operative Work 19–23 March 2011, Hangzhou, China, 123–132. New York: ACM, 2011.

Brubaker J.R. and J. Vertesi. "Death and the Social Network." Paper presented at the CHI Workshop on HCI [human computer interaction] at the end of life: Understanding Death, Dying, and the Digital, Atlanta, GA, 2010.

Bryson, J.J. "Internet Memory and Life after Death." *Bereavement Care* 31.2 (2012): 70–72.

Carroll, B. and K. Landry. "Logging On and Letting Out: Using Online Social Networks to Grieve and to Mourn." *Bulletin of Science, Technology & Society* 30.5 (2010): 341–349.

Davies, J. "One Hundred Billion Dead: A Theology of Death." *Ritual and Rememberence: Responses to Death in Human Societies.* ed. Jon Davies, Sheffield: Sheffield Academic Press, 1994.

DeGroot, J.M. *Reconnecting With the Dead via Facebook: Examining Transcorporeal Communication as a Way to Maintain Relationships.* PhD dissertation, Ohio State University, 2009.

deVries, B. and J. Rutherford. "Memorializing Loved Ones on the World Wide Web." *Omega Journal of Death & Dying* 49.1 (2004): 5–26, available online at http://baywood.com/journals/previewjournals.asp?id=0030-2228 (accessed 2 February 2013).

Douglas, K. "Translating Trauma: Witnessing Bom Bali." *ARIEL: A Review of International English Literatures* 29.1–2 (2008): 147–165.

Douglas, K. and G. Whitlock. Editorials: "Trauma in the Twenty-First Century." *Life Writing* 5.1 (2008) and *Life Writing* 5.2 (2008).

Durante, M. "The Online Construction of Personal Identity through Trust and Privacy." *Information* 2 (2011): 594–620.

Gannes, L. "1000Memories Funded by Greylock, Angels." *Wall Street Journal: All Things Digital*, 2011, available online at http://allthingsd.com/20110216/1000memories-funded-by-greylock-angels/ (accessed 2 February 2013).

Graves, K.E. *Social Networking Sites and Grief: An Exploratory Investigation of Potential Benefits*. PhD dissertation, Indiana University of Pennsylvania, 2009.

Green, J.W. *Beyond the Good Death: The Anthropology of Modern Dying*. Philadelphia: University of Pennsylvania Press, 2008.

Hallam, E. and J. Hockey. *Death, Memory & Material Culture*. Oxford: Berg, 2001.

Howarth, G. "The Emergence of New Forms of Dying in Contemporary Societies." In D. Oliviere, B. Munroe. and S. Payne, eds. *Death, Dying and Social Differences*. Oxford: Oxford University Press, 2011.

Hsiung, R.C. (ed.). *e-Therapy: Case Studies, Guiding Principles, and the Clinical Potential of the Internet*. New York: WW Norton & Company, 2002.

Ibreck, R. "International Constructions of National Memories: The Aims and Effects of Donor Support for Genocide Remembrance in Rwanda," *Journal of Statebuilding and Intervention* 7.2: 149–169.

Ibreck, R. "The Resistance Memorial, Bisesero, Rwanda." In M. Andrews, C. Bagot-Jewitt. and N. Hunt, eds. *Lest We Forget: Rethinking Cultures of Remembrance*. Stroud, Gloucestershire, UK: The History Press, 2011.

i-Shrine. BBC Radio 4, 21 May 2010, available online at http://www.bbc.co.uk/programmes/b00sdd8v (accessed 2 February 2013).

Kasket, E. Continuing Bonds in the Age of Social Networking: Facebook as a Modern-day Medium." *Bereavement Care* 31.2 (2012): 62–69.

Klass, D. "Continuing Conversations about Continuing Bonds." *Death Studies* 30.9 (2006): 843–858.

Klass, D., P.R. Silverman and S.L. Nickman (eds.). *Continuing Bonds: New Understandings of Grief*. Washington, DC: Taylor & Francis, 1996.

Klass, D. and T. Walter. "Processes of Grieving: How Bonds are Continued." In M. Stroebe, R. Hansson, W. Stroebe. and H. Schut, eds. *Handbook of Bereavement Research: Consequences, Coping and Care*. American Psychological Association, 2001.

Kollar, N.R. "Rituals and the Disenfranchised Griever." In K.J. Doka, ed. *Disenfranchised Grief: Recognizing Hidden Sorrow*. Lexington, MA: Lexington Books, 1989, 271–286

McMilan, D.W. and D.M. Chavis. "Sense of Community: A Definition and Theory." *Journal of Community Psychology* 14.1 (1986): 23.

Melnyczuk, L. *Silent Memories, Traumatic Lives: Ukrainian Migrant Refugees in Australia*. Fremantle, WA: Western Australian Museum Publications, 2012.

Metro (UK). "Madame Tussauds: The Place Where Time Stands Still." 15 June 2012, available online at http://metro.co.uk/2012/06/15/madame-tussauds-the-place-where-time-stands-still-467651/ (accessed 1 July 2012).

Pickering, P. and R. Westcott. "Monuments and Commemorations: A Consideration." *Humanities Research* x.2 (2003).

Rheingold, H. *The Virtual Community: Homesteading on the Electronic Frontier.* Reading, MA: Addison-Wesley, 1993.

Roberts, P. "The Living and the Dead: Community in the Virtual Cemetery." *Omega Journal of Death & Dying* 49.1 (2004): 57–76.

Roberts, P. "From Myspace to Our Space: The Functions of Web Memorials in Bereavement." *The Forum* 32.3 (2006): 1–16.

Roberts, P. and D. Schall. "'Hey Dad, It's Me Again': Visiting in the Virtual Cemetery." Paper presented at the 7th International Death, Dying and Disposal Conference, University of Bath, UK, 2005.

Roberts, P. and L. Vidal. "Perpetual Care in Cyberspace: A Portrait of Web Memorials." *Omega Journal of Death and Dying* 40.4 (2000): 521–545.

Ruby, J. *Secure the Shadow: Death and Photography in America.* Cambridge: Massachusetts, MIT Press, 1995.

Schwarts, M., J. Clark and J. Troyer (eds.). *Dead (In)Famous: Memory, Materiality, and Materiality in Culture.* New York, New York University Press, 2013.

Shushan, E.R. *Grave Matters.* New York: Ballantyne Books, 1990.

Smith, B. *Age* (Melbourne). "Historian Out to Explode Our Take on the Anzac Legend." 18 April 2012, available online at http://www. theage.com.au/national/historian-out-to-explode-our-take-on-the-anzac-legend-20120417-1x5oi.html and http://www.theage.com.au/national/historian-out-to-explode-our-take-on-the-anzac-legend-20120417-1x5oi. html#ixzz25GwUejKD (accessed 2 February 2013).

Sontag, S. *Regarding the Pain of Others.* London: Penguin, 2003.

Tal, K. *Worlds of Hurt: Reading the Literatures of Trauma.* Cambridge: Cambridge University Press, 1996.

Valentine, C. and K. Woodthorpe. *Death & Society: A Global Introduction.* London: Sage, 2013.

Veale, K. "Online Memorialization: The Web as a Collective Memorial Landscape for Remembering the Dead." *Fibreculture* 3 (2004), available online at http://three.fibreculturejournal.org (accessed 2 February 2013).

Walter, T. "Why Different Countries Manage Death Differently: A Comparative Analysis of Modern Urban Societies." *British Journal of Sociology* 63.1 (2012): 123–145.

Wertheim, M. *The Pearly Gates of Cyberspace: A History of Space from Dante to the Internet.* Sydney: Doubleday, 1999.

West Australian. "Shrine." 10 September 2012, 55.

Woodthorpe, K. "Grave Goods: Why Do People Leave Things on Graves?" *ICCM Journal* 79.1 (2011a): 70–71.

Woodthorpe, K. "Using Bereavement Theory to Understand Memorialising Behaviour." *Bereavement Care* 30.2 (2011b): 29–32.

Woodthorpe, K. "Sustaining the Contemporary Cemetery: Implementing Policy alongside Conflicting Perspectives and Purpose." *Mortality: Promoting the Interdisciplinary Study of Death and Dying* 16.3 (2011c): 259–276.

Index

Printed in Great Britain
by Amazon